Toward an Urban Vision

Published for the
Organization of American Historians

Thomas Bender

Toward an Urban Vision
Ideas and Institutions in Nineteenth-Century America

The University Press of Kentucky

Publication of this book was assisted by
the American Council of Learned Societies
under a grant from the Andrew W. Mellon Foundation.

ISBN: 0–8131–1326–1

Library of Congress Catalog Card Number:
74–18930

Copyright © 1975 by The University Press of Kentucky

A statewide cooperative scholarly publishing agency
serving Berea College, Centre College of Kentucky,
Eastern Kentucky University, Georgetown College,
Kentucky Historical Society, Kentucky State University,
Morehead State University, Murray State University,
Northern Kentucky State College, Transylvania University,
University of Kentucky, University of Louisville, and
Western Kentucky University.
Editorial and Sales Offices: Lexington, Kentucky 40506

*To my mother and
the memory of my father*

Contents

[Illustrations follow page 180]

Preface

This book examines intellectual and institutional responses to unprecedented urban and industrial growth in nineteenth-century America. My intention is to explore the interplay of thought and experience in the emergence of an urban vision in the United States. I hope the study will also illuminate the general configuration of nineteenth-century American culture.

Consideration of the city in nineteenth-century American thought has been hampered by a tendency, most notable in *The Intellectual Versus the City* (1962), by Morton and Lucia White, to remove thinkers from social history and to classify them as either pro-urban or antiurban. Such a conceptual framework is unnecessarily limiting. More interesting questions may be asked about the complex pattern of experiences, ideas, and values upon which such likes and dislikes are based. How did ideas about the city or America change as Americans confronted the industrial city? What adaptive mechanisms (psychological and institutional) were developed by a people moving from the country to the city? What were the changing meanings of "community"? How did Americans develop new cultural ideals that would give meaning and coherence to their lives in an increasingly urban environment?

What follows is, in part, an inquiry into the relationship between structures of belief, or cultural paradigms, and changes in the social and physical environment. It is not my intention to set ideas and reality in opposition; rather I am trying to explore the ways in which cultural traditions and social developments interact to form a meaningful psychological reality. In this version of cultural history, ideas and social events are mutually entangled in the complex process of historical change.

Cultural ideals provide a vocabulary of symbols or metaphors for interpreting, predicting, and relating to social experience. Sometimes these symbols provide motives to social action; at other times social change forces a reconstruction of these symbols. Ordinarily, cultural paradigms supply men and women with a map of social reality. But just as development can render a road map useless or positively misleading, maps of social reality lose their usefulness in the face of rapid and extensive social change. The resulting dissonance between inherited cultural ideals and everyday experience stimulates the creation of new ideologies seeking to supply the meaning that older symbols no longer provide.

The emergence of the industrial city in nineteenth-century America produced such a situation. Nonurban cultural ideals inherited from Jefferson's generation no longer helped men and women structure their increasingly urban experiences. Obviously, this crisis was felt most intensely by sophisticated thinkers, and Leo Marx's book *The Machine in the Garden* (1964) explores the responses of some of our most sensitive nineteenth-century literary figures. My argument, however, is that this crisis was felt and dealt with by a far wider spectrum of Americans–if still a minority–than his and other studies suggest. Besides sophisticated intellectuals in New York and Boston, I found middle-class gentlemen and reformers and even the "mill girls" of Lowell responding to the imperatives of this cultural crisis.

When I began this study, my intent was to investigate the roots of modern urban thought. After I was well into my research, however, I realized that I had stumbled on to a lost historical tradition that offered an alternative to the dominant pattern of urban thought and development. This mid nineteenth-century urban vision, which I admittedly find appealing, developed out of the interplay of a New England version of early American agrarian ideals and the modernizing forces associated with the industrial city. It sought to bring city and country, and the values they respectively stand for, into a contrapuntal relationship. It found expression in a broad range of thought–from political economy to theology to art and literature–and in a variety of urban institutions. It provided, in other words, a viable symbolic structure for ordering urban experience and for developing urban policies that offer a contrast to the rational-bureaucratic ones that came to prevail.

Writing the kind of cultural history implied by these remarks requires that ideas be placed firmly in their social context. I have therefore relied upon a series of closely analyzed case studies probing the interaction of idea and experience as the foundation of

more general speculations. In selecting my various topics I picked
the most revealing, not the most typical. Collectively, the cases chosen are intended to express the complexity of historical change that
created an urban culture in the United States. If my work gains as
much historical insight through this method as it loses in coverage,
I will be satisfied.

Although the various contexts that I have selected for close study
are not linked by concrete association in time and place, they find
unity in their convergence upon a developing cluster of beliefs that
culminates in the thought and work of Frederick Law Olmsted.
One way of explaining my approach is to say that unity in cultural
history is to be found as much in thematic links as in such external
considerations as personal or institutional connections or geographical proximity. In other words, I have not written a genetic history
of an idea, an institution, or a group of Americans. Instead I am
attempting to illuminate a developing but never complete pattern
of thought in nineteenth-century America by approaching it from
a variety of complementary perspectives.

Chapter resumés as book prefaces are seldom necessary. Yet in a
study considering different kinds of subject matter, it may be well
for an author to explain the structure of his book while reassuring
the reader that the major theme will be sustained–that the following chapters, showing various stages and dimensions of cultural development, are meant to connect the issues and ideas at the heart of
an American urban tradition.

The introductory chapter reconsiders some common (and some
not so common) historical materials to sketch an interpretation of
the changing symbolization of city and country during the first
half of the nineteenth century. The interpretation offered challenges
the notion that American thinkers of that period were simply antiurban. In most areas of thought, it turns out, many Americans
gradually but definitely abandoned agrarianism in favor of a more
complex environmental vision. By mid-century they were seeking
a new understanding of city and country, art and nature, that would
allow them to hold key values identified with each. This reorientation of American social thought describes, in broad outline, the
changing of a map of social reality.

The starting point for the more specific studies is the Jeffersonian legacy. This legacy, whether called agrarianism or the "Puritan ethic," as Edmund S. Morgan has recently defined its New England version, consisted of a belief in republican freedom, community, individual morality and industriousness, and the moral and economic value of turning the land to productive uses. Both Jefferson and early New England industrialists proposed to introduce the machine and the factory under the aegis of agrarianism. While this agrarian ideology of nonurban manufacturing was used to defend early industrialism, by the 1830s and 1840s the concept was becoming less and less useful in explaining personal experience and the course of American development.

The interplay of agrarian ideology and urban-industrial development provides the focus for a case study of a single New England industrial center, Lowell, Massachusetts. The social and intellectual history of Lowell reveals the complex process whereby structural change and urban growth rendered inherited ideals inadequate as guides to experience. The crisis of belief, which urban-industrial growth produced in Lowell, found parallels, with slight shifts in timing and intensity, in other New England cities and elsewhere, but Lowell is an especially fruitful case for historical analysis. It was the first New England industrial city, and it elicited an enormous volume of comment. Its growth was so sudden and rapid that it brought traditional New England ideals and patterns of life into an especially sharp and revealing confrontation with the modernizing forces of the industrial city. Another advantage of Lowell is its articulate factory workers; the stories they wrote for the *Lowell Offering* provide a unique opportunity to learn how working people responded to the transformation of the environment and social relations.

When Lowellians found their nonurban cultural ideals inadequate, they groped toward an urban point of view. This emerging urban consciousness did not, in mid-century Lowell, result in a systematic ideology. Yet the ideas that arose there contained several key themes that became more fully articulated among significant nineteenth-century urban thinkers. Lowellians fully accepted the organization and economic power symbolized by the city, but they saw no reason why they should have to give up entirely the natural beauty and the organic pattern of social relations associated with New England ideals.

Versions of this vague but developing urban orientation can be traced in a host of local sources, both within and outside New England. Of more interest at this point, however, is the problem of translating such ill-defined ideas into a clear urban vision and ultimately into a viable social policy. To pursue this question, I turn from the case study of Lowell to detailed studies of two urban thinkers and reformers of national reputation. Charles Loring Brace and Frederick Law Olmsted, who carried their New England values into the nation's metropolis, developed the suggestions one finds earlier among Lowell's more ordinary thinkers into an urban ideology that provided the basis for national urban reform. The link between the urban spokesmen of Lowell and national urban thinkers like Brace and Olmsted is thematic. Each is expressing, with varying degrees of clarity, an underlying group of urban ideas that are associated with their common experiences in an urbanizing society.

The mid-century response to the city found its most impressive ideological and institutional expression in the thought and work of Brace and Olmsted. The final two chapters, therefore, probe the ideas and careers of these two urban reformers in order to describe and assess the nineteenth-century urban vision at its best.

By the end of the century these ideas and institutions were undoubtedly on the periphery of American culture and soon to be forgotten. Yet they were of central importance in the third quarter of the century when Brace was the nation's most notable urban welfare expert and Olmsted was acknowledged as the finest and most prolific city and environmental planner. Of course, their ideas were not part of urban reality for all Americans. Yet they grew out of a pattern of experience shared by many urban Americans, and an examination of that experience and these ideas is necessary for an understanding of the distinctive urban institutions and policies developed in nineteenth-century America. These mid-century ideas, moreover, have an intrinsic quality that makes them worthy of our study at a time of urban and cultural crisis.

Lest my account, however, seem to make Brace, Olmsted, and

many of their urban contemporaries appear more successful than they actually were, their ultimate failure must be acknowledged at the outset. The mid nineteenth-century achievement was remarkable and deserves our attention, but it was neither complete nor durable.

What follows is no more than a preliminary probe into nineteenth-century urban thought. To deal fully with this subject would be a monumental undertaking. Yet monuments need bricks, and I hope that this study provides a few for future scholars.

I owe much to previous scholars, institutions, and, most of all, to my teachers. As much as is possible in a world where the really interesting ideas quickly become the property of the whole community, I have indicated my debts to fellow scholars in my notes and bibliographical essay.

I wish to thank the staffs at the Library of Congress, the New York Public Library, the New York Historical Society, the Yale University Library, Widener, Baker, and Houghton libraries at Harvard University, the Boston Public Library, the Schlesinger Library on the History of Women at Radcliffe College, the Massachusetts Historical Society, the Massachusetts State Library, the State Historical Society of Wisconsin, the Minnesota State Historical Society, the American Antiquarian Society, the Essex Institute, the Merrimack Valley Textile Museum, and the Lowell Public Library.

Marion Morse, former secretary of the Lowell Historical Society, put the Society's collections at my disposal. Professors Harold Kirker, Kenneth W. Porter, and Dr. Robert V. Spalding kindly aided me in my search for manuscripts in private hands that relate to the early textile industry. I wish to thank Harriet Ropes Cabot of the Bostonian Society for generously allowing me to examine family papers in her possession relating to Francis Cabot Lowell. Ethel J. Lambert of the New York Children's Aid Society arranged for me to examine pertinent early records in the Society's files. Gerald Brace graciously provided me with transcripts of pertinent personal papers of Charles Loring Brace that are in his possession. The interlibrary loan department at the University of California, Davis, deserves special thanks. The New York Public Library allowed me to reproduce an engraving from its I. N. Phelps Stokes Collection. Some of the material in chapter 4 appeared in the *New England Quarterly* 47 (June 1974). A grant from the Chancellor's Patent Fund, University of California, Davis, helped defray the costs of travel to distant libraries.

At different points and in different ways, David Brody, Lawrence Chenoweth, and Wava Haney offered valuable suggestions that improved this book. I owe much to Daniel Calhoun for his penetrating criticisms and for his always illuminating perspectives on American cultural history. My deepest obligation is to Wilson Smith. Combining sympathetic understanding, constant encouragement, and wise counsel with exacting standards, he has been a teacher in the deepest and best sense of that word. Special thanks should also go to the members of his seminar who read and criticized nearly every section of the manuscript in its dissertation form. Had I taken full advantage of all the suggestions for improvement that I have received, the manuscript, I am sure, would have been better. No one, let it be said, should feel responsible for what I have done with his or her ideas.

Finally, although I have many other reasons for thanking Sally Hill Bender, I want to express my appreciation here, not always obvious at the time, for her readiness to tell me when I am simply not making sense.

I.

Introduction:
The Challenge of the City

Your towns will probably e're long be engulphed in
luxury and effeminacy. If your liberties and future
prospects depended on them, your career of liberty
would probably be short; but a great majority of
your country must, and will be yeomanry, who
have no other dependence than on Almighty God for
his usual blessing on their daily labour. From the
great excess of the number of such independent
farmers in these States, over and above all other
classes of inhabitants, the long continuance of your
liberties may be reasonably presumed.

David Ramsay (1793)

Our country has entered upon a stage of progress
in which its welfare is to depend on the convenience,
safety, order and economy of life in its great cities.
It cannot prosper independently of them;
cannot gain in virtue, wisdom, comfort,
except as they also advance.

Frederick Law Olmsted (ca. 1877)

WHEN THOMAS JEFFERSON assumed the presidency, the United States was a rural republic. Although cities had played a leading role in the revolutionary movement and were the cradles of culture in the new American nation, few Americans saw their future as being linked to the progress of cities. There was, in fact, little to suggest the nation's urban-industrial future. As Henry Adams later wrote in his history of the period, "the machinery of production showed no radical difference from that familiar to ages long past."[1]

Only six places had populations of over 10,000 persons. The combined population of these "cities" was only 183,000 in a nation of well over five million persons.[2] All six cities were eastern seaports. They represented mere specks on an immense virgin continent and were easily "lost" in the rural landscape. It was remarkably easy, therefore, for Jefferson and his contemporaries to ignore these 183,000 urban members of the American community.

Although Jefferson was surely expressing personal views in his *Notes on the State of Virginia*, he was also articulating ideas that pervaded his culture when he wrote: "Those who labor the earth are the chosen people of God, if ever He had a chosen people, whose breasts He has made His peculiar deposit for substantial and genuine virtue." Even Alexander Hamilton, in his celebrated *Report on the Subject of Manufactures*, admitted that husbandry is "a state most favourable to the freedom and independence of the human mind . . . [and] has *intrinsically a strong claim to preeminence over every other kind of industry*."[3]

Similar expressions run through the writings of other early American leaders. George Washington warned that "the tumultuous populace of large cities are ever to be dreaded." Urbane Philadelphians also joined in the praise of husbandry. Benjamin Franklin declared that "the great Business of the Continent is Agriculture." Although Franklin readily admitted that his constant residence in "Capital Cities" made him largely ignorant of rural life, he nevertheless designated farming "the most honourable of all Employments." Dr. Benjamin Rush, another civic leader of Philadelphia, agreed that "farmers and tradesmen are the pillars of national happiness and prosperity." Tench Coxe, a Philadelphian more generally known as an early proponent of American manufactures, gave public expression to the opinion that "rural life promotes health and morality" and that farmers constituted "the bulwark of the nation." And George Logan, who as a physiocrat was already committed to giving agriculture precedence in the nation, also praised farming as "of first importance because it brings us near to GOD himself." Finally, were it not for the unmistakable style, the paean to agriculture that John Adams wrote for the *Boston Gazette* in 1763 might have come from the pen of Thomas Jefferson: "The finest Productions of the Poet or the Painter, the statuary or the Architect, when they stand in Competition with the great and beautiful operations of Nature, in the Animal and Vegetable World, must be pronounced mean and despicable Baubles."[4]

Much has been written on the agrarian bias of the founding fathers, especially that of Thomas Jefferson. Actually, early American agrarianism was more than a bias. It was a political philosophy and a definition of a social ideal.[5] Jefferson, and all political thinkers of his generation, transformed what was originally a literary convention–going back as far as Virgil, even Hesiod–into a political theory. The belief that good citizens live and work in the country rather than in the city formed the core of eighteenth-century American political thought.[6] The famous passage in his *Notes on the State of Virginia* wherein Jefferson praises farmers concludes with an assessment of the type of citizens produced by cities: "The mobs of great cities add just so much to the support of pure government, as sores do to the strength of the human body."[7]

Simplicity, farming, virtue, and republicanism were fused into a national ideology. This cluster of American symbols was set off against the luxury, urban vice, and monarchism of the Old World. Closeness to nature distinguished the new republic from the old nations of Europe. The farmer emerged as the dominant symbol for the nation; the occupation of husbandman became "tinged with glory."[8]

Jefferson, who believed that he lived in an "age of experiments in government," was confident that "never was a finer canvas presented to work on than our countrymen. All of them engaged in agriculture or the pursuits of honest industry." The vast extent of fertile land in America would produce a new kind of citizen who would make the republican experiment possible. Such men, Jefferson wrote to John Adams, could "advantageously reserve to themselves a wholesome controul over their public affairs, and a degree of freedom, which in the hands of the Canaille of the cities of Europe, would be instantly perverted to the demolition and destruction of everything public and private."[9] But Jefferson was telling the New Englander nothing new. In *A Defense of the Constitutions of the Government of the United States of America* (1787–1788), Adams had written that "in the present state of society and manners in America, with a people living chiefly by agriculture, in small numbers, sprinkled over large tracts of land, they are not subject to those panics and transports, those contagions of madness and folly, which are seen in countries where large numbers live in small places, in daily fear of perishing for want." Such a people, he reflected, "can live and increase under almost any kind of government, or without any government at all."[10]

Many Federalists agreed with Jefferson's and Madison's contention that "generally speaking, the proportion which the aggregate of the other classes of citizens bears in any state to that of its husbandmen, is the proportion of its unsound to its healthy parts."[11] Professor David Howell of Providence, Rhode Island, for instance, considered "cultivators of the soil" to be the "guardians" of republicanism. Philip Barton Key, a lawyer from Annapolis and later Georgetown, declared in Congress that in time of war or crisis "you would never look to men and boys in workshops for that virtue and spirit in defence that you would justly expect from the yeomanry of the country."[12]

Some urban Federalists, of course, preferred the city to the country. For these men, primarily residents of seaboard cities, America faced toward the Atlantic rather than toward the agrarian West. George Cabot, a leading New England Federalist, was firmly convinced that Boston possessed "more wisdom and virtues than any other part of the world." Harrison Gray Otis shared his fellow Bostonian's outlook.[13] Gouverneur Morris of New York and several of the New England Federalists who went to the Hartford Convention in 1815 had misgivings about western development. Unpersuaded by Madison's argument in the *Federalist* for an extensive republic, this commercial elite feared that geographical expansion might undermine wise government.[14] No doubt, they were also concerned that growing western political power might threaten the national commercial policies they favored. Yet, as Linda Kerber has recently pointed out, Jefferson could easily have found Federalist support for his statements on cities.[15] As late as the State Constitutional Convention of 1821, in fact, when New York Federalists such as Elisha Williams and Chancellor Kent argued against the extension of suffrage, they cited Jefferson in support of their contention that cities produced inferior citizens.[16]

Jefferson and his contemporaries believed that if cities ever exerted a controlling influence upon American life, political morality would decline and the republican experiment would be doomed. Fortunately for them, it was remarkably easy for Americans to dismiss the influence of cities during the early years of nationhood. In fact, they tended to exclude cities from their definition of the "real" America. This tendency was not restricted to farmers; we find it in the thought of Benjamin Franklin, the consummate colonial urbanite. Replying to reports that the increasing luxury in America would ruin the experiment in self-government, he pointed out that the vast uncultivated forest waiting to be cleared "will for a long time keep the Body of our Nation laborious and frugal." He warned that "forming an Opinion of our People and their Manners by what is seen among the Inhabitants of the Seaports, is judging from an improper Sample." Allowing that "the People of the Trading Towns may be rich and luxurious," he asserted that "the Country possesses all the Virtues, that tend to private Happiness and public Prosperity." As for the towns, they "are not much regarded by the Country; they are hardly considered an essential Part of the States."[17]

Thomas Jefferson found it equally easy to exclude the few colonial urbanites living in a half dozen seaport cities from his image of the essential America. He wrote in February 1803 that "the great mass of our people are agricultural; and the commercial cities, though, by the command of newspapers, they make a great deal of noise, have little effect in the direction of the government. They are as different in sentiment and character from the country people as any two distinct nations. . . . Under this order, our citizens generally are enjoying a very great degree of liberty and security."[18]

Two months later, the United States acquired the Louisiana territory, doubling the area of the nation. Jefferson thought that this would surely keep the yeoman in the foreground of the national self-image for centuries to come. The Jeffersonian approach toward cities, in short, was to make them invisible by keeping the farmer at the center of national consciousness.

This agrarian political philosophy rested upon a particular conception of the significance of American history. Since the seventeenth century, Americans had been urged, as Thomas Barnard urged them again in 1758, to "make a *Wilderness*, in a moral as well as a natural sense, a *Fruitful* field."[19] As Barnard's agricultural metaphor implies, Americans celebrated the cultivated or rural, not the wild. This "middle landscape," as Leo Marx has called it, was supposed to be the nursery of good citizens.[20]

From the time when Europeans first set foot on the vast new continent, there had been a persistent fear of lapsing into barbarism.[21] Americans tried to steer between primitivism and what they considered the overcivilization of Europe. Wilderness produced savages, but European civilization corrupted and degraded man. In striving for a middle ground, however, Americans never rejected the idea of civilization itself.[22]

Within this heritage, a social philosophy of the "middle state" emerged. Writing in praise of the new American nation, Richard Price, Jefferson's English friend, described this conception of the "good society." The "happiest state of man," he wrote, "is the middle state between the *savage* and the *refined*, or between the wild and the luxurious state."[23]

Americans sought, in the words of one historian, to "combine the best advantages of nature and civilization." It was assumed that artifice could be "introduced into the natural order [showing] that man has interposed in some way to improve the processes of nature." However, an extreme change could not be accommodated. The balance would then shift from the "cultivated," the good, to the "dissipated and corrupt."[24]

The determinism of this philosophy of nature could lead only to an unhappy conclusion in the rapidly developing United States of the first half of the nineteenth century. The number of people living in places of over 5,000 inhabitants jumped from 597,000 in 1820 to over 5,600,000 in 1860. Nineteen cities had a population of over 25,000 persons in 1860, nine counted a population of over 100,000 persons, and New York (including Brooklyn) reached the one million mark. Moreover, while the urban population was increasing by nearly tenfold between 1820 and 1860, the total population of the nation only tripled.[25] Americans began to fear that instead of improving "nature's nation," such progress might obliterate nature and result in overcivilization.[26] Divorced from nature, would America become artificial, corrupt, and bad–like Europe? Was the democratic experiment paradoxically doomed by progress?

Thomas Cole, the landscape painter, treated this theme in a series of allegorical paintings completed in 1836. The series, entitled "The Course of Empire," consists of five panels–each representing a stage in the history of the American republic. Cole explained his plan for the series to Luman Reed, the New York merchant and art patron who commissioned it: "A series of pictures might be painted that should illustrate the history of a natural scene, as well as be an epitome of Man,–showing the natural changes of landscape, and those effected by man in his progress from barbarism to civilization –to luxury–to the vicious state, or state of destruction–and to the state of ruin and desolation." Accordingly, the first picture in the series is titled "The Savage State," and it presents "a view of a wilderness." The next, "The Arcadian or Pastoral," represents the ideal cultivated state. The third panel, "The Consummation of Empire," shows a "great city" in the "fullness of prosperity." Nature dominates the first two panels, but is nearly obliterated in the third. With nature overwhelmed by artificiality, the fourth panel is predictable. It portrays "a tempest,–a battle, and the burning of the city. . . . This is the scene of destruction." The final picture shows "the funeral knell of departed greatness, and may be called the state of desolation."[27]

The series was immensely popular, and James Fenimore Cooper, who treated the same theme in his novels, considered it "the work of the highest genius this country has ever produced."[28] Yet Cole's gloomy conclusion was not easy for most Americans to accept. "As implications of the philosophy of natural destiny forced themselves upon the more sentient," one historian points out, they "were obliged to seek methods for living in civilization, all the more because civilization was so spectacularly triumphing over the continent."[29]

Cole made one of the earliest attempts to grapple with this problem. In a less celebrated painting entitled "The Architect's Dream" (1840), Cole devised a solution that was prophetic of the mid-century response to the city. His picture showed nature and civilization coexisting on the same canvas in a dynamic tension. One half of the canvas revealed a city of dazzling classical architecture, the other half a dark forest with a Gothic church, of which the latter two were conventional representations of a beneficent nature.[30] Cole's ideal America now included both the culture and power of the classical city and the moral, almost religious, influence of nature.

Social and religious thinkers were traveling along the same path. They no longer felt comfortable trying to preserve the virtuous rural republic by excluding cities from the real America in the manner of Jefferson and Franklin. The urban influence had become too important, too central to nineteenth-century American life. They realized that *the great phenomenon of the Age is the growth of great cities.*[31] The United States was itself becoming a "nation of cities."[32]

Alexis de Tocqueville concluded in his *Democracy in America* that the absence of a "great capital city" was "one of the first causes of the maintenance of republican institutions in the United States."[33] Yet in 1820, a decade before Tocqueville visited America, Samuel Miller, a professor of theology at Princeton University, had pointed out the growing importance of metropolitan influences in American politics and religion. Preaching in Baltimore, then a potential rival with New York as the metropolis of the United States, Miller reversed the Jeffersonian approach to cities. He argued that "a large city . . . forms, as it were, the heart, the most vital portion of the State or Country to which it belongs." If orthodox churches are "established and edified" in the "Metropolis of a State or Nation," their influences "will be extended in every direction." "A happy impulse given here, will vibrate, and be beneficially felt to the remotest bounds of the social body."[34]

After 1825 and the opening of the Erie Canal, most discussion of metropolitan influence referred to New York, but many thinkers were concerned with the general influence of any city upon its environs. Orville Dewey, a New York Unitarian minister, pointed out in 1836 that cities were becoming the centers of political and moral influence in America. They could no longer be ignored. In a sermon on *The Moral Importance of Cities, and the Moral Means for Their Reformation,* he asked his listeners to consider the bearing "upon the political prospects of the country" of the observation that "our cities are not long to be limited to the number of half a dozen, or ten. There are to be congregated masses of men all around us." These urban populations "are the mighty weights in the political machinery, that are to urge every thing onward in a prosperous career, or to hurl everything to destruction."[35] For Dewey, unlike Jefferson, conditions in the city would determine the fate of the nation.

By mid-century, Samuel Miller's assessment of the importance of the city for evangelical religion was being echoed in rhetoric that combined a traditional religious vocabulary with a strikingly modern urban sociology. Recognizing that cities had always been the centers of civilization, Edward Lathrop, a New York Baptist minister, stressed that "the power of *modern* cities . . . is greatly augmented by the increased facilities which the present age affords for multiplying, as well as diffusing the elements of social and moral progress." He admitted that "the city is unfavorable, probably, to the cultivation of personal piety; and benevolent tendencies are more liable to be repressed than encouraged by the contacts and competitions of the crowded metropolis." But he also speculated on the "power of association" to be found in the city. The "*combined* piety and efforts of the benevolent" can make "sympathies and zeal which, in their isolation, would be comparatively inefficient," into a "mighty influence." By taking advantage of the secular means of influence characteristic of modern urban life, religious leaders might make the city the "grande centre" of American religious life. "The prosecution of the work of universal evangelization," he proposed, "must be advanced or retarded, in just the degree that the combined and centralized influence of large cities, is enlisted in the cause of the world's social and religious amelioration."[36]

When ministers at the opening of the nineteenth century referred to cities, their religious symbolism was typically taken from the Old Testament. This imagery, drawn from the language of an agrarian people being persecuted in the Egyptian urban civilization, was basically antiurban. By mid-century, however, American ministers turned more and more to the New Testament for urban symbolism –especially to Paul, who taught Christianity in the cities. The Reverend Richard Storrs, Jr., of Brooklyn, for example, urged the lesson of Paul upon Americans who would meet the challenge of the city. "We must preach Him IN THE CITIES; for nowhere else is the need of this greater, and nowhere else are the opportunities for doing it more numerous and inviting, and from no other points on earth will the influence of it extend so widely."[37]

The trickle of speculation about the moral and political importance of cities became a flood by mid-century. Not only New Yorkers and Bostonians, but men throughout the nation engaged in this discussion.[38] In 1843 Virginian George Tucker discussed the moral and economic importance of cities in his *Progress of the United States in Population and Wealth*. Ten years later and across the continent in San Francisco, William A. Scott delivered *A Lecture on the Influence of Great Cities*. "The tendency of modern society," Scott observed, "is towards building large towns and cities . . . even in our newest States."[39]

Americans began to challenge Jefferson's denigration of cities. James Fenimore Cooper, whose Leatherstocking Tales dramatized the conflict of nature and civilization in American culture, had accommodated himself to the city by mid-century. Observing in 1851 that "it has long been a subject of investigation among moralists, whether the existence of towns like those of London, Paris, New York, etc., is or is not favorable to the development of the human character," he declared that he did not "believe any more in the superior innocence and virtue of a rural population than in that of the largest capitals." Acknowledging that there are "incentives to wrongdoing in the crowded population of a capital town," he insisted that "there are many incentives to refinement, public virtue, and even piety, that are not to be met with elsewhere."[40] Historian Richard Hildreth, in *Despotism in America: An Inquiry into . . . the Slave-Holding System in the United States* (1854), assessed the "comparative progress" of the free and slaveholding states. He judged the rural and slave South by urban standards. In fact, he insisted that cities "are essential to any great degree of social progress" and that they "are the central points from which knowledge, enterprise, and civilization stream out upon the surrounding country." And Francis Bowen, Alford Professor of Natural Religion, Moral Philosophy, and Civil Polity at Harvard University, wrote in 1870 that "cities and towns are the great agents and tokens of the increase of national opulence and the progress of civilization."[41]

"The prevalent error of modern times," M. D. Bacon wrote in 1855, "has been an uncontradicted condemnation or aspersion of all great cities 'in the lump,' as great evils, and as necessarily and inherently evil. The remark that 'great cities are great sores on the body politic' (commonly attributed to Jefferson . . .), is but one current expression of this vulgar and shallow opinion."[42] During the crisis of union, Jefferson's reputation, in the words of one historian, fell under a "dark shadow." Moreover, the war seems to have accelerated American acceptance of the centralizing tendencies implicit in urban industrialism.[43] After the Civil War, Ebenezer Platt Rogers, a New York minister, declared that Jefferson simply "was not right when he said that large cities were ulcers on the body politic." Of course, "dregs and scum of society, and forces that are potent for evil" might be found in cities. "But there is a great deal [said] of the superior virtue of a rural population, which is not warranted by facts. And there is a great deal that is good and great and glorious about large cities."[44]

Mid-Victorian Americans, proponents of progress that they were, believed there was no need for cities to be the "great sores" condemned by Jefferson. They could be reformed.[45] Leonard Kip wrote in 1870 that we have not "hitherto been accustomed to pride ourselves overmuch upon our cities. . . . We have been rather wont to bestow the greater portion of our admiration and affections upon fields and pastures. . . . But of late years it seems as though we were beginning to learn a new lesson upon the subject." Americans, he observed, "are beginning slowly to understand what of itself ought rather to have been accepted from the first as an axiom, that uncleanliness, inordinate disproportion of crime, and a dingy absence of beauty, are not of themselves the necessary concomitants of city life, but are rather mere unholy parasites which long neglect has allowed to cluster around it; and that it is possible, with good management, to retain the advantages afforded by large massing of population, and not necessarily assume its disadvantages also."[46]

In anticipating success for the American government, Jefferson, Franklin, and Tocqueville focused their attention upon the rural districts of the nation. They feared and denied the existence of metropolitan influences in politics. However, by mid-century, and especially after the Civil War, social thinkers realized that cities lay at the heart of American politics and society.[47] Henceforth, no appraisal of the American democracy could ignore urban life. The quest for the good society shifted from the farm to the city.

Frederick Law Olmsted, the "principal theorist and planner" of the nineteenth-century city, observed in 1868 that "the most prominent characteristic of the present period of civilization has been the tendency of people to flock together in great towns."[48] He spoke for his generation, and our own, when he pointed out that the future of democracy in America depended upon the conditions of life in the nation's cities. "Our country," he wrote, "has entered upon a stage of progress in which its welfare is to depend on the convenience, safety, order and economy of life in its great cities. It cannot prosper independently of them; cannot gain in virtue, wisdom, comfort, except as they also advance."[49]

Olmsted realized that his observation "offered a very dark prospect for civilization" to those who regarded the "drift townward" as a "sort of moral epidemic." But he disagreed with their pessimistic point of view. He spoke for an emerging group of urban leaders who believed that "modern science has beyond all question determined many of the causes of the special evils by which men are afflicted in towns, and placed means in our hands for guarding against them."[50]

These introductory comments do not argue that mid-century Americans were "pro-urban." They wished, rather, to establish a balance between city and country. Like Thomas Cole in "The Architect's Dream," Americans were seeking ways of having both nature and civilization. In his recent book on Emerson and the city, Michael H. Cowan observes that "the continuing attempt to

find a way to 'have both,' in spite of the almost impossible difficulties involved, is one of the striking characteristics of the American literature of Emerson's era." Emerson himself "tended to accept a dichotomy of city and nature not as a conclusion, but as a
point of departure" for the development of an artistic strategy of
reconciliation.[51]

Emerson's sometime Concord neighbor, Nathaniel Hawthorne,
was also concerned with this problem. In accordance with the
literary conventions inherited by his generation, Hawthorne established Boston and the natural landscape as opposites in *The Blithedale Romance*, but, as in his other major novels, the movements of
the protagonist between city and country suggest an attempt at a
symbolic harmonization. Miles Coverdale, recalling his return to
Boston from Blithedale (Brook Farm), observes that "whatever
had been my taste for solitude and natural scenery, yet the thick,
foggy, stifled element of cities, the entangled life of many men together, sordid as it was, and empty of the beautiful, took quite as
strenuous a hold upon my mind. . . . All this was just as valuable, in
its way, as the sighing of the breeze among the birch-trees" near
Brook Farm.[52]

One of the most ambitious literary attempts to establish harmony
between city and country was a romance entitled *Big Abel and the
Little Manhattan*, published by Cornelius Mathews in 1845.[53] Mathews, a New York writer prominent in his own time but since
overshadowed by his more talented contemporaries, was one of the
first American artists to perceive the literary possibilities of urban
scenes.[54] Although the structure of *Big Abel and the Little Manhattan* is implausible at best, the relationship between Big Abel and
Little Manhattan represents the symbolic reconciliation of nature
and civilization sought by mid-century writers.

The book opens with a mysterious meeting between Little Manhattan, an Indian descended from the chief who sold Manhattan
Island to the Dutch, and Abel Henry Hudson, the descendant of
the Dutch explorer. They represent the forces of nature and civilization which for generations have struggled against each other for
possession of the island. However, Big Abel and Little Manhattan,
the mid nineteenth-century heirs of this struggle, become friends
and walk the island over dividing up the city. To Big Abel go all

the civilized phenomena (buildings, ships, and such), while Little Manhattan claims the vistas and memories of Indian encampments. The conflicting claims of nature and civilization reconciled, the romance concludes with Big Abel and Little Manhattan hosting a celebration on the roof of the Banking House in Union Square.

It was within the intellectual milieu created by Mathews, we have recently been reminded, that Herman Melville wrestled with the problem of nature and civilization.[55] Melville's greatest treatment of this American dilemma was masked in a narrative of a whaling voyage, but in *Pierre; or, The Ambiguities*, published in 1852, he handled a specifically urban setting, New York. Identifying the city and country with the head and heart respectively, Melville suggests that some ideal mixture might be possible. Although Pierre is ultimately doomed in the novel, he seems at first to have the proper combination of urban and rural experiences. Melville introduces him as having the good fortune "to have been born and nurtured in the country, surrounded by scenery whose uncommon loveliness was the perfect mold of a delicate and poetic mind. . . . But the breeding of Pierre would have been unwisely contracted, had his youth been unintermittingly passed in these rural scenes." He was able to accompany his parents "in their annual visits to the city; where naturally mingling in a large and polished society, Pierre had insensibly formed himself in the airier graces of life, without enfeebling the vigor derived from a martial race, and fostered in the country's clarion air."[56]

Three years later, Walt Whitman published *Leaves of Grass*. Throughout the many editions of this work, as F. O. Matthiessen has written, Whitman "thought of himself as the poet of the city and as the poet of nature."[57] Accepting city and country as separate and contending phenomena, Whitman believed that a symbolic reconciliation of these opposites could be achieved in the poet's imagination.[58]

While artists and writers sought new literary strategies to accommodate themselves to the city, reform-minded urban intellectuals reworked social thought in order to cope with the emergent city. Asking whether these men liked or disliked the city misses the point. Frederick Law Olmsted, the most important of them, ex-

plained that "no broad question of country life in comparison
with city life is involved; it is confessedly a question of delicate
adjustment."[59]

Horace Binney Wallace, a Philadelphia art, literary, and legal
critic, told Americans that urbanization did not imply man's complete separation from nature. It is true, he admitted, that the initial
effect of technological progress "upon the condition of communities" is to "make life more artificial." And "the interest and value
of earlier modes of life," he added, "seem to fade, and civilization
seems to be advancing into a progressive disavowal of all that once
gave it strength and health; and we grow alarmed lest it should
become wholly divorced from all human and spontaneous sympathies." But "these apprehensions," Wallace insisted, "belong only
to the early and undetermined stages of improvement." The passage of time will show that "the appliances of Art and business" are
contributing to a "revival of natural tastes" among city people. The
popularity and accessibility of parks, suburbs, and vacations in the
country, he suggested, demonstrate that "the perfections of Art
always throw us back upon Nature."[60] Writing in support of a
proposed New York park, Andrew Jackson Downing made the
same point in 1851: "because it is needful in civilized life for men
to live in cities, . . . it is not therefore, needful for them to . . . live
utterly divorced from all pleasant and healthful intercourse with
gardens, and green fields."[61]

The Reverend Henry W. Bellows, a New York Unitarian and a
close associate of Olmsted, neatly phrased the issue in 1872: "It is
common enough for moralists of the Jeffersonian type to deplore
the existence of great cities and to describe them as sores on the body
politic, while they enlarge on the superior innocency and happiness
in the country." But the truth is "that city and country are both
necessary, . . . that there is no advantage in either which is not offset
by a corresponding draw back, [and] that each needs the other to
correct, supplement, and complete it."[62]

Instead of emulating the attempts of Jefferson and Franklin
to "lose" the city in the American landscape, mid-century social
thinkers accepted the challenge of urban industrialism. Yet they
did not relinquish their commitment to nature. In fact, the tendency of urban-industrial society to obliterate the landscape made

them all the more anxious to preserve natural sanctuaries within their increasingly urban civilization. Accepting the utilitarian demands of organizational society and the city, Americans attempted to preserve what they could of the spontaneous freedom represented by romantic nature. They began to conceive of art and nature, cityscape and landscape, organization and spontaneity as opposites that would enrich American life if they could be combined. In his own way, Walt Whitman was speaking for this point of view when he sketched "the new aesthetics of our future" in his "Democratic Vistas." "The problem ... presented to the New World," it seemed to him, "is, under permanent law and order, and after preserving cohesion (ensemble-Individuality), at all hazards, to vitalize man's free play of special Personalism." [63]

Referring to this generation of Americans, Lewis Mumford has recently reminded us that for a brief moment in the nineteenth century, "it looked as if the romantic personality and the utilitarian personality might exist harmoniously side by side. ... Many of the leading minds–Audubon, F. L. Olmsted, Emerson, Marsh, Melville, Whitman, among others–could, with a wholeness of response, embrace the scientific and the mechanical and the industrial and at the same time place these within the ample framework of man's natural and humanistic heritage." [64]

My study investigates the background and development of this outlook as it relates to the creation of an urban culture in nineteenth-century America. It is also a commentary on cultural failure: this initial response to urbanization, however creative its initial impulse, was not developed to its fullest democratic and humanistic possibilities nor did it endure.

II.

Agrarianism & Industrialism, 1800–1860

We are inclined to believe that in the
British factories are found disgusting exhibitions
of human depravity and wretchedness. But we
cannot believe that the exercise of industry could ever
be the cause of demoralizing any race of men. . . .
In this country there are extensive manufactories,
and yet no such consequences are observed. . . .
We have, besides, none of those great manufacturing
cities; nor do we wish for such. Our factories will
not require to be situated near mines of coal,
to be worked by fire or steam, but rather on chosen
sites, by the fall of waters and the running stream,
the seats of health and cheerfulness, where good
instruction will secure the morals of the young,
and good regulations will promote, in all, order,
cleanliness, and the exercise of the civil duties.

*The American Society for the Encouragement
of Domestic Manufactures (1817)*

THE DOMINANT agrarian social theory in the new republic was antiurban, but it did not necessarily preclude manufactures. Proponents of domestic industry even considered it possible to present their case within an agrarian context.

Since Thomas Jefferson has stood as the principal interpreter of American agrarianism, during his own lifetime and since then, his attitudes toward cities, commerce, and manufacturing have been subjects of intense interest and often political significance.[1] The American philosophe's response to Paris reveals both his appreciation of the culture of cities and his preference for a society of a middle state in America. "Were I to proceed to tell you how much I enjoy their architecture, sculpture, painting, music," he wrote in 1785, "I should want words." Jefferson particularly enjoyed their music, "the deprivation of which with us cannot be calculated. I am almost ready to say it is the only thing which from my heart I envy them, and which in spight of all the authority of the decalogue I do covet."[2] Yet his total impression of the European metropolis was not favorable. He preferred the rural virtues of America to the vice, misery, and empty bustle that accompanied the cultural achievements of Paris. By 1800 he had completely overcome his envy. "I view great cities," he wrote to Benjamin Rush, "as pestilential to the morals, the health and the liberties of man. True, they nourish some of the elegant arts, but the useful ones can thrive elsewhere, and less perfection in the others, with more health, virtue & freedom, would be my choice."[3]

In spite of this powerful statement—and others could be culled from Jefferson's writings—Morton and Lucia White recently have written that "the American city found in Jefferson a great intellectual defender at the beginning of the nineteenth century."[4] A failure to distinguish, as Jefferson did, between cities, commerce, and manufactures accounts for this incredible statement. In a series of letters written between 1809 and 1816, many of which are noted by the Whites, Jefferson made a ringing defense of American manufactures, but were he alive today he would be amazed, and not a little distressed, to find his statements interpreted also as a defense of cities. Historians and social scientists presently despair of separating the individual components of urban-industrial society, but on the other side of the watershed of nineteenth-century industrialism such was not the case. We must read Jefferson's statements with eighteenth-century eyes and not our own in order to understand them. His propensity to distinguish between cities, commerce, and manufactures provides the key to the Jeffersonian legacy.

During the election campaigns of 1796, the Democratic-Republicans of New York presented Jefferson as a true republican who would unite commercial and agricultural interests.[5] It was one of those rare instances in which political rhetoric correctly characterized the man. His letters and career reveal that Jefferson was completely comfortable advocating American commerce and condemning commercial cities because, for him, commerce was an element of an advanced agricultural economy and was without urban implications. As secretary of state, for example, he declared that European harassment of American commerce "strikes at the root of our agriculture, that branch of industry which gives food, clothing, and comfort, to the great mass of the inhabitants of these states."[6] Overseas commerce, in Thomas Jefferson's political economy, was an agricultural and not a mercantile interest.

His opposition to turning New York or any other American city into a great commercial metropolis was constant. The conduct of "so much commerce as may suffice to exchange our superfluities for our wants, may be advantageous," he wrote, "but it does not follow, that with a territory so boundless, it is the interest of the whole to become a mere city of London."[7] Moreover, he feared that "the wealth acquired by speculation and plunder is fugacious in its nature and fills society with the spirit of gambling." And if the business practices of the merchants threatened their own morals, the foreign luxuries they imported endangered the morals and the republican spirit of the nation.[8] This "Puritan ethic," as Edmund S. Morgan recently characterized it, played an important role in encouraging domestic manufactures during the first years of the republic.[9] It is an indication of how far the world of Thomas Jefferson is from our own that sympathy for domestic manufactures was often linked with antimercantile and antiurban positions.[10]

Jefferson's most famous statements on manufactures are in his *Notes on the State of Virginia* and in his letter to Benjamin Austin of Boston in 1816. He declared in the former that "while we have land to labor ... for the general operations of manufacture, let our workshops remain in Europe." In the latter, he declared that because of changed conditions, he is ready to "place the manufacturer by the side of the agriculturist."[11]

Such is the outline of Jefferson's changing position on manufactures, but the texture of the Jeffersonian legacy is much more complex. Had Jefferson repudiated the agrarian values of the Republican ideology? Was America to have great manufacturing cities as in Europe? Was America to be in any sense an urban nation? The central question is whether Jefferson, in the letter to Austin, was renouncing his earlier agrarian vision of America, or whether he was declaring that the manufacturer could be accommodated within that vision. Every indication points to the second interpretation. There is no evidence that Jefferson ever abandoned his belief that the American people will "remain virtuous for many centuries; as long as they are chiefly agricultural. ... When they get piled upon one another in large cities, as in Europe, they will become corrupt as in Europe."[12]

Jefferson's letter to Austin made public his previous decision to encourage "domestic manufactures" (to use the appropriate eighteenth-century phrase). It is anachronistic to speak of his acceptance of industrialism in the modern sense of the word.[13] Jefferson believed or hoped that manufactures could be introduced without disturbing the nation's rural landscape and its agrarian values.

In the political discourse of the early republic, mention of domestic manufactures in the United States did not conjure up an image of a crowded, dark, and grimy American Manchester. Americans envisioned instead either household manufactures or small workshops, usually in a rural or village setting. Jefferson's conception of American manufactures was undoubtedly shaped, in part, by his own activities as a manufacturer. During the 1790s, he operated a nail factory on his plantation. Although his production was large enough to require retail outlets throughout the state, he always considered the nail factory an integral part of the plantation economy. He would never have thought about this factory in the Virginia countryside in the same terms he used for the industrial operations he saw in English cities.[14]

Manufactures in a rural nation constituted an altogether different matter from the situation of manufacturing cities in Europe. Accordingly, in 1805, Jefferson "had in *contemplation* some particular alterations" in the famous chapter on manufactures in a revised edition of his *Notes on the State of Virginia*. He believed that his strictures against manufactures had been misconstrued. In writing that chapter, he observed, "I had under my eye . . . the manufacturers of the great cities in the old countries." The moral depravity, dependence, and corruption of the population of those cities made them "an undesirable accession to a country whose morals are sound." But nature's bounty of a vast extent of fertile land in America, Jefferson decided, not only made possible virtuous farmers, but also virtuous manufacturers. "My expressions" in that chapter "looked forward to the time when our own great cities would get into the same state" as those in Europe. "As yet," however, "our manufacturers are as much at their ease, as independent and moral as our agricultural inhabitants, and they will continue so long as there are vacant lands for them to resort to."[15]

This early expression of the "safety-valve" theory was a facet of Jefferson's commitment to an extensive as opposed to intensive development of the American economy. To a greater degree than is usually recognized, the controversy between Hamilton and Jefferson was over this issue. Hamilton sought, through assumption, funding, bank stock, and bounties and other aids to manufactures, to solidify a financial elite that would be the bulwark of the new government. This program implied a concentration of wealth and power on the eastern seaboard. Hamilton perceived that the American propensity for extensive development, which tended toward the diffusion of capital, threatened this policy. The Virginian, however, consistently praised western expansion precisely because it tended to prevent the concentration of wealth and capital in the eastern cities and served to distribute political power into the hands of the independent yeomanry. Undoubtedly, Jefferson agreed when George Logan, his political ally in Philadelphia, wrote that the primary danger of the Hamiltonian program was that "the wealth of our country" would be wrested from agriculture and "devoted to support the parade and dissipation of a few idle men, in great cities." If Hamilton had proposed a program of encouraging manufactures in another policy context, Jefferson probably would have supported it.[16]

The shape of the Jeffersonian legacy is clear. A boundless extent of free land distinguished America from Europe, and the success of the republican experiment depended upon the independent and virtuous yeoman who tilled this land. Occasionally, however, Jefferson anticipated the rhetoric of the Jacksonians and included the whole "body of labourers . . . whether in husbanding or the arts" among the ranks of republicans.[17]

On the question of the "true limits of manufactures and commerce," Jefferson suggested "manufactures, sufficient for our consumption, of what we raise the raw material (and no more)" and "commerce sufficient to carry the surplus produce of agriculture, beyond our own consumption, to a market, exchanging it for articles we cannot produce (and no more)." If this political economy, as stated by Jefferson, did not imply cities, the nineteenth-century history of New York and Chicago reveals that the agricultural export trade produced great commercial cities. Jefferson did not anticipate this, probably because agricultural commerce in Virginia was conducted on plantation wharves rather than in urban seaports. And he never overcame his hostility to such cities.[18]

Manufactures offered a possible check to the development of overgrown commercial centers. Instead of being located in crowded, dirty cities, American manufactures would be spread over the green countryside–in farmhouses or along swiftly flowing streams. Under these conditions, and with the safety valve of nearly unlimited land waiting to be tilled, Jefferson felt he could prudently allow the manufacturer into his rural republic.

At the beginning of the nineteenth century, it looked as if the Jeffersonian ideal might work out. Tench Coxe, probably the most active proponent of manufactures in the new nation, proposed in 1794 to "draw a picture of our country" under an economic system encouraging manufactures. "In *the foreground*," he observed, "we should find the mass of our citizens–the cultivators." Then, he continued, "we should see our manufacturers encouraging the tillers of the earth by the consumption . . . of the fruits of their labours, and supplying them . . . [with] the necessaries and conveniencies of life, in every instance wherein it could be done without unnecessarily distressing commerce and increasing . . . the difficulties of changing our remaining wilds into scenes of cultivation and plenty." [19]

Henry Clay delivered his first Senate speech on the subject of manufactures ten years after Jefferson assumed the presidency. "In inculcating the advantages of domestic manufactures," he declared, "it never entered the head . . . of any one, to change the habits of the nation from an agricultural to a manufacturing community. No one . . . ever thought of converting the plowshare and the sickle into the spindle and the shuttle." He complained that "opponents of the manufacturing system transport themselves to the establishments of Manchester and Birmingham, and dwelling on the indigence, vice, and wretchedness prevailing there, by pushing it to an extreme, argue that its introduction into this country will necessarily be attended by the same mischievous and dreadful consequences." The analogy is "erroneous." "England is the manufacturer of a great part of the world," but "if we limit our efforts, by our own wants, the evils apprehended would be found to be chimerical." [20] Henry Clay, like Coxe, was able to present the case for domestic manufactures within the Jeffersonian framework.

American factories in the fields became more than a literary vision of proponents of manufactures during Jefferson's presidency. As secretary of state, a decade before he became president, Jefferson had written to David Humphreys, the American minister to Spain and Portugal, telling him that European disruptions of American commerce "renders it wise in us to turn seriously to manufactures." Humphreys, a moderate Federalist who had been an aide to Washington during the Revolutionary War and had attained fame as one of that group of poets known as the "Connecticut Wits," decided in 1806 "to commence the manufacture of cloth." [21]

He purchased a "picturesque" mill seat at Rimmon Falls on the Naugatuck River in Connecticut. The factory village that he established there soon came to be called Humphreysville. He took every precaution to prevent the evils attending manufactures in European cities. In contrast to Samuel Slater's earlier mills in Rhode Island, there is no indication that Humphreys employed whole families in his establishment. He apparently drew his labor force from New York orphans and the daughters of New England farmers. Housed in groups of ten to fifteen, the factory hands were provided with schools and gardens.[22] The small factory village was characterized by a strict concern for the workers' health and moral influences. Humphreys was commended by the state legislature in 1808 for solving the problem of the "dearness of labor" in a "mode very useful to himself and to the State." By employing persons not formerly productive, the legislators observed, "nothing is drawn from tillage and yet the funds of national industry [are] increased."

According to Timothy Dwight, the factory at Humphreysville "fairly established three points of great importance; one is, that these manufactures can be carried on with success; another, that the workmen can be preserved in as good health as that enjoyed by any other class of men in the country; and the third, that the deterioration of morals in such institutions, which is so often complained of, is not necessary but incidental; not inherent in the institution." Tench Coxe declared in 1813 that "the system, adopted at the manufactory of Humphreysville, in Connecticut, with respect to education, manners, discipline, morals, and religion, is an interesting evidence that the People of the United States may quicken and increase the virtues of the rising generation . . . by a humane and politic system in the large manufactories."[23] Jefferson also praised the Humphreysville establishment. He believed that it offered the possibility of American "manufactures to the extent of our own consumption of everything of which we raise the raw material" without the long chain of evils attending manufactures in Britain.[24]

Jefferson's famous letter to Benjamin Austin was intended as public support for the moderate protective tariff being advocated by Francis Cabot Lowell in 1816.[25] Then, in the next year, Jefferson accepted an honorary membership in the American Society for the Encouragement of Domestic Manufactures. These actions are sometimes taken as important clues to his changing attitude toward manufactures. Actually, this evidence is more revealing of the degree to which advocates of American manufactures shared the Jeffersonian vision.

In its *Address to the People of the United States,* the Society expressed views long held by Jefferson. It warned that reliance upon foreign manufactures threatened American political and economic independence. Further, foreign imports were labeled "serpents" which threatened the virtuous American republic. The Society assured the public that it had no intention of destroying American agriculture or commerce: "we will manufacture, that we may be agricultural and commercial." Neither, they promised, would manufactures interfere with the great work of the nation—settling the vast wilderness and turning it into a garden. Doubters were urged to go to the western part of New York where they "will find that mills and manufactures formed the first rudiments of those almost countless villages and towns which spangle that fertile and beautiful country, emphatically styled, the Eden of the state." While the Society agreed that "disgusting exhibitions of human depravity and wretchedness" were found in British factory cities, "no such consequences are observed" in connection with American factories. This difference exists because "we have none of those great manufacturing cities; nor do we wish for such." Our manufactures are conducted "rather on chosen sites, by the fall of waters and the running stream, the seats of health and cheerfulness, where good instruction will secure the morals of the young, and good regulations will promote, in all, order, cleanliness, and the exercise of civil duties."[26]

There were no manufacturing cities in the United States at this time. Throughout the nation, manufactures were located in the country and carried on in households or small mills. Production was basically for home or neighborhood use. The best figures available to historians show that in 1810 and again in 1820 about two-thirds of all the clothing worn in the United States was the product of household manufacture. The amount of cloth annually produced by household manufacture at the end of the first decade of the nineteenth century added up to twenty times the output of America's few cotton mills.[27] Conditions in New England mirrored the national picture. In 1810 there was virtually no division of labor

in New England's economy. Farmers combined household manufactures with their agricultural occupation, and mechanics usually
combined farming with their trades. More than 90 percent of the
population lived by agriculture.[28]

The Slater mills, which tapped markets far beyond the neighborhood, provided a partial exception to these generalizations. Yet
even the Slater factories remained small, employing only twenty-
five to fifty operatives. The traditional village was not severely disrupted by the massing of population or by the development of
unusually large work groups. The social system in Slater's factory
villages clearly represented an extension of the existing mill-handi-
craft-farm complex of Jeffersonian America and not the first step
in the creation of an urban-industrial social order.[29]

But a great change was impending in lower New England. Only
three towns in southern New England had a population of over
10,000 persons in 1810, and they accounted for only 6.9 percent of
the total population of the three states. By 1860, however, the
twenty-six towns with a population over 10,000 persons represented
36.5 percent of the population.[30] This population shift reflected the
emergence of modern industrial capitalism in New England.[31]
While in 1810 the total annual production of cotton cloth in American factories had amounted to 856,645 yards, by 1845 any four of
the ten large corporations located in Lowell, Massachusetts, could
turn out as much in a single week. Household manufactures had
been eclipsed by the development of industrial production and a
market economy. By 1840, according to Samuel Eliot Morison,
Massachusetts "had become predominantly a manufacturing state."
Its economy and society, particularly in the eastern portion, clearly
pointed toward the nation's urban-industrial future.[32]

The history of this transformation, the emergence of urban industrialism in America, begins with Francis Cabot Lowell. The
whole enterprise of introducing the modern factory system in
America bore the impress of Lowell's mind. He solved the technological problem of the power loom and devised the financial
and executive organization necessary for large manufacturing establishments. And his solution to the labor problem secured mill
hands whose intelligence and virtue formed a sharp contrast with

the "degraded" operatives in European factories. He even won the support of Jefferson and Madison for the protective tariff he successfully advocated in 1816. As one of his associates later put it, he was the "informing soul, which gave direction and form" to the project.[33]

Francis Cabot Lowell was born at Newburyport, Massachusetts, in 1775. His father, Judge John Lowell, moved his family to Boston a year later. Once in Boston, the Lowells quickly moved upward to fill the vacuum at the top of the social structure created by the departure of the loyalist elite. Lowell entered Harvard at the age of fourteen. He excelled in mathematics and graduated with his class in 1793–after being "rusticated" to Bridgewater for a prank. After Harvard, he engaged successfully in the import-export business and in various real estate promotions in Boston. As a speculator, he was involved in the India Wharf Project, the Broad Street Association, and in a land development scheme at Wheeler's Point. He was joined in these projects by Uriah Cotting, Nathan Appleton, and James Lloyd–all of whom would be original investors in his first textile factory.[34]

George Cabot, Lowell's uncle, operated a cotton factory at Beverly for several years. Lowell may have become interested in manufactures during his childhood visits there, but there is no evidence that he ever intended to go into the manufacturing business until his trip to Europe in 1810.[35] Ill health and deteriorating commercial conditions induced him in that year to make a prolonged journey to the British Isles with his wife and children. He decided while there to investigate English textile factories and to study their machinery. The British took great pains to prevent industrial espionage, but Lowell, as a prominent American merchant and importer of cotton goods, was undoubtedly a welcome visitor in the English factories. Meeting Nathan Appleton in Edinburgh, Lowell told him that he had resolved "before his return to America, to visit Manchester, for the purpose of obtaining all possible information on the subject [of cotton manufacture], with a view to the introduction of the improved manufacture in the United States."[36]

Lowell returned from Europe early in 1812. Trade was still seriously disrupted, and he began to consider the possibilities of implementing the plan he had discussed with Appleton. Shortly after the War of 1812 began, he decided to "bring the matter to the test of experiment."[37] He asked Patrick Tracy Jackson, his brother-in-law, to join him. Jackson agreed, and the two enthusiastically devoted themselves to the project. Both men were dynamic individuals, and they were convinced from the beginning that they would succeed. Ralph Waldo Emerson later numbered them among those "persons [who] naturally stand for cities, because they will certainly build them."[38] But Emerson spoke after New England had become transformed.

In 1813 Lowell and Jackson were surrounded by doubters. According to Henry Lee, Jackson's brother-in-law, many of Lowell's "nearest connexions used all their influence to dissuade him from the pursuit of what they deemed a *visionary and dangerous scheme*." Even Lowell's most sympathetic associates, like Nathan Appleton, were originally skeptical of the project. When Lowell and Jackson were in the process of organizing their manufacturing corporation, they went to Appleton and asked him to subscribe for ten thousand dollars of stock. Appleton later recalled his response: "theoretically I thought the business ought to succeed, but all which I had seen of its practical operation was unfavorable; I however was willing to take five thousand dollars of the stock, in order to see the experiment fairly tried, as I knew it would be under the management of Mr. Jackson; and I should make no complaint under these circumstances, if it proved a total loss."[39]

Lowell, Jackson, Benjamin Gorham, and Uriah Cotting petitioned the legislature for a charter of incorporation, and in February 1813 the Boston Manufacturing Company was established. The organization of the company reveals an interesting mixture of the old and the new. Lowell's ideas on financial and executive organization, including a very high capitalization, were a long step toward the modern corporate structure. But when we discover that nearly all the first generation of investors were linked to Lowell either by kinship, long association, or by Essex County backgrounds, it becomes clear that Lowell and his associates were operating in a traditional world where kinship and familiarity were crucial elements in the business system.[40]

Meanwhile, with only a mental picture of what he had seen in English cotton factories, Lowell set out to build a power loom. For this work, he secured the services of Paul Moody, an exceptional mechanic. The two spent several months experimenting at a store in Broad Street, and by the end of summer they were ready to build a full-sized power loom.[41]

The seriousness with which Lowell and Jackson pursued the project puzzled their family and friends. In August 1813 Jackson's sister was surprised to learn "that they really intend to live at the place—certainly Pat and perhaps Mr. Lowell. I had no idea that it was a thing that would decide their future destination."[42] Neither Jackson's sister, nor probably anyone else in Boston, even suspected the magnitude of what they were doing: that they were deciding, to a large extent, the future course of American economy and society.

They purchased an old mill site on the Charles River in Waltham. By late Autumn the power loom was completed. Lowell unwilling that anyone see the loom until finished, then invited Nathan Appleton out to view it. "I well recollect," Appleton later wrote, "the state of admiration and satisfaction with which we sat by the hour, watching the beautiful movement of this new and wonderful machine, destined as it evidently was, to change the character of all textile industry." Appleton was no longer skeptical: "from the first starting of the first power loom, there was no hesitation or doubt about the success of this manufacture."[43] Lowell had put together at Waltham something completely new to America. The Boston Manufacturing Company was the first factory in the country, maybe in the world, in which all the processes of the manufacture of cotton cloth, from the opening of the bale to the finishing of the fabric, were performed under a single roof by machinery.[44]

The question now became whether this tremendously powerful economic organization could be smuggled into American culture under the protective cloak of Jeffersonianism, or whether agrarianism would be frankly repudiated.[45] A resident of Lowell, Massachusetts, recalled the circumstances in a public letter to the agents of the textile corporations in 1827: New Englanders, who had "heard with pain, of the corrupt and profligate state of society in the manufacturing towns of the old world, . . . looked upon the establishment of an exclusively manufacturing community . . . as an act fraught with consequences dangerous to our moral and social character." Before the project could proceed, therefore, it was necessary to overcome "such habits of thought and feeling." The Waltham and Lowell establishments, accordingly, were commenced upon a "liberal plan" with churches, schools, and a strict system of moral police. The founders gave the impression that every effort was being "made to give this population a high character for morality and intelligence." "This single consideration" was more important than any other in dispelling "the prejudices that existed against manufacturing towns" and in "gaining for your establishments the favor of the community." The writer graciously left open the question of "whether the liberal course you have taken was in accordance with the dictates of conscience, as members of a republican community, or from mere motives of policy." The surviving evidence, however, indicates that both motives influenced the early industrialists. In fact, it was no secret among contemporaries that "the sagacity of self-interest, as well as more disinterested considerations" led to the owners' concern for morality and virtue in the mill towns.[46]

Lowell's view of the relationship between Europe and America was similar to Jefferson's. Impressed with the product of centuries of civilization there, but shocked by European poverty, Lowell ultimately declared his preference for American scenes. The English capital struck him as a "great city." He and his wife enjoyed the "business–pleasures–bustle of London."[47] He wrote to his uncle William Cabot soon after arriving in England that the mother country is much more than the picture we have of the "great corruption of the highest & lowest classes, and the great number of beggars & thieves." But as he prolonged his stay he became more and more disturbed by the "distress and poverty" he found, especially in the "manufacturing towns." Eventually, like Jefferson, Lowell was willing to forgo the highest achievements of European civilization for the middle state characteristic of America. "I prefer," he wrote in a later letter to Cabot, "cultivated fields & handsome houses."[48]

Lowell and his associates expressed a "deep interest" in the effect of American manufactures "on the character of our population."

Since the "operatives in the manufacturing cities of Europe, were notoriously of the lowest character, for intelligence and morals," it was seriously "considered, whether this degradation was the result of peculiar occupation, or of other and distinct causes." They concluded that labor in a textile factory, of itself, "should [not] vary in its effects upon character from all other occupation."[49]

Satisfied in their own consciences that with proper precautions manufacturing would be safe in America, they still had to persuade the public. Nathan Appleton believed that some opponents of the tariff secured by Lowell in 1816 went "out of the way, to stigmatize the occupation of a manufacturer as calculated to debase the moral character."[50] The Boston associates recognized, however, that they had to cope with a genuine "opinion which . . . prevailed extensively, that occupation in manufactories were less favorable to morals than other manual labor." The Boston capitalists had more than a theoretical interest in confuting this opinion. "In order to secure workers," Caroline Ware reminds us, "the American manufacturers had to demonstrate that the moral standards of the community would not be impaired."[51] Although the founders of Waltham shared the Jeffersonian fear of manufacturing cities in America, it was the necessity of obtaining a labor force for their factories that compelled them to translate their concern into practical innovations to protect the character and reputation of American factory operatives.

Recruiting factory labor had been less of a problem for Samuel Slater in Rhode Island, or Colonel Humphreys, or other early American manufacturers because they had lacked the power loom. Until Slater developed a workable power loom in 1827, the demand for concentrated factory labor for his simple spinning mills was relatively small.[52] Since he did not weave cloth at his factories, the yarn Slater did not sell outright was "put out" to be woven by farm families located within a sixty-mile radius of the mill. Instead of drawing labor into the factory villages, Slater distributed the yarn from his mill to the under employed labor on New England farms. The prospective growth of his early mills and his demand for factory labor was basically limited, therefore, by the capacity of hand weavers to turn his yarn into cloth.[53]

The invention of the power loom, however, "formed a new era

in the manufacturing business."[54] It brought with it infinite possibilities for growth and created a massive demand for factory labor. Lowell's problem also differed from Slater's in that the complexity of the machinery in his mills ruled out child labor; in fact, it required an exceptionally high level of intelligence and dexterity on the part of his operatives.[55]

Nathan Appleton recalled that when they looked about for suitable factory operatives it occurred to them that "there was little demand for female labor, as household manufacture was superceded by the improvements in machinery." The farm girls of New England could supply "a fund of labor, well educated and virtuous."[56] The problem was how to attract them to the mills. The Boston associates theorized that high wages, well-conducted boardinghouses, and a strict system of moral guardianship would draw the girls from the New England countryside. They were correct. As soon as manufacturing thus was made respectable, young girls flocked to the mill towns from the declining agricultural areas of New England. So effective was the system that there is no evidence of the early factories being at all handicapped by a shortage of common labor.[57]

The early mill girls who came to the factories stayed for a short period and then returned to the country to marry. They were a remarkable group of factory operatives: they read, listened to lectures, joined improvement circles, and even edited a literary magazine that won praise from Charles Dickens and Harriet Martineau. Of course, the few girls who participated in these activities did so after working more than seventy hours per week in the textile mills. Yet the contrast with Manchester, England, apparently was so sharp that the New England mill girls were celebrated throughout Europe and America for their intelligence and virtue.

This reputation was important to the industrialists. If it were besmirched, the "supply of help" would be "cut off."[58] This fact distinguishes the Waltham system from Robert Owen's factory at New Lanark, Scotland, with which it is sometimes compared because both systems were characterized by high wage policies, paternalism, and decent living conditions. Unlike Owen, however, the Boston associates were not moral reformers. They were basically intelligent businessmen who recognized the concessions they would have to make as manufacturers in an agrarian nation. While Owen tried to raise the living standards of his operatives, the Boston associates simply met Yankee expectations.[59]

The Waltham factory was to be a testing ground. The results of the experiment there would determine whether the industrial system would be expanded.[60] It was a brilliant success—both in profits generated and in convincing large numbers of Americans that under the Waltham system manufactures would be morally safe in America. The dividends paid by the Boston Manufacturing Company were phenomenal. From 1817, the first year with tariff protection, until the city of Lowell was founded in 1821, the dividends averaged over 19 percent annually. This is all the more remarkable because during these years business was not generally good in the United States, and a large number of the Rhode Island mills failed.[61]

With Waltham and, later, Lowell and Lawrence as their evidence, the Boston associates developed a litany of praise for American manufacturers that was never effectively challenged. They admitted "that in the old world, no class of the working population is more degraded or worse educated" than the factory operatives, but they claimed that in the United States "none is more respectable and intelligent, or better educated." The reason for this difference, Jackson explained, is that "in Europe, manufactures are established in large cities, the business is followed from parent to child, and wages are miserably low." In contrast, "manufactures are dispersed through the country" in the United States, and "the operatives are, to a considerable extent, females who come into the factories, after having acquired their education, who stay there but a few years" and earn "liberal wages." [62]

Americans welcomed an extension of manufactures on the Waltham model. William Tudor, founder and first editor of the *North American Review*, wrote in 1820 that "there can be no doubt of the practicability of our becoming manufacturers." While he was "not anxious for the growth of large manufacturing towns, and that kind of population that exists in them in Europe," he observed that "our manufacturing population is now blended with that of agriculture; the laborers in the former are drawn from the latter, and frequently return to it for a time. This preserves their health and energy; and in this way we may go on to a great increase of manufactures."[63]

A year later, a writer in *Niles' Weekly Register* praised the Boston Manufacturing Company as the best possible argument for American manufactures. He asserted that whenever anyone claims that America "is not fit for manufactures, we can, with pride, tell them –look at Waltham: that manufactures are injurious to morals and agriculture–look at Waltham." He concluded that "there is not an objection to the encouragement of manufactures among us, that is not put down by an inspection of this establishment." Earlier in the year, the Committee on Manufactures of the United States House of Representatives had come to a similar conclusion. The committee rejected the argument that manufactures drew hands from agriculture. On the contrary, the Waltham mill employed young women who "are able to earn support in no other manner." The fear that large manufacturing establishments would produce vice found no support at Waltham, according to the Committee.[64] The Waltham system of manufactures would give Americans just what they wanted: substantial and productive factories without large manufacturing towns filled with ignorant and depraved operatives.

Although this proposal to achieve industrialization without radically altering the social structure may appear chimerical to the twentieth-century American, recent studies in underdeveloped nations suggest that factories need not imply cities. The Guatemalan factory village of Cantel is an example. The cotton textile factory established there in the late nineteenth century was smoothly accommodated into the existing culture. Social structure and values there today are not substantially changed from what they were before the factory was built. Many of the conditions that accounted for this phenomenon were also present in New England industrial development: only factory production was added to the existing community, the organization necessary for the industrial firm was carried on outside of the local community, no significant part of the labor force was removed from farm work, and the culture and social structure contained elements favorable to industrialization such as regular work habits.

While Cantel thus retained its traditional community structure and values, the establishment of factories at Lowell, Lawrence,

Manchester, and other New England textile towns transformed social relations. Why? There was at least one important difference. The owners of the Cantel factory were either unable or unwilling to convert it into a means of expanding private profits and achieving rapid economic development. The New England textile leaders, however, founded and developed factory towns in pursuit of the speculative profits that could be gained from real estate and machinery sales in rapidly expanding cities. Combined with the characteristic mobility of Americans, this speculative approach to factory-building resulted in a massive influx of population at the factory sites. The traditional social structure in New England was crushed under numbers while the population of Cantel remained relatively stable for half a century after the introduction of the factory.[65]

When Francis Cabot Lowell died in 1817, at the age of forty-two, the foundations for expanding the factory system had already been laid, and Boston capital was being shifted from commerce to manufacturing.[66] With Lowell's death, leadership of the Boston associates was jointly assumed by Patrick Tracy Jackson and Nathan Appleton. Jackson was born at Newburyport, Massachusetts, in 1780. His maternal grandfather, Patrick Tracy, had migrated penniless to America, but rose to become an "opulent merchant of Newburyport." His father, Jonathan Jackson, had a distinguished career in Federalist politics and was serving as treasurer of Harvard College at the time of his death. Jackson attended the Newburyport schools and Dummer Academy before being apprenticed in 1795 to William Bartlett, the richest and most enterprising merchant of Newburyport. Within five years, Jackson was captain of his own ship, and in 1808 he retired from the sea to establish himself as a Boston merchant. In 1812 he became associated with Lowell's manufacturing project, and he devoted his energies to the textile industry until his death in 1847. His services to the industry included organizing and directing the construction of the first railroad in New England. The Boston and Lowell Railroad, opened in 1835, brought the two cities within an hour of each other.[67]

Like the Lowells and Jackson, Nathan Appleton came down

from north of Boston to enter business in the city. Born in 1779, Appleton was the son of Isaac Appleton of New Ipswich, New Hampshire. Instead of entering college, he chose to go into trade in Boston with his brother Samuel. Nathan soon became the senior member of a new firm including another brother, Eben. By the time Lowell approached him about textile manufactures, Appleton was already a wealthy man and had largely withdrawn from active business. After the War of 1812 he became a spokesman for the financial elite of Boston, and his election to Congress in 1830 over Henry Lee, a free trader, marked the political ascendency of the manufacturing over the mercantile interest in Boston. He died in 1861.[68]

In 1821, Appleton later recalled, the immense profits of the Boston Manufacturing Company "made me desirous of extending my interest in the same direction." Since all the water power was already developed at Waltham, the Boston associates had to locate a new site for the company. In November 1821 they decided to build the new factory beside Pawtucket Falls on the powerful Merrimack River at East Chelmsford. The company was organized December 1, 1821, and construction commenced in April 1822 under the direction of Kirk Boott.[69]

The son of a merchant of the same name, Boott was born at Boston in 1790. He was sent to England to attend Rugby, but he later returned to America and entered Harvard—never graduating. In 1808 his father obtained a commission for him in the British army, and he served under Wellington in the Peninsular War. His regiment was ordered to New Orleans in 1813, but Boott refused to serve against the United States and resigned. He then entered a British military academy "where he acquired a thorough knowledge of engineering and surveying arts, which were afterwards of such service to him" in supervising the planning and construction of Lowell. He returned to the United States after the war. While passing a day with P. T. Jackson during the summer of 1821, Boott, whose financial situation had been uncertain since his father's death in 1817, offered to accept "any post of service which Mr. Jackson might assign him." Jackson appointed Boott agent for the new manufacturing corporation to be established at East Chelmsford (later Lowell). Until his sudden death in 1837, Boott, a domineering man by nature and habit, was the central figure in Lowell's history.[70]

On September 4, 1823, Boott wrote in his diary that he went to the factory after breakfast "and found the wheel moving around his course, majestically and with comparative silence." Appleton had come up from Boston to watch Paul Moody put the wheel in motion, and Boott recorded his reaction: "N. Appleton became quite enthusiastic. In the afternoon, he spent an hour looking at the wheel."[71] By the end of the year, "the manufacture of cloth may be said to have been fairly commenced," at East Chelmsford.[72]

The new community provided a spectacular exhibition of the transformation of the New England landscape. Lowell, like the emerging western cities, "sprang into being . . . at a leap."[73] Three years after the big wheel at the Merrimack Manufacturing Company began to move, Lowell had grown from an agricultural village of about two hundred persons to an incorporated town of 2,500 persons. A decade later, Lowell was chartered as the second largest city in Massachusetts. By 1840, with a population of over 20,000 persons, Lowell was the fourteenth largest city in the United States.[74]

The textile city on the Merrimack quickly won the title of the American Manchester and a reputation as the "first instance in America of the development of a city of the primarily industrial type."[75] But Lowell's heyday lasted only until 1848. After that date, the city went into a protracted economic decline caused by over-expansion that resulted in an intolerable cost-price squeeze throughout the New England textile industry. By the beginning of the Civil War, Pittsburgh, which had claimed industrial primacy before the sudden rise of Lowell, resumed its earlier position as the nation's most notable industrial city.[76]

The rapid development of Lowell was so novel that Jacksonian America found it almost incredible. There are repeated references to its "magical," or "miraculous," or "enchanted" growth. According to Edward Everett, who represented Lowell in Congress and was later president of Harvard University, "the change seems more the work of enchantment than the regular process of human

agency." He half suspected that Lowell was "a great Arabian tale
of real life." John Greenleaf Whittier, the poet, was no more successful than Everett in finding words adequate to describe the place.
Lowell, he wrote, is "a city springing up, like the enchanted palaces
of the Arabian tales, as it were in a single night–stretching far and
wide its chaos of brick masonry and painted shingles. . . . Marvelously here has Art wrought its modern miracles." Yet Everett,
Whittier, and nearly all Americans were sure that in Lowell they
were being treated to a glimpse of the future. In the midst of all
this wonderful change, Whittier wrote, the stranger "feels himself,
as it were, thrust forward into a new century."[77]

Lowell quickly replaced Waltham as the focus for discussion
about the implications of manufacturing in America. It became an
axiom of political discourse that Lowell would decide the question
of American manufactures. Henry Clay declared that "Lowell will
tell whether the Manufacturing system is compatible with the social
virtues." Already in 1826, Lowell was being cited by a New York
newspaper as a "favorable specimen" that "removes the fears and
objections of those who apprehend the prevalence of vice, ignorance, and misery, in communities of that kind, so rapidly increasing in the United States." None "of the injurious effects to society so
much complained of in similar establishments in Europe" are present there.[78]

Beginning with Andrew Jackson's visit in 1833, there was a
regular procession of presidents and presidential aspirants traveling
to Massachusetts to see what President Polk called the "chief manufacturing city in the nation."[79] Foreigners were no less curious. No
visit to America during the Jacksonian period was considered complete without a trip to Lowell. A parade of distinguished foreigners,
beginning with Basil Hall in 1827 and including over the years
Harriet Martineau, Michel Chevalier, Charles Dickens, Domingo
Faustino Sarmiento, and Louis Kossuth, made the trek there. "Ni-
agara and Lowell," one Scottish divine wrote, "are the two objects
which I will longest remember in my American journey–the
one the glory of American scenery, and the other of American
industry."[80]

The men and women of Lowell were highly conscious of their
significance.[81] Heirs of the Puritans, they knew that they were

"imperiously called upon to make Lowell, as she is already the focus of all eyes, friendly and unfriendly, a light upon a hill." Lowell, they believed, "will one day, as we may hope, start a work of reform to put away the misery and vice of those [English manufacturing] cities."[82]

In 1845 the Reverend Henry A. Miles, a Lowell clergyman, wrote the first history of Lowell. "The great questions relating to Lowell," he wrote in his preface, "are those which concern the health and character of its laboring classes." He assured the reader that Lowell had been "carefully provided with strong moral and conservative influences."[83] Far from a critical analysis of industrial conditions in Lowell, Miles's book represented the culmination of a generation of myth-making about Lowell.

In his book *America* (1827), Alexander Everett wrote that he saw new opportunities for the youth of New England in the well-regulated manufacturing establishments at Waltham and Lowell. Everett and most Americans accepted the prescriptions for a strict moral police at these establishments as an indication that the young men and women of New England who decided to seek opportunity in the factory village would be just as safe, from the moral point of view, as those who became western farmers. But another argument could be made. And Timothy Flint, minister, literary light, and propagandist for the American West, made it in a review of Everett's book. He argued that the "rigid rules" and "the extreme precautions . . . in these establishments prove, after all, what the wise and provident superintendents think of the natural tendency of things in them. It is only a besieged city," he retorted, "that requires martial law, and the constant guard of armed sentinels."[84]

Flint's attempt to focus attention on the challenge Lowell presented to the predominant agrarian vision of America went unheeded. Political ideology was developing in a different direction. Within a few years, a set pattern of praise for American industrialism emerged alleging that the new technological and economic forces symbolized by Lowell were entirely compatible with American agrarianism.

According to the agrarian ideal, the great drama of American history was the conversion of a barren wilderness into a fruitful field–a cultivated or productive landscape. It was a grand opportunity for the defenders of American industrialism. If they could show that manufacturing in America was close to nature and was, in fact, simply another form of making unimproved nature productive, then the industrial system might be accommodated into an expanded version of the Jeffersonian legacy.

The realities of American industrial development provided the materials necessary for such a strategy. It was relatively easy to conjure up a bucolic image of American factories drawing their power from New England's waterfalls as contrasted with the fiery steam engines that powered factories in crowded European factory cities. But there remained the problem of where manufacturing might ultimately lead in America. Development on the agricultural frontier clearly would not lead to cities, luxury, and vice, but would manufactures bring these evils to America? In order to disarm opposition, spokesmen for industrialism argued that factories in the countryside and nature's bounty of virgin land in the West would preserve American uniqueness.

Waltham and Lowell were interpreted within this context. The Reverend Bernard Whitman of Waltham, for example, appraised and defended the manufacturing system in a Thanksgiving Day sermon of 1828. Whitman asked his listeners whether "our manufacturing establishments" may not "eventually become nurseries of ignorance, and vice, and wretchedness?" He acknowledged that "this is indeed feared by some individuals. But their fears do not appear to me well founded." These apprehensions have "been awakened by descriptions of the worst English establishments; and not by any circumstances which now exist, or ever have occurred in this commonwealth."

The American situation was altogether different from that of Europe. Whitman told his listeners that "the causes which have made those establishments so abandoned need never operate in our manufacturing communities; and consequently the same mental and moral degradation can never be produced." The causes are obvious. "In the first place, there is a wide difference in the numbers of people collected together." Because the English factories rely on steam power, there is a tendency toward concentration into large cities. In America, however, "our machinery is carried altogether by water power." Since nature has blessed the United States with an abundance of waterfalls and fuel is so expensive, steam will never be used. "We shall therefore be delivered from the evils of a crowded manufacturing population; because no stream is sufficiently large to warrant the erection of a great number of factories." If the dominant image of English industrialism was the depressing spectacle of unhappy people crowded around smoke-belching factories, in America there were happy people working in a neat factory alongside a fresh and swiftly flowing stream. American industrialism, according to Whitman, was safe because it would never be linked with urbanization.[85]

Two years after Whitman's sermon, Edward Everett, the brother of Alexander and Lowell's congressman, was selected to be the orator at Lowell's Fourth of July celebration. Everett—whom Perry Miller considers "one of the rewarding witnesses of the time" because "he betrays that he is defending a conservatism, which, by its very dynamism, is transforming the country"—took the occasion to assure Americans that Lowell represented no radical departure from the American agrarian tradition.[86]

Everett opened his address with an observation on the rapidity of Lowell's growth. In ten years it had grown up out of nothing. But what, he reminded his audience, could be more characteristically American. The great "romance" of American history has been the shortness of time required to make a "barbarous wilderness" productive. "With what rapidity the civilization of Europe has been caught up, naturalized, and, in many points of material growth and useful art, carried beyond the foreign standard!" This national drama has been paralleled in Lowell's short history. Before America secured her independence, the restrictive policies of the colonial system had allowed the "natural capital" of America's waterfalls to be wasted. The voice of nature uttered in vain "Let these [rivers] be the seats of your creative industry." Since the achievement of independence, however, American industry has been able to develop in its natural course. The result is most apparent at Lowell where unproductive lands have been turned into a source of wealth. "These favored precincts, now resounding with all the voices of successful industry . . . [formerly] lay hushed in the deep silence of nature, broken only by the unprofitable murmur of those streams which practical science and wisely applied capital have converted into the sources of its growth."

He also assured them that industrial development would not challenge the favored position of Jefferson's farmer. "The population gathered at a manufacturing establishment," he pointed out, "is to be fed, and this gives an enhanced value to the land in all the neighboring region." The effect in each locality where there is a factory may not be great by itself, but the "aggregate effect" is "of the highest importance."[87] Everett used this oversimplified but basically sound economic argument with great force. An advocate of manufactures in a republic that defined itself as agrarian, he sought to persuade his audience that nothing could help the farmer so much as covering the landscape with factories.[88]

Everett found another and vastly more important lesson taught at Lowell. He reminded his listeners that "it is well known that the degraded condition of the operatives in the old world had created a strong prejudice against the introduction of manufactures into this country." Reflecting persons in America "contemplated with uneasiness" the introduction of "a system which had disclosed such hideous features in Europe; but it must be frankly owned that these apprehensions have proved wholly unfounded." The social character of Lowell, he was proud to say, is high, as high as would be expected in any "enlightened New England community."

He attributed this to the nonurban character of American manufacturing centers. Manufacturing establishments in the United States, unlike the steam-driven British ones, are not situated in cities. American factories are located in the forest where they draw upon nature's own source of power, falling water. "In calling this water into action," the country benefits "as much as it would by a gratuitous donation of the same amount of steam power; with the additional advantage in favor of the former, that it is, from the necessity of the case, far more widely distributed, stationed at salubrious spots, and unaccompanied with most of the disadvantages and evils incident to manufacturing establishments moved by steam in the crowded streets and unhealthy suburbs of large cities."[89]

Everett was claiming that the Lowell factories were not a rejection of Nature by the devotees of Art, but rather a joining of the two for the improvement of American life. He drew upon that wellspring of American culture which celebrated the efforts of civilized man to turn lands that in the hands of the savages had been wasted for centuries into productive fields. He artfully placed Lowell, which by 1830 was looking more and more like an industrial city, within the familiar nonurban conventions of the Jeffersonian background. Comparing bucolic American scenes with crowded, old, and feudal Europe was an effective device during the early national period. Even in 1830 Everett's audience applauded and wanted to believe him, but there remained a lingering doubt.[90] Everett's bucolic imagery was becoming obsolete in the face of New England's rapid industrialization.

Nathan Appleton looked toward another aspect of the Jeffersonian legacy to quiet fears of industrialism. Saying nothing about the specific conditions at Lowell in his defense of its manufacturing establishments, Appleton drew upon the heart of the agrarian myth to point out that the existence of a vast extent of cheap land in the West made American conditions unique. "The unlimited quantity of fertile land, placed within the reach of every individual," he wrote, "is the distinguishing peculiarity of our situation, in an economical point of view." Further, this condition "will necessarily continue for one or more centuries." Because of this fundamental difference between England and America, English factory conditions will never be reproduced in the United States.[91]

The comforting, though demonstrably false, idea that the vast extent of free land would make America immune to the evils of European manufacturing cities found wide expression in antebellum America. Even the fledgling labor movement devoted as much of its energy toward influencing federal land legislation as toward the enactment of a ten-hour law in Massachusetts.[92]

A few thinkers, however—some radical transcendentalists, some not—immediately perceived that Appleton's free land argument was two-edged. If it was free land that made Lowell different from Manchester, then when the land ran out, which it must someday, would American society become like Europe? At most, said the critics, the West only postponed the day of reckoning: it "is not a corrective of the evil; it is only a fleeing of it." According to Orestes Brownson, the day of reckoning was nearer than anyone supposed. He agreed that the "proletary population" in the United States "has been and is altogether superior to what it is in any other part of the civilized world," but this is the result of the "original equality of the first settlers" and the "low price of land." These causes, he urgently pointed out, are "purely accidental, and . . . are rapidly disappearing."[93]

Ironically, Brownson and his transcendentalist friends were joined in opposition to Appleton by their great theological opponent, Andrews Norton, the conservative Unitarian. In a long personal letter to Appleton, Professor Norton argued that the existence of a vast extent of fertile land in America is accidental, temporary, and an inadequate protection against the evils of European civilization anyway. The study of history, he pointed out, shows no correlation between the extent of a country and the well-being of its people. The best protection against the mass misery that marks Europe is a system of just laws that widely diffuses political power and allows men to rise and fall according to their talents. The difference between America and Europe, is, "I believe, evidently the result of our political and civil institutions. . . . And so long as they continue, this character will continue." Appleton thanked Norton for his interest, but reaffirmed his conviction that the difference between American and English industrialism "rests substantially and fundamentally on the always available resort to the cultivation of land." The myth of a safety-valve in the West was too powerful to be refuted by rational argument. As Henry Nash Smith has observed, it "was an imaginative construction which masked poverty and industrial strife with the pleasing suggestion that a beneficent nature stronger than any human agency, the ancient resource of Americans, the power that had made the country rich and great, would solve the new problems of industrialism."[94]

Although every conceivable statistical index of industrialism and urbanization in the North shows that this Jeffersonian vocabulary was increasingly anachronistic, nearly all discussion of American industrial development during the antebellum years was carried on within its limiting framework. Industrialism won a permanent place in American culture under the aegis of this myth.

It should not be surprising, therefore, that when Thomas Hart Benton, who considered himself the last Jeffersonian in national politics, came to Lowell in 1856 he had nothing but praise for American industrialism as exemplified there. Nearly thirty years earlier, in a speech that precipitated the famous Webster-Hayne debate, Benton had accused the New England industrialists of wanting "to pauperize the poor of the North" because manufacturing establishments require "great numbers of poor people to do the work for small wages."[95] By 1856, however, Benton was ready to accept Lowell on Everett's and Appleton's terms.

Addressing a public assembly there, Benton observed that when he entered the Senate in 1823 Pawtucket Falls was known only as a fishing place where the Indians had lived for centuries. But under the command of Providence that the Indian "retire before the superior genius, industry, and civilization of the Anglo-Saxon race," massive changes had been wrought on this site. After lying unproductive over the centuries, these falls "under the hand of civilization made Lowell what it now is."

Before his address, Benton had toured the mills, and he later praised the "perfection of their machinery." Like all previous commentators on Lowell, however, Benton was most interested in the moral and social condition of the factory operatives. In 1830, when conditions in Lowell were actually quite good, Benton had been harsh in his criticism. Conditions in Lowell had deteriorated badly by the 1850s, but praise for American industrialism had become a convention of political discourse. And Benton was now lavish with his praise. "Everything here is wonderful," he intoned. "All my ideas were reversed" after touring the working and living quarters of the laborers "for I had before me the picture of the operatives as they are in England, living in small, narrow, confined, uncomfortable buildings, stinted for food and clothing." Astonishingly, the Lowell operatives are "as comfortably and handsomely situated as members of Congress are in Washington city."[96]

Lowell, it seemed, had settled the question of American manufactures. Reviewing Henry A. Miles's history of Lowell in 1845, Ezra Stiles Gannett, a Boston minister, concluded that "the evidences which are here given of good order, virtuous character, and mental culture which prevail among the operatives are such as may astonish, but must convince those . . . who have been disposed to question the possibility of impressing these features on a large manufacturing community."[97] Amos A. Lawrence, speaking for the mill owners, declared that Lowell proved there was no "reason to believe . . . that the character of our people will degenerate, or their true happiness be diminished, while the wealth of our country is increased." "It remained for Lowell," the mayor of the city concurred, "to silence forever the old and oft repeated slander, that a large manufacturing population was of necessity a vicious, corrupt and depraved one."[98]

New England gradually began to regard itself as a manufacturing region.[99] Even Ralph Waldo Emerson confided to his "Journal" that it was a "sensible relief to learn that the destiny of New England is to be the manufacturing country of America." He would "no longer suffer in the cold out of morbid sympathy with the farmer."[100] However, the Quaker poet John Greenleaf Whittier best summed up New England's acceptance of industrialism. He pointed out that when the railroad cars came thundering through the Lake Country, "Wordsworth attempted to exorcise them by a sonnet." "I might possibly follow his example," Whittier observed, "and utter, in this connection, my protest against the desecration of Pawtucket Falls; and battle with objurgatory stanzas, these dams and mills . . . but on the whole considering our seven months of frost, are not cotton shirts and woolen coats still better?"[101]

In *Walden*, the book and the living experiment, Henry David Thoreau dissented: "I cannot believe that our factory system is the best mode by which men may get clothing. The condition of the operatives is becoming every day more like that of the English; and it cannot be wondered at, since, as far as I have heard or observed, the principal object is, not that mankind may be well and honestly clad, but unquestionably, that the corporations may be enriched."[102] But Thoreau's was a solitary voice. Most Americans were less fastidious about such things.

As the progress of industry more and more demonstrated its material benefits for the American people, particularly in the North, the need to defend the system diminished.[103] Nevertheless, the increasing numbers of men and women who were committed to the new economic system emerging in the urban-industrial North were sometimes stung by the anti-industrial taunts of southern critics.

Many of these northerners, in turn, challenged the South with an ideology celebrating free labor, which, of course, implied free men. Some antislavery spokesmen even began to refer to Lowell and her sister cities as monuments to free labor. Whittier, for instance, wrote that the mill girls of Lowell "demonstrate the economy of free paid labor" and the "beauty of freedom and hope-stimulated industry."[104]

By the 1860s, manufacturing had become a "normal" fact of American social and economic life, and matter-of-fact acceptance had become possible. Writing during the Civil War, Samuel Batchelder, who had headed early textile factories in Lowell and Saco, Maine, declared that "the history of the *introduction* of the cotton manufacture may almost be considered a history *completed*."[105] By the end of the war, justification seemed unnecessary, and accounts of industrial cities were no longer justificatory in content and tone.[106]

Americans increasingly recognized that the factory system was shaping their civilization. The national self-image took on an industrial cast. By the middle of the nineteenth century, and especially after the Civil War, the American concept of progress centered as much in manufacturing and technology as it had in agriculture during Jefferson's lifetime.[107] Whereas Jefferson had wanted to export American agricultural products to Europe, men like Abbott Lawrence envisioned exporting manufactured goods and technology to the Old World. Not Jefferson's farmer, but the "Crystal Palace" exhibition at New York City in 1853 seemed to be an appropriate symbol for the American nation.[108]

Americans were developing new images and symbols for themselves, but it is questionable as to whether they were any more prepared on the eve of the Civil War to deal with the new world of the city than Jefferson had been. Many of the strongest advocates of the new economic system failed to examine its urban dimension. Some, like Everett, portrayed American industrialism in bucolic and nonurban terms. Others, like Appleton, averted their eyes from the industrial cities they were building and celebrated western lands as an antidote for the unhappy aspects of urban-industrial civilization.[109]

If some of the major spokesmen for the dominant, nonurban

rhetoric of industrialism were not sensitive to the urban implications of the new economic system, others were. Without looking far, one finds men and women for whom the introduction of the machine production system into New England was not so uncomplicated as the conventional rhetoric suggested. For them, the logic of industrial development seemed to lead to troubling personal problems of adjustment and to disturbing urban questions. In part, the development of this alternative logic of industrialism was the result of more critical attitudes toward the machine than one finds in either Appleton or Everett. Before probing the interplay of social thought and social change at Lowell, therefore, we shall investigate those perceptions of the machine and the factory that, by the 1840s, helped direct social analysis toward a more complex understanding of urban industrialism.

III.

Men, Machines, & Factories:
Toward Urban Industrialism

[The] transition from mother and daughter power
to water and steam-power is a great one, greater
by far than many have as yet begun to conceive—
one that is to carry with it a complete revolution of
domestic life and social manners.

Horace Bushnell (1851)

METAPHORS such as "civilization of machines," or "technological society," or "machine system," so powerful and rich in complexity for the modern man, were completely alien to Jefferson's generation. The "mechanic arts" were accepted unambiguously as benefactions to the human race. Americans on the eve of the nineteenth century, in the spirit of the American Philosophical Society, praised useful knowledge for making the "arts of living . . . more easy and comfortable." Members of the American Society for the Encouragement of Domestic Manufactures considered the advancement of the mechanical arts as an index of "the progress of the human mind."[1] The machine represented an unqualified triumph of mind and civilization. As Perry Miller has observed, "never did any weird notion that the machine might someday dominate . . . men cross their minds."[2]

Yet there is no point in belaboring this failure to foresee the full implications of the machine. It is more appropriate to assess the responses of a later generation, the first Americans actually to live under urban-industrial conditions. My major point in this chapter is that a significant number of these Americans were more sensitive to the problems inherent in the machine production system than we usually give them credit for. First, however, I want briefly to point out that many cultural leaders, who, unlike Jefferson's eighteenth-century contemporaries, were familiar with urban industrialism, continued to discuss technological progress within the narrow bounds of the Jeffersonian vocabulary.[3]

For instance, the industrial transformation of New England was manifest in 1837 when Edward Everett celebrated it, in the language of an earlier generation, as an intellectual as well as an economic feat. The mind that produced the power loom and similar useful inventions, he declared, is "kindred with those which have charmed or instructed the world with the richest strains of poetry, eloquence, and philosophy." Not only a triumph of the individual mind, mechanical inventions were also a victory of civilization itself. Before the cultivation of the "useful arts," Everett pointed out, man was but a savage. "All our civilization resides in these arts," he avowed. "Mind acting through the useful arts, is the vital principle of modern civilized society."[4]

The cotton mill in particular, with its marvelously complex machinery, became a symbol of the American mind. Francis Cabot Lowell was celebrated as a culture hero, virtually an American Newton, for the practical science he displayed in inventing the power loom.[5]

Nathan Appleton, Lowell's associate, was endlessly fascinated by the newly invented machinery. He "sat by the hour, watching the beautiful movement" of the "wonderful machine" that Lowell and Moody had constructed at Waltham. Lowell's invention, Appleton told the state legislature in 1828, was an act of genius. "Seldom has a mind of so much science been turned to this subject, and never was a triumph more complete." Scientific novices such as Appleton were not the only Americans enraptured by textile machinery. Professor Benjamin Silliman, antebellum America's most prominent scientist, praised the "perfection and beauty of machinery" at Lowell. He looked with "admiration and astonishment, at the results of the application of scientific principles to matter" in the manufacture of cotton cloth. The romantic sense of pride and wonder that Americans associated with the cotton factory was expressed by Samuel Griswold Goodrich in his *Enterprise, Industry and Art of Man*. A peek inside a textile manufacturing establishment, he reported, "is certainly calculated to impress the beholder with admiring wonder." "The ponderous wheel that communicates life and activity to the whole establishment; the multitude of bands and cogs, which connect the machinery, story above story; the carding engines which seem like things of life, toiling with steadfast energy; the whirring cylinders, the twirling spindles, the clanking looms— the whole spectacle seeming to present a magic scene in which wood and iron are endowed with the dexterity of the human hand —and where complicated machinery seems to be gifted with intelligence—is surely one of the marvels of the world."[6]

In this age of progress, the machine stood ready to serve man. It would help Americans convert into useful production the natural powers of the virgin continent that had lain in waste for centuries under the untutored eyes of the Indians. With modern machinery, "the great powers of nature are brought under the control of man, which in their turn, compel inanimate and unwieldy things to work with the dexterity of thinking beings—with a rapidity far surpassing human efforts." The mind of civilized man, according to this pattern of beliefs, would make it possible to harness the powers of nature to improve the conditions of life. As Theodore Parker put it, "the brute forces of nature lie waiting man's command, and ready to serve him. At the voice of Genius, the river consents to turn his wheel, and weave and spin."[7]

Mary Shelley published *Frankenstein* in England in 1818, but Americans apparently had no premonition of her nightmare. Tench Coxe, writing in 1813, used many of the elements that would be conjured into a Frankenstein metaphor by later writers, but produced instead a benign image in his praise of machinery: "These *wonderful machines*, working as if they were *animated beings*, endowed with all the *talents* of their *inventors*, laboring *with organs that never tire*, and subject to no expense of food, or bed, or raiment, or dwelling, *may be justly considered as equivalent to an immense body of manufacturing recruits, enlisted in the service of the country*."[8] Although one might at first consider the phrase "organs that never tire" an expression of covert fear, I think that would be a mistake. Coxe has not invested the phrase with that kind of emotional power. He is only saying that the machine can work longer and harder than men. The phrase lacks the chilling sense of determinism that is motivated by latent fear.

Compare it, for instance, with the following passage from John Dix a generation later. Dix, like Coxe, supported American manufactures and is here praising the industrial establishments at Lowell in a book dedicated to Abbott Lawrence. However, his perception of the ultimately deterministic nature of machinery results in an emotionally powerful imagery that expresses covert fear. "What a terrific series of thumpings the great wheel gives as with a slow and stately movement it goes round. The workman has lifted up some planks and we see the mighty machine on its mercantile march, never accelerating nor slackening its pace; dripping as with cool perspiration."[9]

Historians have recently discovered and made much of covert expressions of fear in reference to the machine, but they have insisted that overtly negative responses to the machine in nineteenth-century America are difficult to find.[10] Actually, hostility to the machine was expressed openly in mid nineteenth-century America more frequently than they allow. It is true that in 1830, at the onset of American industrialism, the Jeffersonian equation of the machine with the liberation of man was still forcefully expressed. Timothy Walker, replying to Thomas Carlyle's criticism of "mechanical philosophy," argued that "we see not how we can avoid the conclusion, that the nation will make the greatest intellectual progress, in which the greatest number of labor-saving machines has been devised." [11] But this view was challenged in the middle of the nineteenth century. And after forty years of unprecedented mechanical progress, Ralph Waldo Emerson reflected in 1870 that "we must look deeper for our salvation." Our machines "have some questionable properties. They are reagents. Machinery is aggressive. If you do not use the tools, they use you. All tools are in one sense edge-tools, and dangerous." "The machine," he concluded, "unmakes the man." [12]

The generations following Emerson quickly forgot his warning as they grasped after the machine as a savior. Edward Bellamy, writing *Looking Backward* in 1888, saw the textile factories of the nineteenth century as models for his utopia. Dr. Leete explained the social and economic system in the year 2000 to Julian West:

You used to have some pretty large textile manufacturing establishments. . . . No doubt you have visited these great mills in your time, covering acres of ground, employing thousands of hands, and combining under one roof, under one control, the hundred distinct processes, between, say, the cotton bale and the bale of glossy calicoes. You have admired the vast economy of labor as of mechanical force resulting from the perfect interworking with the rest of every wheel and every hand. . . . Well now, Mr. West, the organization of the industry of the nation under a single control, so that all its processes interlock, has multiplied the total product over the utmost that could be done under the former system. [13]

How easily he melds together "every wheel and every hand"!

With the onset of the twentieth century, Henry Adams celebrated the dynamo as "a symbol of infinity." Admitting that "among the thousand symbols of ultimate energy, the dynamo was not so human as some," he insisted it was, nevertheless, "the most expressive."[14] Adams's speculations hardly affected the course of society, but as he wrote a generation of progressive reformers took up an ideology which often relied upon machine metaphors to define the good society.

During the Progressive Era, for instance, the mechanical concept of efficiency was applied to society. At this time, Samuel Haber points out, "efficient and good came closer to meaning the same thing . . . than in any other period of American history." But the uses of the machine metaphor went beyond the concept of social efficiency. The dominant image of society increasingly mirrored the total rationalization and the functional interdependence that characterized the machine. The parts of a machine, we know, have no meaning and no function outside of the mechanical system of which they are a part. Similarly, Progressive social thought tended to explain a person's meaning and function in terms of his or her contribution to the social organization. Frederick W. Taylor, whose ideas of scientific management nourished this style of thought, put the matter with uncommon bluntness: "In the past the man has been first; in the future the system must be first." Within this pattern of thought, a person becomes a person—gains his or her sense of identity and meaning—by becoming a functioning part of a larger system.[15]

Many of Emerson's contemporaries apparently sensed that even among well-meaning men and women the machine might eventually replace man as a standard of value in America. They tried to warn the nation that the machine was not an unqualified good. They knew, as Lewis Mumford has recently reminded us, that there are two aspects to the machine: "one negative, coercive, and too often destructive; the other positive, life-promoting, constructive." And the second characteristic cannot readily function unless the first is in some degree present.[16]

The modern factory and the social system of the industrial city exposed the negative and coercive aspects of the machine system. By the 1850s, some Americans began to wonder whether the machine might indeed become man's master. With this concern, Henry David Thoreau conducted his experiment at Walden. And

Herman Melville, in his short story "The Tartarus of Maids," directed his attention specifically toward the factory system emerging in New England. His powerful indictment of the new economic order described a New England paper mill:

Machinery–that vaunted slave of humanity–here stood menially served by humans, who served mutely and cringingly as the slave serves the Sultan. The girls did not so much seem accessory wheels to the general machinery as mere cogs to the wheels. . . . Something of awe now stole over me, as I gazed upon this inflexible iron animal. Always, more or less, machinery of this ponderous, elaborate sort strikes, in some moods, strange dread into the human heart, as some living, panting Behemoth might. But what made the thing I saw so specially terrible to me was the metallic necessity, the unbudging fatality which governed it.[17]

Many similar passages could be culled from Melville. Yet it might be argued that he stands as an exception to the general American response to industrialism.[18] His attitude unquestionably represents a minority position; the machine and those who uncritically embraced it were ultimately victorious in American culture. But historians have unwarrantably ignored the losers. Admitting that the most sensitive literary men and artists perceived the potentially dehumanizing effect of the machine, they imply that the remainder of America, the masses, regarded technology as an unqualified triumph.[19]

Historical myopia, not research, led them to this conclusion. Frederick Law Olmsted pointed out the cause of this partial blindness over a century ago. "Men of literary taste," he wrote, "are always apt to overlook the working-classes, and to confine the records they make of their own times, in a great degree, to the habits and fortunes of their own associates, or to those of people of superior rank to themselves, of whose sayings and doings their vanity, as well as their curiosity, leads them most carefully to inform themselves." The "dumb masses" have been "lost in this shadow of egotism."[20]

The early factory operatives of New England, who edited their own literary magazines, were, however, uniquely articulate. We can therefore penetrate the shadow and learn their feelings about the emerging technology as they struggled to adjust to the demands of the machine and the mechanistic organization of society in the industrial city. Because the feeling was so immediate to them, the common men and women who came from the country to work in the new factories often produced moving documents describing the agony of this adjustment.

Lucy Larcom, a mill worker who went on to become a minor New England poet, provides an example in her retrospective description of the machine she tended as a young woman. The machine, she recalled, "seemed to me as unmanageable as an overgrown spoilt child. It had to be watched in a dozen directions every minute, and even then," she lamented, "it was always getting itself and me into trouble." The machine haunted her. "I felt as if the half-live creature, with its great, groaning joints and whizzing fan, was aware of my incapacity to manage it, and had a fiendish spite against me. I contracted an unconquerable dislike to it." This experience drove her to a crushing admission that she expressed with compelling directness: "And this machine finally conquered me. It was humiliating." [21]

The working classes perceived that the machine system had a dangerously coercive potential that could ultimately deprive them of their human qualities. Tools and machines are not the same thing, and the New England factory operatives gradually realized the consequences of this crucial fact. The tool lends itself to manipulation by the worker; the machine is characterized by automatic action. The machine therefore has a functional imperative of its own, and man's relationship to it is shaped, to a degree, by this circumstance. [22]

The machine is thus more than labor-saving; it becomes lifeshaping. The physical aspects of labor become less important than the psychic consequences of the worker's passive relationship to a mechanical production system, particularly under conditions of extreme division of labor. Albert Brisbane made this point in 1846. "In other kinds of industry," he told an audience of workingmen and women in Lowell, "the laborer uses the tools. In the factory, the machines, the tools, command the service of the laborer, demand his constant attention. He must be the ceaseless, servile waiter of an untiring despot of iron and brass; a tyrant that has no heart to feel, no soul to pity."[23]

The working people in New England's factories, entwined in the new method of production, felt threatened by "systems" of production that seemed to force man to sacrifice everything that raises him above a brute "and makes him a MAN." And they were implored by labor leaders to "sit down and seriously reflect upon this subject, before the monster power becomes too unwieldy, so that you are unable to check its destructive operations."[24]

This critical attitude toward machine production, which emerged in the late-1830s, articulated a fear that the influence of the factory system was "brutalizing." Critics argued that the operatives are "mere automaton appendage[s] of machinery, and in the course of time lose almost all that is valuable in moral, intellectual and social character."[25]

Again and again one finds expressions of a fear that the machine system of production will ultimately turn human beings into machines. John Greenleaf Whittier, for example, wrote in 1845: "I grow weary of seeing man and mechanism reduced to a common level, moved by the same impulse." The pages of the *Voice of Industry*, a New England labor newspaper, bristle with similar comments. A letter to the editor declared that operatives in the textile mills "are themselves animated machines, who watch the movements and assist the operations of a highly material force, which toils with an energy, ever unconscious of fatigue, a power requiring neither food nor rest." Another writer complained that "we are regarded as living machines." The "force of habit" imposed upon the working people of Lowell by the industrial system, the *Vox Populi* editorialized, has the effect of changing "a human being to a *mere thing*–a piece of machinery."[26]

In 1848 a mill girl felt compelled to declare that the operatives were not "merely automata, moving to and fro," that they were real "living beings" who bear "hopes of every degree" and "fears of every shade." Three years earlier, Whittier had been similarly moved to affirm the humanity and dignity of the operative. "The mind of the humblest worker in these mills is of infinitely more consequence" in the sight of God "than all the iron-armed and steam breathed engines of mechanism."[27]

The industrial city represented a new style of life. Adjustment to its demands was not easy. There were, however, mitigating circumstances in New England. American farmers, for instance, were more closely attuned to urban culture than were their peasant counterparts in Europe. As early as 1814 Mathew Carey had pointed out that the yeomanry of the United States, and especially of New England, had "a greater degree of genuine native urbanity . . . [than] the yeomanry of any country under the canopy of heaven."[28] There were also rural survivals in the New England industrial cities that eased the transition.[29] The boardinghouses in Lowell, for example, served as an effective adaptive mechanism. It was not accidental that the girls called their landlady "mother" and their boardinghouse group a "family."[30] Indeed, kinship and village connections usually determined what boardinghouse a new girl chose upon arrival in Lowell. She attempted to get a place in the same house in which a cousin, a sister, or a neighbor from her rural village lived.[31] The boardinghouse served as a functional equivalent of the rural family, as a protector from the complex demands of the industrial city. Instead of being overwhelmed by the city, rural migrants were able to adjust and in time to take advantage of its assets.

Many even came to like the city. When Lucy Larcom left Lowell to take up residence in Illinois with a sister, she wrote a poem of farewell:

> Farewell! thou busy city,
>   Amid whose changing throng
> I've passed a pleasant sojourn,
>   Though wearisome and long.
> My soul is sad at leaving
>   The dear ones, not a few,
> I've met within thy mazes,
>   So noble and so true.

She had found the city "a widening of life."[32] The liberating potential of city life was such that several of the female mill workers later became active in the women's rights movement; one, Harriet Hanson Robinson, became an influential leader.

If there were new freedoms in the industrial city, there were also new and unfamiliar forms of coercion. Time, for instance, was measured differently and with more precision in the city than in the country. Life on New England farmsteads, Emerson once wrote, was "timed to Nature, and not to city watches."[33] The farm girls who streamed into the New England industrial cities were unused to the tyranny of the clock with its artificial division of time. George S. White, the first biographer of Samuel Slater, presented to the age of Jackson a highly romantic picture of the "merry notes of the [factory] bell mingling with the sounds of our waterfalls." But the mill operatives found nothing "merry" in the bell that called them daily "to their work before Nature's luminary furnish[ed] them with its necessary light." We, who are so thoroughly accustomed to it that clocktime seems a fact of nature, can hardly appreciate the agony of their adjustment to the "all powerful mandate of the factory bell."[34]

In 1846 Albert Brisbane wrote an article in the *Harbinger*, journal of the Brook Farmers, condemning the "monotonous mode of life" characteristic of factory operatives. Not long after this, Melville penned his devastating attack on factory routine: "At rows of blank-looking counters sat rows of blank-looking girls, with blank, white folders in their blank hands, all blankly folding blank paper."[35]

While Melville was highly sensitive to the psychology of factory routine, industrial promoters typically were conscious only of the outward aspects of the machine production system. The Boston associates, for example, were often genuinely concerned with the physical well-being of their employees, but one looks in vain for evidence that they appreciated the larger psychological issues implicit in man's relationship to machines. They were also concerned with the public life of the workers and provided churches, schools, and literary societies that would allow and support its institutional manifestation. Yet they had no conception of the emerging romantic idea of "self-expression" that affected writers like Melville and, in a less sophisticated way, the factory operatives whose daily lives seemed to offer no opportunity for such expression.[36]

Medical authorities were no more able to grasp the inner feelings of the operatives. Dr. Elisha Bartlett, in a study of the "moral, intellectual, and physical condition" of Lowell's operatives, concluded that the "*manufacturing population of this city is the healthiest portion of the population.*" He attributed this to the regularity of their habits, which presumably conformed to some general law of health. "Their fare," he wrote, "is plain, substantial, and good, and their labor is sufficiently active and sufficiently light to avoid the evils arising from the two extremes of indolence and over-exertion. They are but little exposed to sudden vicissitudes and to the excessive heats or colds of the seasons, and they are generally free from anxious and depressing cares." The bland routine that had so irked Melville became, for Bartlett, a positive life-shaping force. The particular psychological consequences that concerned Melville were beyond the limits of Bartlett's professional imagination. While the modern reader may find Melville's perspective more convincing, the apologists for industrialism quoted Bartlett's analysis.[37]

Many of the female operatives who supposedly benefited from the strict regimen described by Bartlett were, in fact, disturbed by the pattern of life he praised. It seemed to elevate them to the level of the machines they tended. Their human uniqueness, their sense of personal autonomy seemed threatened. The external regulation of their lives under the factory system especially distressed them. When a mill girl "shall take her exercise, in what modes, in what places," one complained, "are not with her matters of choice and rejection. She must eat when the iron tongue bids her, or not at all. She must take her outdoor exercise then, or not at all, whatever may be her inclination or the requirements of her individual system."[38]

"Industrial discipline" constituted a new and unfamiliar form of authority.[39] Sometimes critics used a traditional vocabulary to describe this "boundless and detestable power over labor." It was, they said, a new feudalism, an "industrial feudalism."[40] Often, however, their language has a modern ring. As many have done in our own time, they turned "machine" into a complex metaphor signifying nonorganic forms of authority and the regimented social organization emerging in the industrial city. Albert Brisbane warned that the industrial system will make laborers "but parts of the machines which they ply, or *dependents* and *tools* of the executives who employ them."[41]

Workers often found a specific symbol for the new society in the factory bell. "The corporations, in order to drill it into the wearied heads of the operatives ... how completely every instant of time is at *their* control, ring their bells every hour in the night." A mill worker wrote in the *Lowell Offering:* "I am going home, where I shall not be obliged to rise so early in the morning, nor be dragged about by the ringing of a bell, nor confined in a close noisy room from morning till night. I will not stay here." Admitting that Lowell had schools, lectures, and meetings of every description for moral and intellectual improvement not available to the farmer, she insisted that still the farmer did not have to respond to the "bell, with its everlasting ding-dong." "Up before day, at the clang of the bell–and out of the mill by the clang of the bell–into the mill, and at work in obedience to that ding-dong of a bell–just as though we were so many living machines." Yet the young woman who wrote these anguished lines did stay in the factory: she had to work, and factory wages were about as high as a woman could expect to earn in 1840.[42]

During the Jacksonian period, we begin to find fulminations against the "soulless corporation."[43] More often than not, however, these expressions looked backward to a Puritan world of personal accountability rather than forward to a modern critique of bureaucratic organization. The meaning of the epithet is revealed in an alternative version: "soulless conscienceless corporations." A generation raised on ideals of personal accountability in private and public affairs found it difficult to adjust to an economic system where the corporate form removed "personal responsibility to conscience."[44]

For Everett and those of his generation who were concerned with outward appearances and who acknowledged only discrete evils, the manufacturing *system* established in New England presented no challenge to American social and political institutions. Others, however, began to see important general social implications in the machine production system.

It was Alexis de Tocqueville who first used an idiom appropriate to industrial society in advising Americans that large manufacturing establishments with a strict division of labor "may possibly ... bring men back to aristocracy." Going beyond other critics of industrialism during the period, he specifically linked the mechanization of work in the industrial city to the problem of a democratic community.

The workman in a modern factory, he reflected, is constantly engaged in a single productive operation. He does his work with "singular dexterity; but at the same time he loses the general faculty of applying his mind to the direction of the work." It may be said that "in proportion as the workman improves, the man is degraded." Under these conditions, the workman "no longer belongs to himself, but to the calling that he has chosen." He is reduced to the level of a machine. Democratic laws and customs opening "a thousand different paths to fortune" cannot overcome "a theory of manufactures" that "binds him to a craft, and frequently to a spot, which he cannot leave."

While it degrades the workman, the modern factory system simultaneously "raises the class of masters." The differences between the master and the workmen "increase every day." The one "resembles more and more the administrator of a vast empire," the other "a brute." And unlike the aristocracies of Europe, these manufacturing aristocrats "have no feelings or purposes, no traditions or hopes, in common." The old territorial aristocracy felt bound (by law or usage) to take care of the poor in their neighborhood. With the new aristocracy, however, "there is no real bond between them and the poor." The business aristocracy "rarely settles in the midst of the manufacturing population which it directs." The new aristocracy "first impoverishes and debases the men who serve it and then abandons them to be supported by the charity of the public." Real association between the master and workman is lacking. "The manufacturer asks nothing of the workman but his labor; the workman expects nothing from him but his wages."

The result of this newly emerging industrial system, Tocqueville warned, could be the destruction of the social equality that makes democracy in America possible. "The friends of democracy," he concluded, "should keep their eyes anxiously fixed in this direction; for if ever a permanent inequality of conditions and aristocracy again penetrates into the world, it may be predicted that this is the gate by which they will enter."[45]

Blanchard Fosgate, an Auburn, New York, physician, claimed

in 1843 that "the present system of manufacturing, is adverse to our social and political institutions." In an analysis that closely followed Tocqueville's argument, Fosgate declared that the extreme division of labor in America's factories was "brutalizing" the workingman "by transforming human beings into machines. While the thoughts and desires of the workingman were being increasingly "restrained within . . . narrow limits," capitalists were becoming a distinct class at the top of the body politic.

The degradation of the worker, he further asserted, has been facilitated by the movement of factories from "*naturally* healthy locations . . . in unsettled parts of the country . . . to densely-populated cities, less salubrious, but affording greater facilities for procuring workmen." And Lowell, which has been "held up as an argument, to refute all the physical and intellectual injuries imputed to the system," is not immune to the malevolent influences inherent in the industrial system. Challenging the apologists of Lowell, Fosgate pointed out that it was too early to evaluate the significance of the textile city on the Merrimack. It has been only twenty years since the first factory was erected there. The effects of factory labor will not be known until a full generation passes. Lowell's population has so far derived entirely from the "healthy, moral and energetic sons of New England. . . . Not until the manufactories of Lowell shall be supplied with a progeny of the operative . . . can they be justly used as an argument against the depressing tendency of the whole system."[46]

Factories in the forest, drawing their help from the country, might be accommodated into the Jeffersonian vision, but an industrial city with a proletarian population could not. And Fosgate, by raising the question of generations of factory operatives, exposed precisely this disturbing development. Machines and factories in America could no longer be discussed without considering the problem of urbanism.

In 1793, when Jefferson learned of Eli Whitney's cotton gin, he told the inventor that he anticipated the gin would be a great aid to "*household* manufactures."[47] In 1812, as Francis Cabot Lowell set out to reinvent the power loom, Jefferson, who had one hundred spindles in operation on his plantation to make cloth for his "family," predicted that the textile machinery being developed in the

United States would lead to "small scale" manufacturing as opposed to "company establishments . . . in the towns."[48] Three decades of technological and economic development proved Jefferson wrong. If the social pattern of the early factory village had represented a mere extension of rural society, the newer manufacturing centers pointed toward industrial urbanism. The operatives drawn to places like Lowell were becoming urban residents instead of returning to the country, and they were raising their children in the city.

A watershed in American history had been crossed. "This transition from mother and daughter power to water and steam power," Horace Bushnell remarked in 1851, "is a great one, greater by far than many have as yet begun to conceive—one that is to carry with it a complete revolution of domestic life and social manners."[49] The transition brought urban industrialism. And as both the agony and the possibilities of this transformation were impressed upon Americans, they gradually abandoned agrarianism in favor of an urban point of view.

IV.

Urban Industrialism & the American Landscape: Lowell

Here and there stood a solitary house—the little
country hamlet at the falls formed a striking picture
of rural loveliness. . . . Look at the extraordinary
transformation effected in the quarter of a century.
The spirit of speculation waved its wand,
powerful in its magic, over the scene, and ere a
generation passed away, each trace of rural beauty
and simplicity had vanished—the current of the
Merrimack was diverted from its channel and
metamorphosed into a mighty commercial agent.—
The genius of mechanism assumed the sway—vast
edifices sprung up like exhalations in every
direction—rows of dwellings gradually gathered
together—order rose from chaos—the form
and impress of a city made itself visible—increasing
multitudes thronged the thoroughfares . . . and lo
and behold! a city was there in all its din and
turmoil, and ever-increasing agitation.

Lowell Courier (1842)

THE EVENTUAL ACCEPTANCE of urban industrialism implied a redefinition of the American landscape. Earlier American cities had been easily comprehended within the Jeffersonian vision of a rural republic largely because they were all seaports clinging to the edge of a vast continent. Owing to their gradual and fairly orderly rate of growth, they did not seem to threaten the dominant agrarian national self-image. Likewise, the first factories had been associated with rural rather than urban life. In the second quarter of the nineteenth-century, however, industrialism and urbanism became linked, and cities multiplied across the landscape. With their powerful and expansive economies, they grew at unprecedented rates. This urban and industrial growth shattered earlier images of the American environment. What definition would Americans give to the new relationship between cityscape and landscape? How would people moving into the city adapt to their growing separation from the green fields of their former rural homes?

If, as Asa Briggs observes, "every age has its shock city," a city with such a prophetic impact upon its culture that it challenges observers to develop a new vocabulary to describe it, then we might consider Lowell, Massachusetts, the "shock city" of the Jacksonian Era.[1] The transformation that urban industrialism brought to the New England landscape was first impressed upon the American mind by the example of the explosive growth that occurred there. An investigation of changing environmental perceptions at Lowell promises to illuminate the dynamics of this problem of redefinition and adaptation.

At first, it seemed that the factory villages being established in New England could be blended into the dominant rural image of the nation. Timothy Dwight, president of Yale College and Jefferson's antagonist, shared the Virginian's belief that the meaning of American history lay in the "conversion of an immense wilderness into a fruitful field."[2] This bucolic conception of the American landscape did not, however, rule out factories. Dwight was quite comfortable using this pastoral vocabulary to describe the "scenery" at Humphreysville as "delightfully romantic." "The Fall is a fine object," and "the river, the buildings belonging to the institution [the factory], the bordering hills, farms, and houses, groves and forests, united form a landscape, in a high degree interesting."[3] Just as the art of the cultivator combined with nature to turn the wilderness into a fruitful field, so the introduction of the factory into the forest produced, figuratively, a united, harmonious, garden scene.

For a generation after Dwight, Americans tended to discuss industrial development within the nonurban context he used. A new vocabulary that admitted the urbanity of the place was not developed at Lowell until around 1840. As urban growth forced Lowell out of the interpretative framework that blended art and nature together to the enhancement of both, a vision of city and country as distinct but abutting each other emerged. By mid-century, cityscape and landscape were treated as counterpoints.

In 1825 the editor of the *Essex Gazette* traveled up the Merrimack River from Salem to view the new manufacturing city that had such "immense prospects of increasing extent and boundless wealth." He used pastoral imagery to contrast the barrenness of the wilderness before the introduction of the machine with the plenty that followed. It "reminds us of a Russian spring which starts, as it were, from the silence and desolation of winter into all the luxuriance and life and motion of summer." His metaphors emphasized the harmony and blending together of the factories with the natural landscape at Lowell (then still called East Chelmsford). "The roar of the water falls is intermingled with the hum and buz [*sic*] of the machinery." "Sometimes," he observed, the machinery "would raise its voice above the roar of the waters and then die away and be lost and mingled with them in harmony. It seemed to be a song of triumph and exultation at the successful union of nature with the art of man, in order to make her contribute to the wants and happiness of the human family."[4]

Three years earlier, in 1822, a group of local promoters had drawn up a prospectus with which they sought to attract investors who would establish more factories on the banks of the Concord and Merrimack rivers. The prospectus devoted as much space to landscape description as to what we would call hard economic issues.

Part of the writer's appeal to the landscape should be familiar to us: he is advising investors to consider projects in "beautiful situations" because people are more willing to live and work in such places. But more than this is involved. A defensive animus shapes his whole discussion of the landscape. He appears self-conscious and uncomfortable about having factories intrude upon the landscape.

This concern should not surprise us. Early American industrial development was more than a simple economic problem: it involved the whole meaning of America–and this ideological debate was often phrased in terms of the American landscape. Thus the prospectus repeatedly tells the reader that the existing factories enhance the natural beauty of the site. The "manufacturing works" are "interspersed with groves and woodlands," and they "form a handsome village." In combination with the various elements of the landscape, they "afford a prospect at once sublime and beautiful." It all forms "as delightful a landscape as can well be imagined."

As a promoter, however, the writer of the prospectus was more interested in prospective growth than in what had already been achieved at the site. This raises a further question. Does the prospect of continued growth strain the pastoral vision? He assures us that it does not. The works of the Merrimack Manufacturing Company "make a handsome appearance at present; but when the works are completed they must exhibit a noble prospect." And again, "the beauties of the views cannot be obstructed or diminished by the town which may, and in all probability will grow up in consequence of these manufacturing establishments. . . . [This development] may rather be supposed to add to the beauties of the scenery."[5]

The passage of time multiplied the difficulties inherent in this stance toward development. Nearly a decade later, Edward Everett, in a Fourth of July oration at Lowell, considered the impact of industrialism upon the American landscape from the same perspective. He relied upon a bucolic imagery to assuage popular fears of urban industrialism. It was a difficult task then; very soon it would be an impossible one.

Everett reminded agrarian critics of American industrialism that the uncultivated wilderness was unproductive. And before the factories were built, he declared, Lowell was such a wilderness. Although available evidence indicates that the farmers and artisans living and working at the preindustrial site of Lowell were quite prosperous,[6] Everett portrayed them as being impoverished, so that he might accommodate the factories established there within the context of early American beliefs about the landscape. Everett asked his listeners to "contrast the condition of the villages in the neighborhood of Lowell with what it was ten or twelve years ago, when Lowell itself consisted of two or three quite unproductive farms. It is the contrast of production with barrenness; of cultivation with waste." The bountiful Merrimack River, he added, was only an "unprofitable murmur" until "practical science and wisely applied capital" converted it into a source of growth and progress.[7] By stressing the pastoral image of Lowell, Everett ultimately denied that it was a city at all.[8]

Even as Everett spoke in 1830, the realities of urban expansion in Lowell were on the threshold of turning his image of Lowell into an anachronism. The first clear signs of urbanism there were perceived during the years immediately following 1830. Writing in 1856 Charles Cowley observed that "in 1830 . . . the once rural hamlet began to wear a decidedly urban aspect." Dr. John O. Green, who arrived in Lowell and commenced practice in 1822, is less precise. He dates Lowell's shift from a "rural community" to a "city" in a social as well as a political sense, sometime between 1826 and 1836. Visiting Lowell in 1834, Michel Chevalier wrote: "Here are all the edifices of a flourishing town in the Old World."[9]

By 1835 an anonymous writer, possibly Freeman Hunt, suggested in the *American Magazine of Useful and Entertaining Knowledge* that the industrial city on the Merrimack River had outgrown the middle landscape imagery. He wrote that "the spirit of enterprise and improvement came, and its touch, like that of the magic wand, has turned this seeming wilderness, not simply into a fruitful field, but into a busy, enterprising and prosperous city."[10] The transformation was tacitly admitted by Lowellians in the following year when the town form of government was abandoned in favor of a city charter. By the mid-1840s, when Lowell boasted thirty-three mills, extensive steam power, and a population of nearly thirty thousand persons, there could hardly be any doubt of its urbanism.

A comparison of two editions, fifteen years apart, of Theodore Dwight's travel book, *The Northern Traveller*, reveals the emerging sensibility to these changes. Dwight's description of Lowell in the 1826 edition merely noted its factories and pointed out that it "is one of the principal manufacturing places in the United States." In the edition of 1841, however, he felt compelled to add that "the place now presents the aspect of a large and busy town." Clearly an industrial city by the 1840s, Lowell was sharply distinguished from a factory village in the country. Lowell's urban image is reflected in an editorial printed in the *Voice of Industry*, a labor newspaper established in Fitchburg, Massachusetts, but now moved to Lowell. "Instead of the picturesque hills, and white cottages of Fitchburg, we find ourself among the massive walls and smoking factories of the 'City of Spindles.' "[11]

The passage of time in rapidly developing New England exposed the rather obvious limits of the Jeffersonian pastoral imagery. In the 1830s and 1840s Lowell was a city, not a "middle landscape"– or nature improved by a modest intrusion of man and the machine. Historians, particularly Leo Marx and John William Ward, have criticized the "middle landscape" ideal as being too static to accommodate urbanization and industrialization.[12] Their criticism is valid, but they overlook the landscape imagery that emerged around mid-century in response to these social changes. Close investigation reveals that important, if subtle, shifts in the mid-century approach to the landscape better enabled urban dwellers to cope with the transformation of their environment.

A wide range of contemporary sources reveal that urbanization was overwhelming the arcadian image of Lowell in the 1840s. As early as 1834, in an anonymous newspaper poem entitled "Lowell," the feeling was expressed that the intrusion of the machine into nature brought not improvement, but annihilation. The writer claimed that in former years he enjoyed sitting on the banks of the Merrimack River "When the sun went down for a night's repose, ... And the nightingale's song on the hill arose." But such pleasures were no more:

> And a few years pass'd, and the forest dark
> Was turned to a full business city quite;
> And the nightingale's song, and the note of the lark
> Were heard no more—nor the beautiful sound
> That sung in the grass of the meadow ground;
> And the pale lamp lighted the lonesome night.

A newspaper editorial a year later complained that the "march of improvement is as destructive in its course, of everything verdant in nature, as the passage of an army of locusts over a field of grain."[13]

Concern over the course of change increased during the 1840s. Industrialization and urbanization seemed to mean the destruction of the natural landscape rather than its enhancement. A poem contributed by A. R. A. of Lowell to the *Literary Repository* in 1840 expressed reservations about yoking "the nameless blessing nature gives . . . with cunning art."[14] And in 1841, a young woman employed in the mills penned this couplet: "Who hath not sought some sylvan spot/ Where art, the spoiler, ventures not."[15] Now art's relation to nature is that of a cunning spoiler. How different from Everett's praise of using art to place the "unprofitable murmur" of the Merrimack River at the service of man.

Harriet Farley, writing over the pseudonym of "Ella," published a story in the *Lowell Offering* that artlessly and poignantly describes the crushing effect of progress upon the middle landscape ideal. The story is an account of the changing view from her window. She opens with praise for the middle landscape image: "I had a lovely view from my window. . . ; it was neither city nor country exclusively, but a combination of both." It "was like a beautiful picture." The window provided constant pleasure and instruction, but one day "my window told me that there was to be laid the foundation of a mighty structure." When the foundation was completed, "the walls [were] commenced." Boats came up the river laden with brick, "and huge piles arose upon its banks. The red walls arose—red, the color of the conqueror—and they proclaimed a victory over my pleasures." With one story completed, the pleasant dwellings were "screened from me" and the "early sunrise was gone." But "I clung more fervently" to the views that were left –"the more tenaciously as I saw them departing." "Then I began to measure . . . and to calculate how long I would retain this or that beauty." I hoped that the "brow of the hill" would remain when the structure was complete. "But no! I had not calculated wisely." It "began to recede from me—for the building rose still higher and higher." Will anything be left? "One hope after another is gone . . . one image after another, that has been beautiful to our eye, and dear to our heart has forever disappeared." "How has the scene changed! How is our window darkened!"[16]

About the time Harriet Farley wrote this story, her friend Harriet Hanson revealed a similar concern for the future of the natural landscape when she marked these lines in her copy of Sir E. L. Bulwer's *The Pilgrims of the Rhine:* "The wheels of commerce, the din of trade, have silenced to mortal ear the music of thy subjects' harps. And the noisy habitations of men, harsher than their dreaming sires, are gathering round the dell and vale where thy comates linger;—a few years, and where will be the green solitudes of England."[17] These demonstrations of concern by Harriet Farley, Harriet Hanson, and their anonymous predecessors reveal the degree to which urban Americans, even relatively unsophisticated ones, were beginning to recognize the inadequacy of the pastoralism that envisioned America as steering a middle course, blurring art and nature together.

The urban generation of the 1840s sought new approaches to the landscape that honestly reflected their urban experiences while also satisfying powerful yearnings to preserve a link with their rural past. Mid-century Lowellians, and Americans in general, abandoned the factory-in-the-forest imagery and began to visualize the cityscape and natural landscape in close proximity, but clearly demarcated. Cities would be granted their essential urbanity, but easy occasional access to nature would be sought for and by the urbanite. Instead of a continuous middle landscape, America would be defined as a counterpoint of art and nature, city and country.[18]

This reinterpretation of the landscape is reflected in surviving views of early Lowell. Benjamin Mather's painting of Lowell, done in 1825, places the city within the context of the middle landscape. There is no clear distinction between cityscape and landscape. The buildings are partially blocked by artfully placed trees, and they are in general subordinated to the natural features that dominate the

painting (Plate 1). E. A. Farrar's view of Lowell from across the
river at Dracut in 1833 shows the emerging division between city
and country. The dominant feature of the engraving, however,
seems to be the thrust of the pastoral scenery toward the city and
the consequent weakening of the distinction between the natural
and artificial (Plate 2). The separation of cityscape and landscape
is revealed in John Warner Barber's engraving of Lowell in 1839.
Once again, the river serves to set the city off from nature, but in
this view it is the division rather than the effort to bridge it that
dominates. The stark architectural features of the cityscape are
shown in marked contrast to the pastoral elements in the foreground (Plate 3). Barber's use of shading in this engraving to
accent the distinction between city and country fits the conventions
of antebellum aesthetic theory. Urban artificiality was often con-
veyed by whiteness, and nature was usually associated with darkness or muted tones.[19] Finally, a view of Lowell in 1845 shows the
complete separation of cityscape and landscape. The compact city
is encircled by the natural landscape (Plate 4).

A curious cultural phenomenon of mid nineteenth-century
America, the rural cemetery movement, provides further insight
into the new understanding of cityscape and landscape.[20] Literally
a misnomer, "rural cemetery" denoted a burial ground that was
located on the outskirts of a city and that was designed according
to the romantic conventions of English landscape gardening. Although historians have noted the development of these cemeteries,
they have ignored their ideological background and their place in
the emerging urban culture.[21]

John W. Reps, in his history of American city planning, expresses
surprise that the cemeteries were used more as pleasure grounds
than for burial places, and he concludes that this "must have as-
tounded and perhaps horrified their sponsors."[22] On the contrary,
they were neither surprised nor outraged. A visit to the local cemetery was considered *de rigueur* for the tourist, and the popular
press carried numerous articles on these romantic burial grounds.
Guidebooks were published for the cemeteries, and many accounts
and engravings depict middle-class families resorting to these park-
like cemeteries, empty or nearly empty of graves for many years, as
pleasure grounds. America's rural cemeteries were explicitly de-

signed both for the living and for the dead, and the assumptions underlying their widespread popularity were central to mid nineteenth-century ideas about the relationship of cityscape and landscape in an urbanizing society.

America's first rural cemetery was Mount Auburn, outside Boston. Dr. Jacob Bigelow was the driving force behind its establishment, and many of Boston's elite supported the five-year campaign which culminated with the opening of Mount Auburn in 1831. Bigelow's motives are not entirely clear. His familiarity with European medical literature probably alerted him to the potential public health menace of cemeteries in the center of densely populated cities. He was undoubtedly also moved by a traditional desire to express respect for the dead through an appropriately serene burial site.[23]

Whatever Bigelow's motives, the consecration addresses and other commentary on the cemeteries reveal that rural cemeteries were intended to offer far more than resting places for the dead. Mount Auburn and its imitators were expected, from the beginning, to serve the needs of the living. A month after the consecration of Mount Auburn, Henry Bellows, in his oration at the Harvard Exhibition on October 18, 1831, declared that rural cemeteries "are not for the dead. They are for the living."[24] And the *Boston Courier* predicted that Mount Auburn "will soon be a place of more general resort."[25] Writing in 1849, Andrew Jackson Downing asserted that thirty thousand persons visited Mount Auburn in a single season.[26]

Clearly, rural cemeteries had some larger significance for mid century Americans. But what is the relationship between the cemetery movement and more general changes in American society? How was the American attitude toward the rural cemetery related to thought and feeling about America's changing and increasingly urban environment?

The consecration address delivered by Joseph Story at Mount Auburn suggests the nature of these relationships. After explaining that the "magnificence of nature" in the rural cemetery would be more comforting to the mourner than the "noisy press of business" surrounding a city churchyard, Story made broader claims for the significance of Mount Auburn. "All around us," he observed, "there breathes a solemn calm, as if we were in the bosom of a wilderness."

Yet "ascend but a few steps, and what a change of scenery to surprise and delight us. . . . In the distance, the City,–at once the object
of our admiration and our love,–rears its proud eminences, its
glittering spires, its lofty towers, its graceful mansions, its curling
smoke, its crowded haunts of business and pleasure." Refining
these images of cityscape and landscape into counterpoints, Story
reflected that "there is, therefore, within our reach, every variety of
natural and artificial scenery. . . . We stand, as it were, upon the
borders of two worlds; and as the mood of our minds may be, we
may gather lessons of profound wisdom by contrasting the one with
the other." Looking at the city, Story explained, encourages us to
"indulge in the dreams and hope of ambition." The influence of
the cemetery's natural landscape, however, serves as a counterbalance: "The rivalries of the world will here drop from the heart; the
spirit of forgiveness will father new impulses; and selfishness
of avarice will be checked; the restlessness of ambition will be
rebuked."[27]

For a people who celebrated both moral virtue and material
progress, Story's address must have been reassuring. Free rein
might be given to hope and ambition because the influence of rural
cemeteries promised to keep urban commercial drives within the
bounds of propriety. Story sketched an image of cityscape and landscape that seemed to preserve rural virtues without compromising
the urbanity or material opportunities of the city. The city of the
dead would purify the city of the living.

Americans gradually began to visualize the cityscape and natural
landscape in terms of the imagery adumbrated by Story. Instead of
trying to blend city and country, they admitted the existence of
compact cities. Yet they also insisted upon easy periodic access to
nature as an essential condition of urban life. If municipal governments were not yet willing to spend public funds to establish large
parks for their citizens, Andrew Jackson Downing pointed out in
1849 that rural cemeteries, financed by subscription, might serve
the same purpose until the city governments assumed their proper
obligation.[28]

Mount Auburn's success had encouraged imitators even before
Downing offered his advice. Following the Boston example, Philadelphia established Laurel Hill Cemetery in 1836, and New York

opened Greenwood Cemetery in 1838. By 1842 New England had several rural cemeteries, including the one opened in Lowell, Massachusetts, in 1841.[29]

The leading spirit in founding Lowell's rural cemetery was Oliver M. Whipple, a self-made Lowell gunpowder manufacturer and civic leader. The Proprietors of the Lowell Cemetery were incorporated on January 23, 1841, and through Whipple's generosity a scenic forty-five-acre site on the outskirts of the city was acquired.[30]

The cemetery was laid out in the romantic style by George P. Worcester.[31] He had been influenced by the famous French cemetery Père-Lachaise, and some commentators believed that Lowell Cemetery, as well as Mount Auburn, were imitations of it. The American cemeteries had indeed imitated the French one to a certain extent, but there was an important difference in their relationship to nature. Père-Lachaise was an old garden dedicated to a new purpose when it was opened as a cemetery. Mount Auburn and Lowell cemeteries, however, were established on sites of natural beauty with the intention of conserving the original character.[32] They were to be enclaves of natural beauty adjoining the artificial urban environment.

The significance of a rural cemetery for a rapidly growing industrial city is illustrated in the Reverend Amos Blanchard's consecration address at the Lowell Cemetery on June 20, 1841. Blanchard was ordained at Lowell's First Baptist Church on December 5, 1829. The young minister undoubtedly attended Lowell's Fourth of July celebration seven months later and listened to Edward Everett define Lowell as an element in the American middle landscape. Now, ten years later, Blanchard abandoned Everett's increasingly unsatisfying perception of Lowell and gave expression to a new ideology more nearly in tune with the feelings and needs of his urban audience.[33]

Although he touched upon such expected themes as the need for a new burial place in rapidly growing Lowell and the respect that ought to be shown for the dead by making burial places beautiful, Blanchard also addressed himself to larger questions. Midway, he began to explain the role of rural cemeteries in enhancing the urban environment. The thrust of Blanchard's remarks was that America's rapidly growing cities, marked by visual monotony and social chaos, generated distress that could be assuaged through the influence of romantically designed cemeteries.

Blanchard characterized Lowell and, by implication, other American cities as "cities of strangers." Life in the city was impersonal, ever in flux, and more concerned with the next commercial opportunity than with a proper attention to the permanent roots of community life. Urban living seemed more like hotel life than the traditional community of fond memory. Blanchard and his generation were jarred by the discovery that even the bones of the dead, man's sacred link with his communal past, were not safe from the next wave of residential and industrial expansion or financial promotion. With a shudder he informed his audience that "a tomb-stone, in one of our large cities, was lately seen covered with gairish [sic] handbills, announcing schemes of business, and of the idlest of fashionable amusements and follies."[34]

The physical removal of burial places from downtown locations would reduce the opportunity for such desecration. The sources of the problem, however, were "the aspirations of vanity, and pride of distinction in place, wealth, and power," and Blanchard hoped that with a rural cemetery they would "receive an effectual rebuke." Possibly a rural cemetery would remind a society busily uprooting itself, conquering a continent, and covering it with cities that the communal past could not be entirely ignored. Blanchard also revealed his "secret wish that when death shall have torn his beloved ones from his embrace, and when [he] himself shall have died, they might repose together, where they should never be disturbed by the encroachments of a crowded and swelling population of the living." In a dynamic, expansive society, the rural cemetery could plausibly serve as a focus for the "cultivation of home attachments towards the city of our abode."[35] Six months after Blanchard's address, the *Lowell Courier* echoed this sentiment, assuring its readers that the cemetery will provide "a new and more sacred and binding tie to this city as our home."[36] In this sense, the rural cemetery movement reflected an anxious search for a sanctuary from the "go a-head" spirit of the age.

But the attraction of the rural cemetery went beyond the conflict between memory and desire in an age of progress. Blanchard explicitly linked the rural cemetery to a complex of beliefs about the landscape that was emerging in the middle of the nineteenth century in response to increasing urbanization. The key elements of this urban ideology were expressed three months before Blanchard's consecration address in a poem entitled "Alone with Nature," written by a Lowell factory worker who signed herself "Adelaide."

> Alone with nature—will not ye
> Who all her beauties daily see,
> Beneath your native, "house-hold tree,"
>   Enjoy them for the roving stranger!
> I can not relish half her sweets
> Till taught by bustling, crowded streets,
> To sigh for nature's calm retreats,
>   Then task them for the city-ranger.[37]

In the poem, and in the mid-century American mind, the city is sharply distinguished from the natural landscape, and natural beauty is more apparent and more necessary for urbanites than for rural dwellers.

As the nation became increasingly urban, city people tended to romanticize nature. Only an urban society can afford such romanticizing: in a frontier society trees are not scenic; they are potential houses. Roderick Nash argues that urban "literary gentlemen wielding a pen, not the pioneer with his axe" romanticized nature.[38] The example of "Adelaide," the pen-wielding mill girl, suggests that the urge to romanticize nature came from more than heavy draughts of Byron and Wordsworth in a New York or Concord library. An intensely felt need was causing a broad spectrum of urban dwellers, gentleman and mill girl alike, to turn to the conventions of romanticism to cope with the distressing social and visual manifestations of the emergent city.

As the urban environment became paved over, more hurried, dirtier, and uglier, a change of scenery, something reminiscent of the supposed calmness and beauty of the rural past, seemed necessary for city dwellers. A romantic landscape, a readily accessible natural sanctuary, was sought as a counterbalance to the disturbing aspects of the cityscape. This longing was at the heart of the movement to establish rural cemeteries on the outskirts of most American cities.[39] Blanchard understood this when he said that the

Lowell Cemetery is "accessible at all times, yet so remote from the marts of business as not to be liable to be encroached upon by the spreading abodes of the living: sequestered from the din and bustle of active life."[40]

Throughout his address, Blanchard endeavored to set off the solitude and romantic beauty of the rural cemetery against the bustle and aesthetic barrenness of the city. He contrasted the praiseworthy Roman custom of burials along country highways with the modern notions that until very recent times preferred the location of cemeteries "by the city church-yard, crowded, noisy, and grassless, and never visited by the dew, and sunshine, and the showers of heaven."[41]

This imagery was noted by the editor of the *Vox Populi*, Lowell's liveliest nineteenth-century newspaper. He found the passage so striking that he checked his copy of William Wordsworth's "Essay on Epitaphs," where he found remarkable parallelism, if not outright plagiarism. Continuing his investigation, he found numerous other expressions in Blanchard's address nearly identical with passages in the standard romantic authors. Although the course of the ensuing debate in the *Vox Populi* is interesting, it need not detain us. Blanchard explained the instances of parallelism by asserting that the boy who had set the type for the printed text must have omitted the quotation marks.[42] The incident has a different significance. It illustrates the manner in which social thinkers like Blanchard turned to a corpus of romantic writings, largely British, borrowed selectively from the vocabulary of romantic nature, and used it to cope with uniquely American cultural problems.[43]

Americans had been using European romantic conventions to celebrate America as nature's nation for nearly a half-century. By 1850, however, they were using them with an important difference. Formerly, they had used the language of romanticism to identify America as a rural republic, but now romantic nature and the city counterbalanced each other in the national image.[44] The American landscape was no longer visualized as of a piece. For mid-century city dwellers, there was an urban "inside" and a rural "outside." From the broad question of city life in comparison with country life, Americans turned to the problem of the relationship between cityscape and landscape. They developed a conception of city and country that seemed to allow a commitment to nature in an urban and industrial nation. Americans avoided the unpalatable choice between city and country by choosing both.

A visitor to Lowell in 1843 focused on the cemetery to describe the city within the context of this new urban vocabulary. From the city's "busy streets" he passed "through romantic woods" into the cemetery grounds where he was filled with "deep peace." "You stand as it were, beyond the world, beyond its cares, its strifes, its false, ignis fatuus hopes, and its griefs. You have entered a realm of quietude, melody and beauty." Two years later, John Greenleaf Whittier, who lived in Lowell for nearly a year as editor of an anti-slavery newspaper, expressed similar feelings about the American Manchester's rural cemetery. In contrast to the city's "crowded mills, its busy streets and teeming life," the poet found the cemetery, "hidden from view," to be "a quiet, peaceful spot." Not only the "aged and the sad of heart," but also the "young, the buoyant" relaxed under its "soothing" influence.[45] Twenty years later, J. W. Meader, in his history of the Merrimack River Valley, again portrayed the romantic cemetery as the link to America's rural past that was so necessary in an urban-industrial society. The Lowell Cemetery, he wrote, is "a symbol of the solitude, though now adorned and beautiful, which [once] covered all this realm around the fine falls of Concord, when it was invaded by the all-subduing and all-conquering Divinity of Mechanism."[46]

Meader's use of *invaded* and *all-conquering* suggests the defensive nature of the counterpoise concept as manifested in rural cemeteries and, later, parks. Initially, Americans treated the introduction of machines and factories into the forest as an enhancement of the American environment, as a sort of technological sublime. By mid-century, however, the dynamic of the machine and the industrial city's capacity to obliterate the natural landscape prompted Americans increasingly to use metaphors suggesting conquest instead of conciliation to describe the machine in the garden. Nevertheless, the new vision did not imply an attempt to roll back technology or even to prevent further progress; it was hoped only that total victory by the "wizard of mechanism" could be prevented. Mid-century Americans attempted to preserve as much of nature as was possible in a nation of cities and machines.

The counterpoise concept was quickly expanded beyond its connection with the rural cemetery, and it became the foundation of the American park movement.[47] Dr. Elisha Huntington, several times mayor of Lowell, provides an early example of a public official who recognized that the attractions of cemeteries for the living could be provided in the form of a public park. In his annual address for 1845, Huntington declared: "We have grown up to a city of twenty-six or seven thousand inhabitants, and with a fair prospect of increasing numbers;—we are being hemmed in by walls of brick and mortar, shutting out the pure air of heaven." It is possible, he observed, to walk out of the city "and seek the green shady fields on our outskirts," but too often one is met with a sign reading "No trespassers allowed." This situation demands the establishment of a "public mall or promenade" near the central part of the city. "The value of such, I will not say luxury, but such a necessary of life, as free, open public grounds, is incalculable; we cannot estimate it."[48]

In urging quick municipal action, the mayor pointed out that the proprietors of the Locks and Canal Company had decided to divest themselves of lands that would suit the city's needs. A month later the City Council responded by authorizing the purchase of the land at each end of the city where North and South Commons, parks of nine and twenty acres respectively, were subsequently established.[49] The idea of a common, going back to the seventeenth century, took on an added dimension in the mid-nineteenth century. No longer simply the physical and symbolic center of the community, the common now served as a counterbalance to the visual monotony and social routine of emerging forms of urban life. As the city continued to grow, however, these small parks were unable adequately to perform this function. Soon after the Civil War, a movement developed to establish a large park that would be for Lowell what Central Park was for New York and Prospect Park was for Brooklyn. The result was Rogers Fort Hill Park. It was surrounded by the city, but was itself laid out in a natural style "avoiding anything resembling mathematical regularity and everything suspicious of geometrical preciseness."[50]

This mid-century approach to the American landscape did not always find, nor did it always require, such institutional realization.

While Henry David Thoreau agreed with Mayor Huntington on the value and necessity of municipal parks, his account of a journey down the Concord River to its junction with the Merrimack River at Lowell in September 1839 suggests that before the age of urban sprawl the contrapuntal relationship of city and country could be appreciated even without the development of rural cemeteries and landscape parks.[51]

Rowing past Lowell with his brother, Thoreau noticed two men leaving the city. The language Thoreau used to describe the situation emphasizes the completeness with which the urban artificiality of Lowell was distinguished from the natural scenery abutting the city. The two men "had just run out of Lowell . . . and [they] . . . now found themselves in the strange, natural, uncultivated, and unsettled part of the globe . . . a rough and uncivil place to them." Thoreau–whose definition of wilderness was generous enough to comprehend both Walden, which was a mere saunter from Concord, and Mount Katahdin in Northern Maine– added that even the city's "busiest merchant" might easily find himself in a situation to experience nature.[52]

He returned to the theme of the relationship between urbanism and natural scenery in his account of the next day's journey. The wilderness, he observed, is "near as well as dear to every man." He meant "near" literally and not figuratively: cities and towns "are indebted to the border of wild wood which surrounds them. . . . There is something indescribably inspiriting and beautiful in the aspect of the forest skirting and occasionally jutting into the midst of new towns, which . . . have sprung up in their midst. . . . Our lives need the relief of such a background, where the pine flourishes, and the jay still screams."[53] Thoreau believed that man could not be happy permanently confined in either the wilderness or the city. A balance between the natural and the artificial was necessary. For an optimum existence, "one should alternate between wilderness and civilization."[54]

Visitors and residents alike shared Thoreau's image of a compact and clearly demarcated city.[55] They also recognized that the natural landscape marking the urban perimeter could make their urban experience more satisfying. Writing retrospectively of Lowell in the 1840s, Lucy Larcom recalled that "nature came very close to the mill-gates . . . in those days." The factories "were in the midst of open fields, and in sight of the tree-bordered river." While praising Lowell as a "beautiful City of Toil," she was quick to "thank God for a glimpse of the hills!"[56]

These first generation city dwellers, learning to live in a strange environment, looked to the natural landscape surrounding the city for temporary relief from the anxieties of urban life and as a link to their rural past. Whittier expressed this feeling when he described a beautiful grove of oaks on the outskirts of Lowell lifting "their sturdy stems and green branches, in close proximity to the crowded city." Whittier realized that the past could not be called back, that "neither in polemics nor in art can we go backward in an age whose motto is ever 'Onward,'" but, he implored: "Long may these oaks remain to remind us that, if there be utility in the new, there was beauty in the old."[57]

Residents of Lowell made their periodic and appreciative contact with the natural landscape in a variety of ways. Besides using the cemetery and public park, they sought nature through flights of fancy, through views from their windows, by walking out of the city (despite the no-trespassing signs complained of by Mayor Huntington), and through summer visits to the country.[58]

If the stories published in the *Lowell Offering* are any indication, dreaming of nature was a preoccupation of Lowell's working population.[59] Harriet Farley, editor of the *Lowell Offering,* was asked by a friend: Why do the factory girls write so much about the beauties of nature? She answered with another question: "Why is it that the desert-traveller looks forward upon the burning, boundless waste, and sees pictured before his aching eyes, some verdant oasis?" When you answer this, then "I will tell why the factory girl . . . thinks not of the crowded, clattering mill, nor of the noisy tenement which is her home, nor of the thronged and busy street which she may sometimes tread,–but of . . . still and lovely scenes." Whittier agreed that "in the midst of the dizzy rush of machinery" the mill girls "hear in fancy the ripple of brooks, the low of cattle, the familiar sounds of the voices of home."[60]

Other Lowellians maintained their contact with nature by observing the natural scenery within view of an upper window in their boardinghouse or at the factory. In contrast to the situation of the modern metropolis, it was relatively easy in the mid nineteenth-century city to gain a view of the natural landscape. One operative found such a spot in the factory room where she worked. "I can stand at my window, and scc the Merrimack river . . . as it moves quietly on. . . . Far across it I can see the hills and groves. . . . Then, in another direction, I can look over the busy city."[61]

Temporary escape from the city could be achieved by walking out to the surrounding greensward. "In the glad intervals of the holy Sabbath," the Reverend Uriah Clark of Lowell urged, "let not the toiling sons and daughters, whose week-day life is imprisoned within grey walls, be denied the light, the beauty and the freedom of Nature." Clark's advice evidently was often heeded. "Wearied with the dull monotony" of the city, Lydia S. Hall, a mill operative, regularly "sought relief from the flying machinery" and "walled enclosure" of Lowell by walking in the nearby woods where she beheld the "many-toned sweetness of nature's melody."[62]

The bulk of Lowell's working population during the early 1840s was made up of single girls from New England farms. The opportunity to visit the homes of their parents or relatives in the country provided them with a readier acccss to a summer vacation than was available to the immigrants who later filled America's industrial cities.[63] A visitor to Lowell in 1845 claimed that during the month of August, when the mills usually cut back because of a shortage of water power, "there is an average of one hundred [operatives] leaving the Factories daily."[64]

By 1850, however, over one-third of Lowell's total population and one-half of the operatives were foreign born.[65] Without kinship ties to the New England countryside, the newer Lowellians were unable to leave the city for summer vacations. Although letters in Lowell newspapers at mid-century suggest that some middle- and upper-middle-class Lowellians were taking summer vacations in the country, the Lowell School Committee reported in 1852 that most of the community's families were unable to travel in the summer and most children had to spend the whole summer in the city.[66] It was not until the late-nineteenth and early-twentieth centuries that the summer vacation became a mass urban custom.[67] Mid-century urban Americans were particularly concerned, therefore, to preserve the natural landscape within close proximity of the city.

The rural cemetery, the park, the landscape painting, the vacation, the rural walk, and the romantic imagination all offered the attractions of rural life without any of its liabilities: the beauty and freedom of the country without the arduous labor, the loneliness, or the cultural poverty of farm life. The young women who wrote for the *Lowell Offering* repeatedly praised nature, but they also complained bitterly that farmers' wives and daughters lacked sufficient time "for rest, recreation, and literary pursuits."[68] We are dealing here with a highly romantic conception of nature and rural life. It is an urban image of the country.

By mid-century, a new vocabulary for describing the American environment had been developed. Thoreau described New England as a series of towns and cities surrounded by nature.[69] He felt one could readily find relief from urban artificiality on the outskirts of his city. For once, Thoreau was not alone; his urban contemporaries were developing a similar perception of the relationship between cityscape and landscape. They began to visualize their environment in terms of an urban "inside" and an integrally related nonurban "outside." Moreover, they began to see in city parks, such as Boston Common, a relief from the feeling of oppression imposed by "the monotonous dominion of brick and mortar." The cityscape, or artifice generally, could be enhanced by a contrapuntal association with nature. A Bostonian writing of urban improvement declared that "nowhere is the magnificence of art more imposing than when surrounded by that of nature. It is not degraded by the contrast, it is ennobled."[70]

Instead of denying the existence of cities, Americans began to counterpoint the increasingly visible cityscape with a familiar, comforting, and easily accessible natural landscape. The newer attitude seems to have taken hold at mid-century and enjoyed success not only in Lowell and Boston, but throughout America—most notably in Frederick Law Olmsted's Central Park in New York. Within this context, the acceptance of urban culture was easier for mid-century Americans.

This new perception of the relationship of the city to the American landscape allowed Americans to reap some of the benefits of industrial urbanism, but it also implied new responsibilities. Acceptance of industrial cities also meant that Americans could no longer avert their eyes from the social problems festering in them.

V.

The Discovery of Urban Society: Lowell

A dozen years ago, it was considered all desirable
to discourage families of operatives from settling
in the city; as, in times like these, the starvation
and riots of the manufacturing towns
of the old world would be our inevitable lot.
But the families would come and must come by a
natural law. And the prophesied times have come
without a thought of disturbance or a murmur
of complaint; because of the influence of religion, the
universality of school education, and the chances
of life open to all.

Horatio Wood (1862)

THE NEW and distinctly urban social patterns that emerged in the second quarter of the nineteenth century stimulated the discovery of urban society in American social thought. Men and women became more sensitive to the urban context of their lives; they began to explore the nature of their urban communities. In their explorations of urban society, Americans were struck by the increasing visibility of poverty in their communities. In fact, most of the urban "problems" typically associated with a later period had already made their appearance in American cities well before the Civil War. Antebellum cities exhibited festering slums marked by poverty, violence, sickness, and despair. These conditions were disturbing enough in their own right, but even more serious to the new city-dweller was what they represented: the fragmentation of the traditional community.

The problem of poverty challenged accepted notions of community life and encouraged civic leaders to seek means of overcoming the "estrangement of men from men, of class from class." With a nostalgic look at the New England town tradition, men like William Ellery Channing and Joseph Tuckerman of Boston hoped that an infusion of Christian spirit into American cities would "knit" urban-dwellers together into a "common weal."

"It is the unhappiness of most large cities," Channing told a Boston audience in 1841, "that, instead of union of sympathy, they consist of different ranks, so widely separated as indeed to form different communities." The "happy community" that he urged upon his listeners is one "where human nature is held in honour, where, to rescue it from ignorance and crime, to give it an impulse towards knowledge, virtue, and happiness, is thought the chief end of the social union." Imbued with this Protestant impulse, civic leaders throughout the North turned to the related problems of poverty and community in the industrial city.[1]

Once again, Lowell provides an illuminating case study. "The factory, the railroad, and the slum," which, according to Lewis Mumford, are the main elements of the nineteenth-century industrial city, came to Lowell with the suddenness characteristic of the American boom town.[2] At the same time, however, Lowell's role as an industrial model and the attachment of Lowellians to traditional forms of New England community life quickened civic concern. Consequently, Lowell offers the historian an instance where both the impact of urban industrialism and the reform impulse were particularly intense.

The city in early nineteenth-century America, as Richard Wade has written, was before all, if not necessarily above all, an economic institution.[3] This crucial fact provides a key insight into the creation of an urban society at Lowell and in America generally. Founded as a nonurban economic enterprise, Lowell gradually evolved a complex social organization and a civic identity. Schematically stated, Lowell was transformed from a formal economic organization into an urban society.[4]

This circumstance had important implications for thought and society in Lowell. During the 1820s, the pattern of life in the new community was shaped by an amalgam of the founders' memories of traditional hierarchical communities and of their understanding of the dictates of economic organization. As Lowell developed into a full-fledged city, these formulations were abandoned and a new configuration of social thought developed. By mid-century, this new point of view was sufficiently well developed to form the basis for ameliorist reform efforts sponsored by established elements of the community.

The founders of Lowell saw their project as an investment opportunity.[5] This is hardly surprising. These men, who migrated to Boston from the North Shore after the Revolutionary War, tended to organize their lives in New England's metropolis largely around business. The older Tory Province House elite that was replaced by them had given the city cultural, religious, and political meaning, but business enterprise and economic growth were the controlling images of Boston for the new entrepreneurial elite. In their pursuit of investment opportunities, these men were associated with the speculators who transformed the face of Boston during the age of Bulfinch: they built India Wharf, organized the Broad Street Improvement Association, and scraped off the top of Beacon Hill. Although much of Boston's charm is a legacy of their projects, we must admit that their approach to the city implies a rather narrow conception of the nature and purpose of urban life.[6]

Our first industrial city was built in the same spirit. The speculative motives underlying the founding of Lowell were remarked upon by Michel Chevalier after his visit there in 1834: "It is not like one of our European towns that was built by some demi-god ... or by some hero of the Trojan war, or by the genius of an Alexander or a Caesar, or by some saint attracting crowds by his miracles, or by the whim of some great sovereign. . . . It is one of the speculations of the merchants of Boston."[7]

As originally conceived, the project at East Chelmsford undoubtedly involved merely the erection of a factory similar to the Boston Manufacturing Company at Waltham.[8] "Manufacturing establishments," not a city, were being constructed at the confluence of the Concord and Merrimack rivers. Nathan Appleton summed it up in a letter to his brother describing the project: "We are building a large machine I hope at Chelmsford."[9] The Boston associates never recognized that they were laying the foundations of a complex civic organism, a city, at Lowell. Their conception of what they were building was extremely narrow: "merely an aggregate of individuals" who lived in substantial buildings. Architectural historian John P. Coolidge observes that they "could dream only of a group of well-built factories, of a settlement of tidy cottages growing up between them, and of profits resulting from the whole."[10]

Aware of the immense water power available at Pawtucket Falls, they quickly realized that their factories would be more extensive than the Boston Manufacturing Company. Yet they never translated this perception into an urban vision. Even Patrick Tracy Jackson, who accurately predicted that Lowell would have a population of over 25,000 by 1845, always thought of Lowell as a large business venture rather than as a city. He visualized 25,000 operatives instead of a city of 25,000 citizens. Even after the town was incorporated in 1826, the distinctions between town and company, citizen and employee, were seriously blurred in Jackson's mind. Town policy was merely an extension of company policy. Of course, since the Lowell corporations had the economic power to dominate any community, Jackson and his partners might be expected to attempt it. But there is a great difference between assuming an identity of town and company, as Jackson did, and conceiving of a complete community dominated by industrial corporations.[11]

The basic plan devised by Kirk Boott, who was hired to plan and supervise the construction of the project, suggests that he understood his task to be the laying out of a business enterprise. He simply plotted out the site in halves or zones: one for the corporation, and one for the bourgeoisie. The dominant conception of Lowell as an economic enterprise is revealed by the strikingly different considerations that guided development in the two portions. The industrial section, including the factories and company housing, was carefully planned according to functional principles. Once this portion was completed, the bourgeois portion was allowed to grow up in the area left over. Here functionalism was abandoned; land use decisions were made primarily on the basis of the speculative profits to be earned. Lowell, like other nineteenth-century cities, was shaped, or misshaped, by decisions made in the marketplace. In other cities, where land ownership was fragmented and the institutions of public authority were weak, the marketplace may have been the only mechanism available for making decisions about land use. In early Lowell, however, the corporations owned nearly all the land. They could have planned the development of the bourgeois as well as the industrial section of Lowell, but this community planning opportunity was lost in the pursuit for speculative profits.[12]

If the specific economic content of Lowell's early imagery came from the business objectives of the founders, the idea of cities with specialized functions as opposed to complex urban communities was typical of this period in American history. When Americans looked at European cities they saw them as conglomerations of diverse activities and types of persons. They were places where ugly poverty existed in the shadow of magnificent splendor and luxury. The image of American cities was much narrower on both counts. The early imagery of Lowell was in part a result of a desire not to duplicate European cities in America.

A revealing similarity between the founders of Lowell and Thomas Jefferson, a major contributor to the plan of Washington, D.C., emerges in this context. Jefferson and Francis Cabot Lowell were both disturbed by the poverty and degradation they found in Europe's political capitals and manufacturing cities. Consequently, when Jefferson planned America's political capital and Lowell planned the nation's industrial center neither wished to duplicate their respective European counterparts, Paris and Manchester, in all their complexity. Believing the urban rabble characteristic of Paris and Manchester to be an unwelcome addition to American society, they simply blotted these aspects of city life out of their plans. Jefferson's plan for Washington made provision only for the political activities to be undertaken there. His plans reserved very little space for the general economic activities ordinarily present in a city the size of Washington. Further, Jefferson apparently gave little consideration in his original plans to the housing needs of the cartmen, bakers, artisans, and day laborers who made up the typical eighteenth-century urban scene, since he intended that every house built in the national capital be constructed of stone. A regulation that "all Houses in the said City, shall be of Brick or Stone" was promulgated in 1791. Although a city of prosperous republicans housed in substantial (and fireproof) stone houses would have formed a favorable contrast to the squalor that surrounded the splendid palaces of European capitals, reality soon forced a modification in the regulation. It would be a prosperous day laborer indeed who could afford a stone house.[13]

Similarly, the founders of Lowell, who did not want any urban proletariat in their manufacturing center, made their plans as if there would be none. Although Boott made ample provision for those employed in the actual production process in the mills, he never made any preparations for housing the essential day laborers who dug the canals and constructed the mills. As a result, the "lords of the spade and shovel" were forced to live in hovels in a section of town known as the "Acre."[14] One cannot help thinking that the founders of Lowell planned the city in terms of the organizational chart–to use an anachronistic term–of their manufacturing corporation.

By 1830 change was impending. Until 1828 population growth in Lowell depended entirely upon the manufacturing enterprises. After that date, however, the social and economic foundations of community life became more diversified.[15] An urban identity increasingly separate from, and even sometimes in conflict with, the manufacturing corporations began to develop.

The foundation of this civic identity was the emergence of a

middle class with relatively strong attachments to the local community. This class consisted of ministers, lawyers, doctors, editors,
merchants, local manufacturers, and some corporation executives
who lived in Lowell. It is difficult to say how large this class was,
but clearly it was substantial. The city directory for 1851 lists seven-
teen clergymen, sixty-two physicians, and thirty-three attorneys.
There were dozens of small merchants and shopkeepers, nineteen
insurance agents, and two real estate agents (see Appendix A).
The city was served by eight newspapers and six banks. There were
also twenty-four locally owned manufacturing establishments employing more than 550 men with an annual product valued at more
than $860,000. A final indicator of the development of Lowell's
middle class is the number of taxpayers assessed fifty dollars and
over. In order to be thus taxed in 1850, a resident had to own property valued at $7,575 or more; 177 Lowellians qualified.[16] The civic
leadership of Lowell was drawn from this pool of prosperous and
respectable citizens. They formed a substantial urban elite who
accepted responsibility for local affairs and presumed to speak for
the community.

These men were not hostile to the corporations: they realized
that the corporations were still the lifeblood of the city. But if they
acknowledged the preponderance of the incorporated companies
in the community, they rejected Patrick Tracy Jackson's assumption that the corporations were identical with it. Elisha Bartlett, a
doctor, Lowell's first mayor, and a frequent defender of the factory
system, reminded the citizens of Lowell in his inaugural address in
1836 that the highest interests of the community are not always
identical with those of the corporation. A weekly newspaper, the
Vox Populi, was established in 1841 specifically to give expression
to Lowell's developing self-image "as a separate municipality."[17]
The developing urban consciousness in Lowell during the middle
of the nineteenth century is also revealed by the increasing proportion of space devoted to the city's general social as opposed to
industrial history in historical accounts of the city written between
1833 and 1880.[18]

One must be careful not to exaggerate the speed with which this
civic identity developed, but its first clear expression can be dated.
It appeared in a school controversy in 1832 that pitted the newly

self-conscious community against Kirk Boott and the corporations. The Merrimack Manufacturing Company had set up a school in 1824 for the children of its operatives. It was placed under the supervision of the Reverend Theodore Edson. When Lowell was incorporated two years later, this school became a part of the town's district school system. By 1832 Edson and other members of the Lowell School Committee concluded that while the district system was fairly well adapted to rural communities, it was "quite unsuited to a compact, rapidly growing community like Lowell." At a meeting in April 1832, the committee proposed that the small district schools scattered through the town be abolished in favor of a partially graded system. If the new system were adopted, it would be necessary to build two new grammar schools. The cost would be $20,000, and this was the nub of the controversy between the School Committee and Boott. Speaking for the corporations, who would have to pay a large portion of the taxes to be raised for the schools, Boott declared that the community should not spend such a large sum for education. After all, Lowell was only an industrial "experiment," and a "traveller visiting the place in a few years might find only a heap of ruins." Edson, speaking for the bourgeois community, replied that if the visitor examining those ruins "found among them no trace of a schoolhouse he would have no difficulty in assigning the cause of the downfall of Lowell." Edson carried the meeting, and the voters of Lowell established the new schools against the will of the corporations.[19]

The men who gradually replaced the founders as managers of the corporations also began to reappraise the relationship between industrialism and urbanism. They began to appreciate the urban setting of their factories. As American mores became more industrial and urban, the elaborate precautions taken by the founders of Lowell no longer seemed important to the corporate managers. The founders and early spokesmen for Lowell had assured Americans that manufactures would be safe in the United States because they were dispersed through the countryside instead of being in crowded cities as in Europe. By mid-century, however, American industrial promoters apparently forgot earlier American reservations about the moral and political consequences of manufacturing cities. "The tendency of manufacturing," John A. Wright of Philadelphia wrote in 1847, "is gregarious: it is so in England, and we see the tendency here. The advantages overbalance the disadvantages." By turning to steam power and by taking advantage of the labor pool and transportation facilities already existing in America's large commercial cities "we have no Lowells, Nashuas, Merrimacks to build."[20]

Seven years earlier, Charles T. James of Newburyport had made the same argument against the Lowell rationale. The Lowell factories, he admitted, "are as favorable specimens of manufacturing by water as our country can furnish," but "proprietors of water mills . . . in the interior, are under the necessity of purchasing land, and erecting dwellings for the accommodation of their operatives. . . . In seaports, this necessity does not exist." While Lowell has to offer high wages to attract help to the mills, "in maritime places," he pointed out, there is already available "an abundance of help, of nearly all descriptions wanted in the mills." And better, "they will readily and gladly go into the mills . . . for less wages than would command their services abroad." He argued, in short, that capitalists in seaports would do well to forget the nonurban model associated with Lowell and "employ their capital at home."[21] The concerns that had motivated the founding of Lowell were largely abandoned in America after about 1850. Factories were increasingly located in the larger cities.[22]

Henry A. Miles, Lowell's most articulate public spokesman during the 1840s, had replied to James that "it will deserve the serious consideration of those old towns which are now introducing steam mills, whether, if they do not provide boarding-houses, and employ chiefly other operatives than resident ones, they be not bringing in the seeds of future and alarming evil."[23] But even as Miles wrote, the policies developed by Francis Cabot Lowell a generation earlier were being modified and gradually adjusted to new conditions in Lowell itself. Manufacturers in Lowell perceived that they no longer needed to rely upon the labor policies devised by the founders to attract labor from the countryside. They too might draw their labor from an urban proletariat.

The Waltham-Lowell system originally included boarding-houses, high wages, and a high turnover rate for the essentially rural operative population. However, increasing acceptance of industrialism, urban growth, and the advent of immigrant labor eroded each of these policies. Irish immigrants, who gradually replaced the daughters of Yankee farmers as the principal source of labor, made up about one-third of Lowell's population and nearly one-half of the factory operatives by 1850.[24] Since the Irish typically did not live in boardinghouses, the corporations were no longer required to invest in housing.[25]

Urban growth brought even more important changes to wage policies in the Lowell factories. Francis Cabot Lowell had insisted that high wages were essential in order to draw labor from the countryside and to prevent its degradation while working in the factories. In 1839, however, the editor of the *Boston Daily Times* accused the corporations of exploiting an urban proletariat in Lowell. This population, "incapable of getting away with advantage," was liable to the kind of exploitation Lowell, Appleton, and Everett had claimed could never happen in America. Realizing in 1834 "that a large number of girls could be relied upon to remain and work, because they could do nothing else, . . . the corporations by agreement, and simultaneously, reduced wages–the same operation has taken place once since [in 1837]."[26] There is no question about the wage cuts: they had indeed taken place. Our interest is in whether the development of Lowell into a full-fledged city had in fact precipitated the abandonment of Francis Cabot Lowell's labor policies.

The interlocking Boards of Directors of the corporations, meeting in Boston, decided that a severe downturn in the economy in 1834 warranted a wage cut. The action was unprecedented. Many Americans from Jefferson onward had opposed the introduction of manufacturing corporations in America precisely because they understood that bad times would force down the wages of the factory operatives. Francis Cabot Lowell, however, had disarmed these opponents. He explained that wages could not be cut and workers exploited because the operatives could simply quit their factory work and return to the farm. Thinking within this framework, William Austin, agent for the Lawrence Manufacturing Company in Lowell, at first opposed the 25 percent reduction proposed in 1834. He feared that it would adversely affect the recruitment of good operatives. Once the policy was implemented on order from Boston, however, Austin realized that conditions had changed in Lowell. He perceived that high wages were no longer necessary to keep the operatives in the factories. He wrote to the treasurer in Boston that "the reduction of 25% may judiciously be insisted upon and it can be enforced without stopping the mills more than three weeks."

The operatives struck or "turned out" in response to the wage cut. The abortive strike is less important than Austin's reaction to it. He said that he had originally opposed the reduction because he "felt in common with many other[s] that the more respectable females might be induced to work in the mills by receiving higher wages." Their decision to "turn out," however, convinced him that a lower class of workers than was already in the mills could hardly be found. The ideal operative according to Jefferson and to Lowell had been one with a sufficient sense of independence to refuse to work for low wages. For Austin in 1834, docility seemed to be the most important quality in a good employee.[27]

The lesson the managers learned in 1834 made them all the more ready to cut wages when hard times came again in 1837.[28] Instead of relying upon a steady flow of farm girls who took up temporary industrial employment, the mills began to draw upon an emerging urban proletariat such as the founders had hoped would never develop in Lowell. A great social transformation had taken place.

The roots of this change extend back to the year of Lowell's founding. The first Irish arrived there on April 6, 1822, when a gang of thirty laborers under the leadership of Hugh Cummiskey came in search of work. Kirk Boott, needing laborers to construct the canals and factories, treated them to "refreshments" at a nearby tavern and hired them on the spot. As news of abundant jobs at East Chelmsford spread, more workers followed. First single men came, then families arrived. Since the companies had made no provision for housing common laborers, these workers were forced to provide for themselves. They established "rude habitations" on a piece of land known ever since as the "Acre." By 1830 there were about five hundred Irish Catholics living in "cabins, from 7 to 10 feet in height, built of slabs and rough boards, a fireplace made of stones in one end, topped out with two or three flour barrels or lime casks."[29] While foreign and American commentators celebrated Lowell for its absence of poverty, many Irish lived in squalor there. Seth Luther, a radical labor leader, declared in 1832 that "at Lowell 72 persons (Irish) were found 'in one half of a *small house.*'"[30]

Tensions quickly developed between the Irish and native-Americans in Lowell. These animosities were manifested in personal squabbles, street fights, and finally a general "riot" in May 1831. One person was killed and several "were much injured." A year later, the Selectmen of Lowell reported that "a disturbance of the peace is of almost nightly occurrence."[31] Conditions on the "Acre" and these breaches in the public order during the 1830s alerted some to the possibility "that in a place having such an accumulating and diverse population there should . . . be before many years a great increase of paupers."[32] Yet the dominant image of Lowell as an industrial utopia without any poverty or disorder continued to prevail.

By mid-century, however, the whole community had discovered the existence of widespread urban poverty. The number of poor reported by the Overseers of the Poor and the expenditures on pauper relief in Lowell rose dramatically in 1847. The available statistics on pauper relief reveal that immigrants do not themselves account for the large increase. Since local governments in Massachusetts were reimbursed by the state for relief supplied to foreigners, the number of state paupers in Lowell provides a rough measure of the immigrants helped. While the total number of paupers receiving aid in Lowell rose from 451 in 1846, to 1,723 in 1847, the number of state paupers only increased from 130 to 353.[33] The ranks of the poor, in others words, were swelled by older residents, the sons and daughters of New England, as well as by impoverished immigrants.

The meaning of these statistics for the poor is obvious, but they also affected the established citizens of Lowell who for the first time saw widespread begging in their city.[34] Poverty became even more visible during the early 1850s, and concern deepened. Civic leaders wondered about the consequences of poverty for the community. What could and should be done about it?[35]

The mythic pastoralism that had earlier dissuaded Lowellians from admitting or even considering the existence of any urban evils was eroded by continued urban development and by the increasing visibility of urban poverty. The emerging urban awareness lent a realistic quality for the first time to discussions of urban problems in Lowell. For example, when the editor of the *Boston Daily Times* had claimed in 1839 that many of the girls who came to the mills eventually turned to prostitution, he had been roundly rebuked for libeling the character of Lowell's female operatives. A decade later, however, when Judge Nathan Crosby of Lowell testified before a legislative commission that many New England farm girls were "ruined" in Lowell and became prostitutes, his statement was welcomed as an important contribution to the campaign to establish a state reformatory for girls.[36]

Similarly, and more importantly, by mid-century the medical profession had begun seriously to discuss public health issues in Lowell. During the 1830s and early 1840s, the medical men of Lowell had flatly denied any suggestion that the condition of public health in Lowell was any lower than in the rural districts of Massachusetts.[37] The first sign of a changing attitude came in Dr. John O. Green's presidential address before the Massachusetts Medical Society in 1846. Green, who had practiced medicine in Lowell since its founding, drew the conventional sharp contrast between English industrial cities and Lowell. But instead of categorically denying the existence of any evils, he admitted many and urged reform. Three years later, Dr. Gilman Kimball, head of the Lowell Hospital, went much farther. Americans, he said, could no longer think of Lowell as being immune to the consequences of urban industrialism. "The same evils that so glaringly and deplorably affect the sanitary conditions of the manufacturing towns of Europe, are gradually making their appearance in our own."[38]

Later in the same year, another Lowell physician, Dr. Josiah Curtis, made an important report to the newly formed American Medical Association. His study, one of a series of investigations of urban health and sanitation undertaken by several medical authorities under the sponsorship of the committee on public hygiene, argued that conditions of life in dense cities like Lowell were deteriorating. Instead of continually celebrating the superiority of

American cities over their European counterparts, Americans, he suggested, might study recent British experiments in sanitary reform in order to improve urban life in their own country. And since "few cities are so crowded as Lowell," he thought that his own city ought to be among the first to experiment with the English sanitary reforms. "Various obvious reasons" have drawn a large laboring population to Lowell and filled "every habitable tenement to an unhealthily dense degree." Lowell needed a "health officer" who "should visit [the] cellars and hovels, now crammed with filth, and degradation, and disease, which are so numerous in our city." He predicted that "the faithful report of such an officer would astonish the public, for very few are aware of the hundreds of places now inhabited by a horde in a horrid condition."[39]

The conditions publicized by Curtis could not be ignored. The changing character of the community received official recognition in 1852 when Elisha Huntington made the great increase of urban poverty one of the major points of his inaugural address as mayor.[40] Nathan Allen, who served several times as city physician of Lowell, reported in 1858 that "there is reason to apprehend [poverty] may increase from year to year here after in Lowell."[41]

Was Lowell, the city founded as the answer to English industrial cities, going to be cursed with the evils of class and poverty after all? Lowellians readily admitted that it was futile to reiterate that Lowell was a bucolic noncity with no poor. Yet they were not ready to admit that Lowell was just like Manchester. After all, urban poverty was different in America because in the United States it was only a temporary condition. America, unlike Europe, was an open society.

Urban Americans adapted a tradition reaching back to the nonurban era of Franklin and Crevecoeur, if not farther, to cope with the problem of urban poverty. They persuaded themselves that the poor man in America would soon raise himself to a position of respectability and even wealth. Such social mobility would ensure the integration of the newly visible urban poor into the community. The fragmented community thus would be melded together and the revolutionary potential of an impoverished underclass would be removed. This ideology underlay mid-century approaches to the problem of poverty and community.

Before this new complex of ideas emphasizing mobility on a massive scale could be adopted as the framework of an urban ideology, however, social thought in Lowell had to evolve beyond the hierarchical formulations of the founders.

As late as the 1820s, many Americans defined the ideal social order in terms of deference and proper stations.[42] Although this ideal was based upon the image of a rural gentry much like Jefferson's natural aristocracy, the early leaders of Lowell tried to adapt it to the conditions of the manufacturing society growing up along the Merrimack River. They visualized the social organization of their factory village in terms of a "hierarchy of clearly defined groups."[43]

The founders' assumptions about the various statuses in the social system of a factory village are revealed in the manner in which their agent, Kirk Boott, laid out the town. Boott, who was known for his "almost parental solicitude" about the well-being of the operatives, lived in a large house surrounded by a beautiful garden. While standing prominently apart, it was located near enough to the employees so that the paternalistic agent could watch over them outside the factory as well as inside.[44] The overseers came next in the hierarchy. An operative later recalled that they were the equivalent of a "gentry" in Lowell. Each block of company housing included an overseer's residence. This pattern enabled the overseers to watch over the operatives boarding on their block. Finally, there were the "operatives" who worked in the factories. They lived in boarding-houses supplied by the company.[45] The numerous Irish day laborers were neither part of the traditional New England community nor part of the organizational chart of the corporations, and, it will be recalled, they were not provided for in Boott's plan.

Ithamar A. Beard, paymaster of the Hamilton Manufacturing Company of Lowell, articulated the social ideas underlying this scheme. In an address before the Middlesex Mechanics Association meeting in 1827, Beard spoke of the proper arrangement of society in a factory village. Like many Americans of his time, Beard was concerned with the question of the social order and what held it together. He was firmly convinced that "the first thing in every society is order; without it nothing can be done." One of the "most prominent evils in society," he told his audience of workingmen, is "a want of proper subserviency in subordinate stations, and an overbearing contumely in exalted ones." Speaking on the eve of an era noted for its emphasis upon individualism,[46] Beard urged a more traditional standard for social relations. "Entire independence," he declared, "ought not to be wished for. . . . We are abundantly more happy for our being bound together by our mutual dependencies." These mutual dependencies, in Beard's view, were vertical rather than horizontal, and they had a particular relevance for places like Lowell where large numbers of persons gathered together into a society. "In large manufacturing towns, many more, in proportion to the inhabitants, must fill subordinate stations, that is, must be under the immediate direction and control of a master or superintendent, than in farming towns." Some critics, he admitted, fear that this may lead to aristocracy, but he believed that a modest subserviency is the foundation of a stable society wherein "both the master and the servant [are] lasting friends." "Let those who fill subordinate states," he concluded, "be in due and quiet subjection to those who have the charge over them and let those who are placed to rule and direct, do it with prudence and discretion" and they will all serve "the general good of society."[47]

Yet even as Beard expounded this New England Federalist philosophy, urban industrialism was eroding its social foundation. A new vocabulary was needed to describe the volatile urban and industrial society emerging in nineteenth-century America. The Reverend Amos Blanchard was the first Lowellian to bring a new perspective to this problem. "One thing is certain," he wrote in 1836, "we are to be a manufacturing country." In New England, where "populous towns, cities in all but the name, occupy the soil," manufacturing "will henceforward compose an important feature of our moral and social scenery." Although many worried that this implied a degraded and potentially revolutionary urban proletariat, Blanchard discounted such fears. In America, he observed, "the elements of society, like the particles in a mass of boiling liquid, are constantly changing places." This social theory, so different from that of the founders of Lowell, was the basis of mid-century confidence that the urban poor could be assimilated into the community.

Blanchard himself sketched the outlines of what became the

American "success myth." Because of "the constant though noise-less revolutions which [American] society is undergoing," it is pos-sible to expect the "industrious tenants of our mills . . . to become themselves at no distant day proprietors" and to achieve a "com-petent, if not affluent wealth." In America, he said, "we cling to the hope that, under the operation of our social system, manufacturers will never become a distinct *caste*, doomed *as families*, to mere mechanical toil, and aspiring to no higher education for themselves or their children than is requisite to make them convenient ap-pendages of the machinery which they work."[48] Lowellians no longer felt compelled to deny that their community was a city. The new complex of ideas adumbrated by Blanchard assured them that the emerging urban proletariat would never become so demoralized as in Europe.

In 1849, after his return from a tour of England's industrial cities, John Aiken, a Lowell mill agent, elaborated upon the difference between Europe and America. Among the working classes of Eng-land, he found "a general indifference to the miseries of their condition, or despair of being able to escape those miseries." In America, however, hired laborers do not exist as a class. Of course, there are large numbers of relatively poor urban wage earners in Lowell, but while young men and women often "begin life in this way" they have no "intention of following it permanently." Aiken explained that "their object is to gain a capital, with which to estab-lish themselves in business on their own account." And in the "vast majority" of cases this is precisely what happens. "He who five years ago was working for wages, will now be found transacting business for himself; and a few years hence, will likely be found a hirer of the labor of others." Americans could rest assured that "the poorest boy, if he be industrious and frugal, when attained to man-hood, may be found a man of substance, and in his old age, a man of wealth." For Aiken, a corporate manager, the promise of upward mobility went beyond reassurance on the possibility of community integration. Revealing an acute perception of the function of the success myth in an expanding economy, Aiken explained that the American belief in equal opportunity "has stimulated [individual] industry in a very high degree."[49]

Historians are still testing the validity of this "rags to riches" story as a believable and usable myth. Clearly, not very many men from working class backgrounds achieved national prominence as businessmen. And few leaders in the textile industry were the sons of "working" men. After studying the mobility experiences of three hundred unskilled laborers in Newburyport, Massachusetts, Stephan Thernstrom concluded that there was enough upward mobility *within* the working class to make the myth seem plausible.[50] Of course, it could be argued that the small degree of progress he found for the mass of workers is evidence against the myth's credibility. Yet there is still another approach to this problem. Perhaps a few local successes were more important than the actual experience of the bulk of the working class in convincing nineteenth-century urban Americans of the promise of upward mobility.

Mayor Jefferson Bancroft of Lowell was just this sort of success. He had begun life in Lowell as a factory operative in 1824. He soon became an overseer in the Appleton Mills. After serving as deputy sheriff and tax collector of Lowell, he entered elective politics when he won a seat on the Common Council in 1839. The next year he was elected to the first of four terms as representative to the state legislature. And in 1846, twenty-two years after he arrived in Lowell as a common laborer, he was elected mayor of the city.[51] During the 1840s, Lowellians saw in this self-made man assurance that the opportunity for mobility in America protected their city from the evils predicted by opponents of urban industrialism.

Bancroft, who realized the symbolic importance of his career, made a brief reference to the "success" theme in his inaugural address as mayor.[52] Then, a year later, he elaborated upon it when he welcomed to Lowell President James K. Polk, a man Lowellians considered an opponent of American industry. In welcoming the president to "the great manufacturing city of this great nation," Bancroft reminded him that only twenty-five years earlier there were but a few farms where now stands a city of "more than thirty thousand inhabitants, engaged in the industrial pursuits of life." Under the stimulus of manufacturing, the area "has been built into a handsome city of mills, workshops, dwellings and public edifices." This, he continued, has been achieved in a community composed of many persons, like himself, who from humble beginnings rose to become respectable citizens. "Many, very many of those who will greet you here to-day, came poor and penniless to our city, in its infancy, and here, by the hard labor of their own hands, have been able to purchase stock in the mills in which they labor, and have become owners of permanent property throughout the city."

Polk's response indicates that he also understood the significance of Bancroft's career and the mobility ideology. The president declared that he was "happy to learn" that the mayor "had risen from the occupation of an operative in one of the factories to the office of the chief magistrate of such an enterprising city. . . . To obtain this position he had undoubtedly been influenced by the lesson taught by the success of Franklin." Polk concluded by observing that "in all parts of the country such men often rose to commanding stations, and were the best calculated to illustrate the working of our free, republican institutions."[53]

Clearly, a belief in the possibility and value of social mobility was an important aspect of the emerging urban consciousness in Lowell. Moreover, this belief unquestionably made the adjustment to an urban-industrial society easier. However, we must press our inquiries further. We must ask how the mobility ideology influenced institutional responses to the problems of poverty, disorder, and community integration in the industrial city. Was the ideology merely a rationalization and justification for inaction, as Orestes Brownson charged in 1840 and as others have alleged since? Or is there a more humane interpretation of the creed? In the case of many Americans, probably most, the mobility ideology undoubtedly encouraged complacency. But as Richard Weiss and Stephan Thernstrom have pointed out, it could also become a powerful stimulus to reform.[54] And many of Lowell's civic leaders were touched by this impulse.

A more serious question yet remains. The rubric "reform" has become a difficult one for historians to handle. For an earlier generation of liberal historians, the appellation "reform" implied a movement for human betterment.[55] But the progressive assumptions underlying this interpretation have been eroded by the discovery that many of yesterday's reforms are facing us as today's problems. Historians, as a result, are beginning to pay more attention to the specific social and ideological contexts and social functions of institutional innovation. Likewise, our consideration of the influence of this emerging urban ideology upon reform in Lowell leads us to a close investigation of the assumptions underlying reform and the exact nature of its institutional articulation.

Civic leaders in Lowell believed that the maintenance of social order depended upon their success in assimilating the floating proletariat into the community. Since they assumed that the pattern of mobility described by Bancroft would play an important role in achieving this stability, it is important to determine precisely what mobility meant to mid-century Americans. Looking back at Bancroft's address, we see that beyond occupational mobility, he spoke of property mobility–the opportunity laborers had to "become owners of permanent property throughout the city."[56] The role of property in the developing urban ideology was complex. First of all, like occupational mobility, it was seen as an indicator of the improving social status and economic well-being of the laborer.[57] According to the civic leaders of Lowell, however, the ownership of property had another even more important function in the urban community. Disturbed by the unsettled character of the urban population, they hoped that property ownership would help stabilize the population and foster the local attachments they believed were necessary for the development of civic culture.

The population turnover in nineteenth-century American cities was extremely high.[58] And Lowell was no exception. A sample of 205 names (every twentieth listing) was taken from the Lowell city directory of 1840. Eighty-five persons or 41 percent of the sample had left the city before the next edition of the directory came out in 1841. Only 43 percent of the sample (eighty-nine persons) could be located in the directory for 1845, and by the end of the decade (1849) only seventy-one persons or 35 percent of the original sample of 205 persons remained in the city.[59]

The rate of geographical mobility was so high in nineteenth-century cities that two historians studying the phenomenon have raised the question of how any cultural continuity–or even the appearance of it–was maintained.[60] This was a question pondered by the civic leaders of Lowell who feared that their city resembled a railroad station or a hotel more than a community.

The founders of Lowell, it is true, had favored a form of geographical mobility in which unmarried young men and women who were born and bred in virtuous rural homes would accept employment in the mills for a few years and then return to agricultural pursuits. But the founders were not interested in developing a community spirit; their objective was the successful operation of a business enterprise. For them, geographical mobility offered a plausible way of avoiding the industrial evils besetting England and promised to facilitate the introduction of manufactures into an agrarian and antiurban nation. Yet even in this case it was not geographical mobility per se, but the rural beginning and end of the journey that was praised. It was a way of making Jefferson's farmer the foundation of American industrialism.

By mid-century, however, the characteristic geographical mobility of the laboring population seemed ominous rather than reassuring. It had become increasingly difficult for factory operatives to return to farming, and factory labor was no longer merely a brief episode in an essentially agricultural life cycle. The highly mobile urban working class was beginning to look more and more like a potentially dangerous floating proletariat.[61]

Although mid-century Lowellians continued to talk about how geographical mobility served as a safety valve in "hard times," the implications of this mobility for the development of civic culture increasingly disturbed them.[62] They could not find in Lowell "that sense of local pride" that marks a "municipality, in the older and better sense of that word." Any signs of change in this situation were applauded by civic leaders. In 1844, for example, Mayor Elisha Huntington happily noted that instead of being "mere birds of passage . . . taking up a transient abode" in the city, more and more of "our citizens are becoming residents and proprietors of the soil, and, instead of being tenants at the will of another, the lords and masters of their own castles, thus identifying themselves with the permanent interests of the place."[63] It was assumed (correctly in light of recent studies) that as men acquired property and achieved higher status in the community they were more likely to remain there. This would, civic leaders hoped, improve the "social feeling" of the community and "set on foot projects for public good."[64]

Community leaders accepted the idea that environment and institutions could significantly affect the chances of the poor for achieving such a situation of competence and respectability. Although improving the general environment was important, the reformers were particularly concerned with developing specific institutions that would help individuals raise themselves. Mayor Huntington expressed satisfaction that "those who bring with them steady, industrious and virtuous habits, do almost uniformly succeed in obtaining a comfortable living." But, he observed, "many who come do not possess these attributes, and some even of those who do, in consequence of sickness or other unforeseen calamity" are obliged to appeal for charity.[65]

The municipality, of course, provided for poor and dependent persons. When Lowell was incorporated, a city almshouse and poor farm had been established. The almshouse was intended to be "a workshop for the able bodied, a hospital for the sick, a school for the children, and a house of reformation for all." Supposedly, outdoor relief was extended only to the "sick who cannot be safely removed, and in a small number of cases where the aid needed is trifling in amount, or likely to be required for only a limited period."[66] Yet, during the early years, between 10 and 15 percent of municipal expenditures for poor and dependent persons were expended on persons not living in the almshouse. Such expenditures were either in the form of outdoor relief or payment for the care of dependent persons in private homes. By the 1850s, however, very little public charity was available in Lowell outside of the almshouse, now taken over by the state.[67]

This situation caused Mayor Huntington to raise the question of outdoor relief in his address for 1856. "Everyone at all acquainted with the condition of our population," he declared, "is aware that there is here a pretty large class of persons ... who are utterly unable ... to support their families, without aid from some quarter. The question at once arises, is it right and humane to compel such persons, indiscriminately, to go to the State Almshouses, when a little

assistance rendered for a short time, added to what their own industry can produce, will enable them to live at home?" The issue
extends beyond political economy to "moral and religious duty."
Warning that "the general effect" of sending persons with "any
pride of character" to the almshouse "is to break it down and render
them incorrigible and hopeless paupers," Huntington pointed out
that "the same persons, by a little encouragement and timely relief,
would often become self-supporting, and no longer a burden upon
the community." Although he urged the city to provide additional
help in this line, Huntington observed that the Ministry at Large
already "does an excellent work in rendering material aid, while
laboring to elevate and purify the minds and hearts of its bene-
ficiaries, and to encourage habits of economy, thrift and self-
dependence."[68]

The Ministry at Large was a nondenominational charity organization. Although not the first charity established in Lowell, it was
the largest and most important until the formation of the Associated Charities in 1881.[69] A group of prominent Unitarians, sensing
that there were "hundreds of unfortunate persons" in Lowell who
needed help, decided in 1844 to shift the focus of the newly formed
Lowell Unitarian Missionary Society from "Missions in the Western
States" to "the poor, neglected and sinful of Lowell." The society
resolved to drop the word Unitarian from its title and to establish
a nonsectarian Ministry at Large. The Reverend Horatio Wood,
who as a Harvard College student had been much impressed by the
Reverend Joseph Tuckerman's work with the poor of Boston,
agreed to serve as Lowell's Minister at Large.[70]

The Minister at Large, Wood believed, "had the whole city for
his field–the poor to relieve, the degraded to raise, the well-to-do
and benevolent to bring into communication and sympathy with
the poor." Wood was convinced that by judicious material aid, accompanied with counsel and sympathy from the middle classes, the
large class of poor people in Lowell would "soon reach a comfortable livelihood, and make good members of society." He agreed
with those who believed that public charity and indiscriminate
almsgiving had "the dreaded effect of multiplying the poor and
making permanent poverty." But he also thought that charity
accompanied by thorough investigation of the poor and kindly

intercourse with them would "foster an ambition . . . to be self-dependent."[71] Disturbed by the separation between the classes that was "daily becoming wider," Wood hoped that the ministry and its programs would narrow "the breach between the rich and the poor."[72] His own work and the work of volunteers in the free evening schools, which he organized for poor youths and adults, would establish sympathy and personal ties between the classes.

Yet Wood remained ambiguous on the problem of community. Echoing Channing's "common weal" ideal, he said that the more fortunate as well as the poor would benefit from the mixing of the classes. But this reciprocal ideal was often overshadowed by his concern for social control. He sought to integrate the poor into the dominant middle-class culture. "Near intercourse" with their betters, he wrote of the poor, will "influence them to raise themselves."[73] Wood, a kindly, humane, and indefatigable laborer among the poor, was, after all, a representative of the established order in Lowell.

After a career lasting nearly a quarter-century as Minister at Large in Lowell, Wood concluded that his system of charity had "raised hundreds to a condition of comfort and thrift." Despite this success with adults, however, Wood believed that "beginning with the young is . . . the right place to reform society." There was a limit to how much could be accomplished with "those advanced in life and fixed in their habits." "The young are our hope." It is difficult to arrest the "full passion of matured wickedness," but Wood was confident that "we can do much in giving direction to the pliant twig."[74]

The issue of the child in the city grew in importance as the people of Lowell realized that the rising generation would henceforth be reared in the city instead of on virtuous New England farms. During the early years, Lowell's labor force was made up primarily of single persons who had been raised in the country and who returned to the country when they married and established families. In the decades after 1830, however, a substantial and constantly increasing percentage of the work force was married. Consequently, the proportion of children in the city's population mounted steadily (see Table 1). Civic leaders worried about the urban working class families whose "children are reared in the city, in constant exposure

TABLE 1. The Changing Age Distribution
of the Population in Lowell

Year	Total population	Persons under 15 years	%	Persons 5 to 15 years	%
1830	6,463	1,423	22.1	805	12.5
1840	20,742	5,285	25.0	3,050	14.7
1850	33,383	n.a.	—	5,415*	16.2
1855	37,554	10,374	27.6	6,562	17.5

SOURCES: U.S. Census, *Fifth Census of the U.S., 1830* (Washington, 1832), pp. 16–23; U.S. Census, *Sixth Census of the U.S., 1840* (Washington, 1841), pp. 35–49; U.S. Census, *Seventh Census of the U.S., 1850* (Washington, 1853), p. cxi; Lowell School Committee, *Annual Report*, 1851, p. 11; and Massachusetts Secretary of the Commonwealth, *Abstract of the Census of the Commonwealth of Massachusetts, 1855* (Boston, 1857), p. 82.

*The published materials for the U.S. Census of 1850 do not break down the population by age for cities (it is broken down by counties). I have taken this figure from a census taken on June 11, 1851, to ascertain the number of children between 5 and 15 years of age in Lowell. It is reported in Lowell School Committee, *Annual Report*, 1851, p. 11.

to all its corrupting scenes."[75] Many of these children, moreover, were being raised by foreign parents who knew nothing of New England religious and educational traditions. The "moral character" of the city, it seemed, was "receding" because urban working class parents had neither the time nor the knowledge to rear their children properly.[76]

Failure of education in the home was bad enough, but close observers in Lowell realized that the city itself was a worse teacher of evil. Horatio Wood warned that "to receive the education of the streets, and of low influences, must make miserable citizens for a republic." Amos Blanchard was more specific. "The influence of manufactures on education and morals," he observed, "is to be one way or another tremendous." "The constant contact of mind with mind" gives the youth in a manufacturing city like Lowell "a degree of intelligence perhaps above the average intellect of an agricultural community." One will find "little stagnation of thought" in the city. "Their ignorance, if they be ignorant, will not be that of torpid, vacant minds. It will be ingenious, passionate, prurient; putting itself forth in forms of bold, reckless, destructive error."[77]

For many, the only solution was the development of "a practically religious spirit" in Lowell. In an increasingly secular society, however, more and more men turned to an "enlightened and improved system of public education." As Dorus Clarke put it in his *Lectures to Young People in Manufacturing Villages*, "next to the conservative power of the gospel, we must look to *education* to give perpetuity to our republican institutions, and to preserve our cities and villages from riots, incendiarism and blood." Ambrose Lawrence, mayor of Lowell in 1855, agreed: "Next to the benign influence of religion, the cause of education should be cherished, as essential to the well being of the community."[78]

Responding to the challenge of the city, community leaders and educators committed public education to an ambitious task of social reform. The schools were intended simultaneously to save the city from disintegrating into immorality and to acculturate the young so that they could perform effectively in an urban-industrial society.[79] The Lowell School Committee reported in 1846 that the expenditure for the school system is "the largest appropriation made by the City." However, "it dwindles into insignificance in comparison with the intrinsic value of a correct moral and intellectual education to any community, but especially to a manufacturing one, where the great problem is to be solved whether we have virtue enough to save us from the moral and physical degradation which have overtaken similar pursuits in other places."[80]

Schools did not suddenly abandon intellectual purpose with the rise of cities. Historically, schools have been concerned with society as well as with the minds of children. The simple fact of schools accepting responsibility for important social functions is neither new nor particularly significant. The specific character of the social functions undertaken by the new urban school systems, however, is interesting and important.

It was characteristic of mid-Victorian elites to believe that although they were capable of the self-discipline necessary amidst the "temptations of a crowded population," the ordinary men and women in the city could not be trusted in this respect.[81] The elites, who developed their own "inner check," assumed that the urban masses must have discipline either externally imposed upon them or inculcated in them by more subtle means.[82] The first approach found institutional articulation in the establishment of professional and efficient police forces. However, less formally repressive means were preferred. The schools, since they reached most children, seemed to be particularly well suited to instill the essential self-restraint in the masses.[83] In the schoolroom, where the "first lessons of subordination and obedience" would be taught to many scholars, the "baser passions" would be "shut out" and replaced by nobler sentiments. Writing about the high school in 1841, the Lowell School Committee expressed the dual purpose of the schools: "In this school should be developed, not the powers and faculties of the mind only, but the better feelings of the heart."[84]

The schools could also inculcate qualities that would enable the young to fit into an industrial society, successfully advance themselves, and contribute to the communal wealth. School Committee members thought that previous generations of young men and women had acquired traits of order, self-discipline, and responsibility on virtuous New England farms. These traditional rural, or more generally "Puritan" qualities, they believed, produced good urban citizens and effective industrial workers.[85] Now the public school system would have to assume the task of instilling these traits in the urban youth.

It was considered especially important for the children of Lowell's foreign population to enter the public schools to learn these old New England virtues. Children of the impoverished foreign born would acquire the knowledge and develop the character that were necessary to raise themselves higher in the social scale than their poor parents. Lowell would thus avoid the development of a permanent underclass in which poverty and vice are passed from one generation to the next. "Every intelligent foreigner," the School Committee pointed out, "should understand that his sons will never be able to successfully compete with our own sons" unless they are trained in the common schools.[86]

But it was not easy to persuade Irish Catholic parents to send their children to public schools. The School Committee admitted that the Irish had "a natural apprehension" about "placing their children under Protestant teachers." If the schools were to perform their task of raising the poor and bringing them into the community, the School Committee realized that some way must be found to "extend the benefits of our public schools more fully to our Irish population." The committee devised a bold innovation to meet the problem. They arranged with the Roman Catholic pastor, Father Connolly, to provide public funds for the operation of special schools for Lowell's Catholics. These special schools, established in 1835, were taught only by Catholics and used textbooks that "contain[ed] no statement of facts not admitted by that faith, nor any remarks that reflected injuriously upon their system of belief." The School Committee nominally retained the power to supervise the general policy of the Irish schools, examine teachers, and prescribe the course of study, but never used it to challenge the autonomy of the special schools.[87]

School attendance among the Irish children quickly improved. In the first year of operation, the School Committee reported, the "punctuality and regularity" in the Irish schools was "fully equal to that of our other schools." The social effects were noticed immediately. The School Committee declared after one year that "the advantages of this arrangement must have been obvious to every observer . . . in the improved condition of our streets, in their freedom from noisy, truant, and quarrelsome boys." And the committee "confidently hoped" that the long-run results would "soon be equally obvious in the improved condition and respectability of these children." Five years later, benevolent old Amos Lawrence wrote that in twenty years, as a result of the special schools, the children of Lowell's Irish homes will "be mingled with our mass of population, an active, enlightened and fine spirited body."[88] The concern for achieving social order through the schools unquestionably distorted educational goals, but it also produced a notable experiment in educational pluralism which lasted until 1851, when nativist pressure forced closure of the special schools.[89]

Lowell High School was the capstone of the public education system. Established in 1831, it was soon enlisted in the battle against urban disintegration. It was to be a "place where the rich and the poor may meet together." There both classes would "insensibly forget the distinction which difference of circumstances would otherwise have drawn between them." The "children of our wealthier citizens will have an opportunity of witnessing and sympathizing ... in the wants and privations of their fellows." More importantly, "the indigent may be excited to emulate the cleanliness, decorum and mental improvement of those in better circumstances."[90]

"In a population like Lowell," the School Committee declared, the value of a high school is "incalculable." Every part of the community will benefit, but it is "eminently and chiefly beneficial" to the poor. "This alone enables them to bring their talents and industry into the market, and thus, to rise by dint of merit, to those trusts and that influence, which otherwise will fall exclusively into the hands of the rich." The school system, and in particular the high school, they said, will keep the path of opportunity open for the generation of children now growing up in the city.[91]

However, the high school was not all it was purported to be. Several sons of New England apparently began their upward climb toward success in the Lowell High School, but very few of the Irish at mid-century even entered its doors (see Table 2). The apparent failure of the schools to foster upward social mobility for the Irish did not go unnoticed. Yet the School Committee was able to explain it without admitting the limits of educational reform. Some Irish scholars "who were qualified for the High School," the committee reported, "did not wish to go." Instead, "a very large number of scholars in this school [the Irish Grammer School] enter the mills."[92] The committee failed to acknowledge the social and economic circumstances that influenced the decision of Irish youth to go into the mills instead of to the school house.

The civic leaders of Lowell were more disturbed by the knowledge that in any given year over a third of the school-aged children in the city were not being reached by any public schools. "No language of ours," declared the School Committee in 1846, "can convey too strongly our sense of the dangers which await us from this source."[93] This concern resulted in the establishment of the House of Reformation in 1851. Officially known as the House for the Instruction and Employment of Truants from School and Juvenile Offenders in the City of Lowell, the institution was the third of its kind in the state, the earlier ones having been the Boston House of

TABLE 2. Irish Students Continuing from
Grammar School to High School*

Year	Schools	No. Students	No. to H.S.	% to H.S.
1838	Irish Grammar Schools	157	2	1.3
	All other Grammar Schools	964	88	9.1
1839	Irish Grammar School	290	0	0.0
	All other Grammar Schools	1,501	81	5.4
1843	Irish Grammar School	391	6	1.5
	All other Grammar Schools	2,211	98	4.4
1846	Irish Grammar School	191	11	5.7
	All other Grammar Schools	1,330	119	9.0
1847	Irish Grammar School	175	3	1.7
	All other Grammar Schools	1,299	118	9.0
1848	Irish Grammar School	338	0	0.0
	All other Grammar Schools	2,442	107	4.4

*A complete answer to this question would require a quantitative study of individuals, but this aggregate data published in the School Committee's *Annual Reports* leads me to my conclusion. The reports indicate how many students from each of the eight grammar schools went on to high school. It is possible to identify the Irish grammar school (there were two in 1838) and to compare the percentage of its graduates who went on to high school with the combined percentage for the other seven schools.

Reformation, opened in 1827, and the State Reform School opened at Westborough in 1848.[94]

Truant, vagrant, and delinquent children formerly had been placed in the almshouse, but it was increasingly thought best to separate "children from the adults, in order that the children might be kept free from any intercourse with adults, whose influence on tender minds was deemed to be very injurious and pernicious."[95] So a new wing was constructed at the almshouse to serve as a separate and distinct institution for children.

Juvenile offenders were placed in the new institution to be "employed and instructed in such a manner as to prepare them to become useful and respectable citizens." The House of Reformation was also "a very suitable place to be assigned for the reception of all such truant and wayward children as shall be found in our city, without any regular and lawful employment and occupation, growing up in ignorance and vice, and thereafter to become pests to society." The average number of inmates in the House of Reformation in 1856 was about eighteen, and they were subject to a strict disciplinary code. This discipline was thought to have "had a highly reformatory influence over many of its subjects." Mayor Huntington even supposed that its good influences were not "confined within its walls. To some extent, at least, it is believed that it inspires many without, with a salutary fear of its discipline, and operates as a restraint upon truancy and other offences."[96]

Reformers in mid-century Lowell sought a cultural consensus on middle-class values. Reform was sponsored by a conservative Protestant middle class. Their assumptions were elitist in the sense that they felt free unilaterally to define cultural standards for the entire community. They often spoke of Channing's "common weal," but they were largely concerned with the problem of social order in the city. Moreover, being themselves newcomers to the city, members of this elite were immediately concerned with the self-discipline that was part of the emergent urban culture. Intensely conscious of their own yearnings and the restraint demanded by middle-class respectability, they were disturbed, even challenged, by the seeming disorderliness in the lives of the poor.[97] They responded by defining the life-style of the urban poor as pathological and by prescribing their own newly adopted values as an antidote.

Committed to an ideology celebrating upward social mobility, civic leaders acted on the belief that institutions could and should be devised to inculcate into the poor, especially the children of poverty, qualities that would enable them to raise themselves to middle-class respectability. Although extensive poverty remained in Lowell after this first wave of urban reform, the effort did produce an impressive network of educational and charitable institutions.[98]

Finding such an elaborate institutional response to the problem of poverty and community in the city so early in our history leads one to expect a relatively simple pattern of augmentation and development toward the professional welfare bureaucracy that characterized the Progressive Era. In fact, there was no such linear development of formal welfare organizations. The institutional methods devised in antebellum cities for the care of poor and dependent persons, especially children, were under attack on the eve of the Civil War.

Horatio Wood provides an example of this unexpected shift in policy. Having praised the State Reform School at Westborough in 1849 and having at that time proposed the establishment of a similar institution at Lowell, Wood changed his position by 1860. "A great error had been committed" in gathering juvenile delinquents in "one mammoth structure." In "very many cases," it would be better simply to remove the "troublesome, burdensome" juvenile from "discordant and corrupt influences" and to place him in a Christian family. Such a change "will take all the obstinate, disobedient, truant, vagrant, thievish dispositions out of a lad. It has been proved in a thousand cases." Wood was convinced that "the free spirit comes into regulation gradually and naturally without the confinement and arbitrary rules, deemed needful in reformatory establishments, which not unfrequently depress youth and clip the wings of their ambition." "Reformation in the midst of society, and through the influence of good society" as opposed to reliance upon "expensive side agencies ever so systematically and wisely conducted" was more likely to develop "the young into strong, self-dependent, thrifty men–into better citizens of the republic."[99]

In 1865 Nathan Allen, a Lowell physician and a member of the newly created Board of State Charities, defended reformatories against Wood's charges. Allen agreed that children ideally should be placed in family situations, but he nevertheless argued that reformatory institutions were necessary "in order to cleanse them [the children], to train them and educate them, to some extent to fit them to go out into good families." Wood replied that it was precisely the idea of the children's being fitted *before* placement in a good home that bothered him. He wondered "whether the process is *necessary and wise*, except in very few cases; whether it harmonizes with the free play and affection of a child's nature; with the laws of influence, domestic, social and general; whether it is best calculated to fit for a respectable and high stand in society." Allen left the issue hanging by observing that this "train of thought" was currently causing much agitation and discussion among charity leaders, including the members of the Board of State Charities.[100]

 The issue caused much controversy indeed, and its significance extended beyond the problem of juvenile delinquents. Wood was using an argument developed by Charles Loring Brace, and it implied a new conception of community that combined the power of formal organizations in community life with the organic pattern of social relations associated with the New England town tradition. The various dimensions of this debate will, therefore, repay deeper investigation. The problem cannot, however, be pursued adequately through examination of Wood's relatively undeveloped ideas or in Lowell, which began its decline into relative economic and cultural insignificance during the 1850s. But we may appropriately turn to New York where Brace was developing these ideas into a new urban vision and policy.

VI.

The Idea of Community & the Problem of Organization in Urban Reform

Charity in cities may rear her monumental piles, and
endow them with the munificence of princes.
Yet she, too—warm, impulsive heaven-born
Charity—may degenerate into a cold, mechanical,
political economy. Her life may be crushed
beneath a system.

Anonymous writer,
The Knickerbocker (1840)

Routine may be carried so far as to make the aiding
of misery the mere dry working of a machine.

Charles Loring Brace (1872)

THE DEVELOPMENT of large-scale formal institutions in nineteenth-century cities raised difficult questions about the relationship of spontaneity and organization in urban life. By mid-century perceptive social thinkers asked what place organic patterns of community and social relations had in an organizational society. Since the issues of social order, proper or natural social relations, and organizational style were closely related, the study of urban reform and philanthropy involves a consideration of ideas of community as well as the structure and ideology of charitable institutions.

An emerging urban culture in America led all manner of men and women to reformulate their relationships to the community. Artists, writers, and academics were redefining their own and others' connections to institutions and to society at large. The focus of the traditional professions was being shifted from the local community toward metropolitan and national organizations. Immigrants were developing the sense of political community that provided the foundation of the urban "boss" system. And various utopian groups were seeking an entirely new basis of community.

More important for our purposes, however, an older sense of community as a nonabstract, direct, personal experience was being abandoned. It was replaced in time by the more abstract and formal conception of community that provides the basis for modern urban politics.[1] Although it is tempting to assume a uniform progression from the first to the second view of community, it would imply a historical inevitability and an absence of alternatives that is unwarranted by the historical record. In fact, a complex version of community standing between these two poles but distinct in itself emerged in the middle of the nineteenth century.

By mid-century, the characteristic tendency of the industrial city to segregate rich and poor into separate residential and social spheres had forced the problem of community to the center of urban thought.[2] Two points became apparent to urban thinkers: the total rejection of urban industrialism seemed out of the question, and the older view of community inherited from colonial New England was evidently inadequate to the demands of urban-industrial society. Yet many of these thinkers were not willing to sacrifice that heritage entirely to the emerging organizational society. They sought to preserve opportunities for organic and natural relations within the new social order. They attempted to link spontaneity and a commitment to organic forms of community with an acceptance of the increasingly constraining formal structures of organizational society. For a brief period in the nineteenth century, this approach seemed to offer possibilities of significantly improving the quality of urban life.

Charles Loring Brace provides an illustration of this response. Using New England community life as his standard, Brace judged urban society to be unnecessarily fragmented. The nineteenth-century city, it seemed, was divided by geography, class, and feelings. The poor were isolated from the other half of society. The "better classes" of New York, he complained, do not even suspect that in a city "so prosperous and wealthy as this there should be multitudes of people without the very first conditions of civilization." Brace, whose philanthropic goal was the absorption of the "multitude of the unfortunate into the community," felt that both the fortunate and the unfortunate suffered in their different ways from this fragmentation of community.[3]

Seeking to develop philanthropic organizations that provided a mutually edifying "link of sympathy" between the classes, Brace advocated an extensive reliance upon volunteers along with professionals in urban charity.[4] Without volunteers from the respectable classes in personal contact with the unfortunate, community was impossible. Brace feared that the formal organizations established by the immediately preceding generation of urban reformers threatened not only this communal ideal but also the spontaneous patterns of personal experience that defined an organic structure of community life. The situation at mid-century demanded innovation in organizational style. The problem was to devise large-scale forms of organization capable of meeting the challenge of the city while still preserving, even enhancing, community.

The formal organizations that disturbed Brace dated from the 1820s. When that generation of reformers first noticed the divisive force of nineteenth-century urban development, they began to define poverty and dependency, a normal and accepted part of American colonial life, as a challenge to community. Physical separation made the lower class alien and even threatening. Living in an age when men and women were moving in and out of cities and up and down the social ladder, they realized that neither the sense of localism nor the sense of hierarchy that had stabilized colonial communities would hold together their volatile and fragmented society. Moreover, the church and the family, traditional keystones of social order, seemed unable to counterbalance the forces of urban disorder and disintegration. If the church and family were failing in their traditional roles, how could social chaos be avoided in the future? What could be expected of children reared in such a society? Anxious Americans wondered what new mechanisms of social order might be devised. Ironically, their search for new sources of cohesion in an urbanizing society led them out of the city; it led, in David Rothman's phrase, to "the discovery of the asylum."

Fearful of urban life and relying upon an environmentalist social philosophy, Jacksonian Americans believed that deviant and dependent persons were the product of the disorder and temptations of the city. Optimistic about the essential goodness of people, reformers believed that they could be rehabilitated by placing them in "well ordered" institutions, typically in rural settings, where a regular regimen would inculcate the discipline that the urban church and family were failing to provide. Here the order so lacking in existing forms of society might be found. Persuaded by this logic, antebellum Americans proceeded to construct penitentiaries, almshouses, insane asylums, and houses of refuge or reformation.[5]

Brace and his predecessors, perhaps revealing a characteristic American preoccupation with the rising generation, shared an overriding concern for the homeless, disorderly, or criminal children who had suddenly become so visible in the nation's cities. But their approaches to the problem were radically different. While the earlier reformers relied upon isolation from society and regimentation for reformation, Brace sought ways of preserving and using natural and spontaneous influences of family and social life as vehicles of reformation. These two styles of response imply different conceptions of the social order, and comparison illuminates the idea of community being developed at mid-century.

America's first juvenile reformatory was created in 1825, when

the Society for the Reformation of Juvenile Delinquents established
the New York House of Refuge. A year later, a House of Reformation was established in Boston. By 1860 there were reformatories in
nearly every large American city, and in many of the smaller ones
as well. Most of them, including the ones in Massachusetts criticized by Horatio Wood, were directly or indirectly modeled upon
the New York institution.[6]

The House of Refuge was founded by the same group of men,
who, in 1825, had organized the Free School Society of New York
to provide "for the education of poor children, who do not belong
to or are not provided for by any religious society."[7] They had
implemented Joseph Lancaster's monitorial system of teaching in
the Free School, and the mechanistic assumptions of the Lancasterian system later found exaggerated expression in the House of
Refuge that they established. Although few other reformatories
achieved the degree of discipline and control that characterized the
daily routine in the New York House of Refuge, managers in other
institutions strove for it. The children were engaged in continuous
activity during their waking hours, and they were subjected to a
strict discipline and regimentation. After spending an average
period of sixteen months in this orderly, almost militaristic, environment, the reformed children either were returned to family and
friends or were indentured as sailors, as tradesmen, or as laborers
on western farms. The Society for the Reformation of Juvenile
Delinquents claimed that 75 percent of the children placed under
its care were reformed.[8]

Yet it apparently was not meeting the city's needs. When Brace
arrived in New York in 1848, he was appalled to hear George W.
Matsell, New York's police chief, report that there were several
thousand vagrant children in the city. Soon thereafter, in January
1853, Brace and twelve prominent New Yorkers founded the Children's Aid Society. More than a simple addition to the city's
child-saving agencies, it specifically challenged the emphasis upon
institutional care for children represented by the House of Refuge.[9]
Brace believed that placing a child under the artificial and mechanical discipline of a reformatory institution would never result
in improved character. In fact, *"the longer he is in the asylum, the
less likely he is to do well in outside life."* Admitting that there were

"exceptional cases" for whom "a half-prison life may be the very best thing," Brace insisted that the "majority of criminals among children" are not "much worse than the children of the same class outside, and therefore need scarcely any different training." He preferred placing them in farmers' homes where natural family influences would allow them more opportunity than in a reformatory to develop their talents fully and freely.[10]

The House of Refuge, it is true, also placed children in farmers' homes. The year preceding the establishment of the Children's Aid Society, for example, the Society for the Reformation of Juvenile Delinquents disposed of children under its care primarily through indenture to farmers and others. Yet there is a crucial difference between the approaches of the two organizations. Unlike the Children's Aid Society, which took children from the streets and immediately placed them in suitable homes, the managers of the House of Refuge placed children in homes only after the discipline of the institution had made them trustworthy.[11] The reforming, in other words, was to be done within the "well ordered" institution safely removed from the stresses and temptations of society. Brace, in contrast, argued that withdrawing children from society and placing them in the artificial environment of a reformatory would actually hamper their ability eventually to assume roles as full and responsible members of their communities. According to Brace, reformation of character could most effectively be accomplished in society through the natural influence of family life. From the founding of the Children's Aid Society until nearly the end of the century, the major issue in child care was between the institutional and family methods.[12]

Brace's philosophy of reform was based upon a particular conception of community. When his predecessors in the asylum movement were faced with the erosion of traditional patterns of social cohesion and increased levels of social and geographical mobility, they were unable to project any new vision of community. Rather, the rigidity of the asylum represented an effort to impose an idealized version of the orderly and peaceful eighteenth-century village onto the disorderly nineteenth-century city.[13] Ironically, their quest for a sentimentalized pattern of order and authority produced a concern for regularity, punctuality, and uniformity that resembled the modern factory more than the eighteenth-century village. Brace, however, was far enough removed from the village of fond memory to feel comfortable with the fluidity that had developed in the nineteenth-century American social structure. The new patterns of social and geographical mobility seemed to enhance rather than threaten social stability. In fact, Brace was less concerned with the looseness of American society than he was with the mechanistic assumptions of earlier reformers. He was confident that allowing a certain looseness in social relations would strengthen rather than weaken the organic community.

This confidence undergirded the commitment of mid nineteenth-century reformers, clearly exemplified in Brace's thought, to naturalness and spontaneity within the framework of an increasingly urban-industrial and organizational society. Their belief that unity is the natural state of a community and their concern for preserving spontaneity in urban society distinguished Brace and his generation of urban reformers from those who developed the welfare bureaucracy during the Progressive Era.

In the course of articulating the philosophy of the Children's Aid Society, Brace quickly earned a national reputation as an urban reformer.[14] He became the principal spokesman for a small but influential group of reformers who advocated the anti-institutional position taken by Horatio Wood against Nathan Allen. This group of anti-institutional reformers ultimately failed to reverse the trend toward bureaucratization that they opposed, but their mid-century challenge slowed its development and suggested an important alternative style in urban reform.

Brace was born in Litchfield, Connecticut, in 1826, but he spent most of his boyhood in Hartford. His family attended North Church there, and on Sundays Brace listened to the sermons of Horace Bushnell, probably nineteenth-century America's most important theologian. In 1842, the year Brace entered Yale College, Bushnell preached a sermon on "Unconscious Influence." Brace later wrote that it "influenced my whole life."[15]

That sermon represents only a fraction of Brace's intellectual debt to his pastor. Bushnell's ideas on the importance of the family in Christian nurture and in the transmission of culture as well as his preference for naturalness in child-rearing clearly provided the theoretical basis of Brace's campaign to place poor and homeless children in families as opposed to institutions. Bushnell argued in "Unconscious Influence" that efforts to influence a child "by teaching, by argument, by persuasion, by threatenings, by offers and promises" count for infinitely less than the "sympathetic powers, the sensibilities or affections" that are "not immediately rational." The character of a child is formed by his imitation of these "unconscious influences."[16]

Bushnell expanded upon these themes in *Christian Nurture*, published in 1847. He maintained there that no "purposed control whatever" can affect the child as much as the "organic *working* of a family." Given this conception of Christian nurture, no artificial institution, with its formal and articulated purposes, could perform the task of the Christian family. In fact, Bushnell recommended on a limited scale what Brace eventually carried out on a massive scale: the placing of badly reared children in virtuous families.[17]

On a more abstract level, Bushnell stated the terms on which Americans might reconcile themselves to the constraints of urban and organizational society.[18] Hoping to bridge the gap between traditional New England religious life and the emerging urban culture in which he and many other Americans found themselves, Bushnell undertook a massive revision of American Protestantism. He discovered that he could accommodate his inherited New England theology to newer American tastes, increasingly affected by Romanticism, by emphasizing the imprecision of language.[19]

He claimed that language is "two stories high, being first a language of sense or fact and next a language of thought or truth." The first level referred to definite things and was relatively precise. The second level drew its imagery from the first, and it referred to thoughts, abstractions, and relations. Words on this level were "hints or images" that might elicit different thoughts according to the "personal contents" of the receiver's mind. The language of theology, the second level of language, was therefore poetic or symbolic.[20]

The implications of Bushnell's theory of language go far beyond nineteenth-century linguistics or even Protestant theology. That words defining the relations among individuals, institutions, and ideas were inevitably imprecise was critically relevant to a society increasingly characterized by large-scale organizations—from factories in Lowell to educational and charity organizations in New York. The inexact coercions communicated to individuals by organizational society inevitably allowed important areas of private freedom.

Although Bushnell criticized the "extreme individualism" of Jacksonian America, the looseness he assumed in the individual's relationship to ideas and institutions suggested a conception of urbanism that favored spontaneous impulses amidst the artificial constraints of city life.[21] It is difficult to trace Bushnell's practical influence in the popularization of such an approach in the middle of the nineteenth century, but it is significant that the two most important spokesmen for such a version of urbanism, Charles Loring Brace and Frederick Law Olmsted, were raised in Hartford and belonged to Bushnell's church.

Brace went to Yale with the intention of following Bushnell into the ministry and writing. He began his theological studies at Yale Divinity School, but in 1848 he left New Haven to continue them at Union Theological Seminary in New York. Attracted to liberal religion, which in New York seems to have drawn upon Ralph Waldo Emerson as well as upon Bushnell, Brace apparently discovered Emerson's ideas in the city. He reviewed Emerson's works for the *Knickerbocker* in 1850 and later acknowledged the influence of the Concord thinker's ideas.[22]

Brace quickly achieved some prominence as a writer, but the promise of literary culture and a conventional ministerial career ultimately failed to satisfy him. In common with numerous young men of his generation, Brace was looking for a satisfactory social role in the expanding urban culture at a time when many traditional roles, like the ministry, were losing their attraction.[23] He found the religion expounded in the seminary too technical and intellectualized. He was driven to doubt by it. He preferred a "practical piety" concerned with justice and "brotherhood between the classes." Christians, he thought, ought to be laboring "for those who have no helper." Possibly his religious doubts would be relieved if he could "give up every nerve and pulse to my work for humanity."[24] Brace's decision for a career in philanthropy, then, is explained in part by religious doubt and by his commitment to "man-helping."[25]

Besides this "subjective necessity," however, Brace was also impelled toward philanthropy by objective conditions in New York.[26] His religious and social experiences in New York profoundly affected his attitudes toward poverty. At Yale, before coming to the city, he had written that "my heart is wrong and my tastes are all set against sympathizing with the low and vulgar." He even admitted that he had difficulty realizing "that some men are my brothers." It seemed to him that "heaven was not made for the low, dirty undressed Christian." In the city, however, he developed a genuine sympathy for poor people. He received his introduction to urban poverty and misery while preaching to paupers on Blackwell's Island. "I never had my whole nature so stirred within me, as at what met my eyes." It was, he informed his father, the "saddest, most hopeless sight." But he was particularly affected by the condition of the city's street children. He wrote to his sister: "You can have no idea, Emma, what an immense vat of misery and crime and filth much of this great city is! Think of *ten thousand children* growing up almost sure to be prostitutes and rogues!"[27] It quickly became evident, he later recalled, "that what New York most of all needed was some grand, comprehensive effort to check the growth of the 'dangerous classes.' " On his return from a trip to Europe in 1850–1851, where he studied various charitable institutions, particularly in England and Germany, Brace decided to undertake some kind of work in behalf of the unfortunate of the city.[28]

He joined the Reverend Lewis M. Pease, who had opened the Five Points Mission in 1850. There he began a lifelong study of urban poverty that shaped his career as a philanthropist. What Brace learned about the causes of poverty led him to concentrate more upon helping than blaming.[29] While he occasionally wrote about inherited criminality and the transmission of vice from one generation to another through the "gemmules," he took, in his own words, a "singularly hopeful" view. He had high praise for Robert Dugdale's still interesting study of intergenerational criminality and vice in the "Juke" family, but he did not, as many early social scientists erroneously did, accept it as a brief for hereditary as opposed to environmentalist explanations of vice and poverty.[30] The important point about poverty for him was that New York's "crowd of poor" was "made up of individuals debased by their own fault, or made wretched by circumstances, *who can be influenced.*"[31]

Brace recognized the massive obstacles facing those urban dwellers who were trying to preserve their morals, dignity, and physical health while caught in the degrading environment produced by overcrowding, poverty, poor housing, and want of work.[32] Although he claimed that his foremost concern with the poor was religious, what he saw in the Five Points district, Water Street, or the Fourth Ward made him urge that "Material Reform and Spiritual Reform ... must mutually help one another." "Preaching sermons to the prostitute, who has to choose between starvation and the brothel, is of very little use."[33]

He challenged those who discounted the problem of poverty in American cities. Admitting that the "*mass* of poverty and wretchedness" is far greater in European metropolises than in the United States, Brace warned Americans, who "boast that in this happy Society" no such class division exists, that there has been "gradually growing up in New York during the last twenty years" a degraded, impoverished, and isolated class of "immense numbers."[34] He pondered whether the passage of time would bring a "fixed and hereditary 'lower class'" to New York. When he described his work among New York's poor in *The Dangerous Classes of New York*, he offered his hopeful opinion that "one of the remarkable things about New York, to a close observer of its 'dangerous classes,' is ... that they do not tend to become fixed and inherited, as in European cities." Yet for all the differences between American and European cities, between New York and Paris, Brace insisted that those who believed that Paris alone is exposed to the mob were mistaken. Writing soon after the Paris Commune, he declared: "there are just the same explosive social elements beneath the surface of New York as of Paris." And for any who doubted it, he recalled the Draft Riots of 1863.[35]

The children of poverty particularly fascinated Brace. The stimulating influence of the American urban environment developed in these rootless children a keenness and an independence of spirit that Brace simultaneously admired and feared. Their quickness and fundamental sense of justice won his respect, but he also saw in them a greater threat to American cities than their more degraded counterparts posed to European cities. "The intensity of the American temperament," he reflected, "is felt in every fibre of these children of poverty and vice. Their crimes have the unrestrained and sanguinary character of a race accustomed to overcome all obstacles." He feared that "they are far more brutal than the peasantry from whom they descend." While the timid European may pick a pocket, the audacious American will plan and execute a robbery.[36]

If the city displayed distressing forms of vice and poverty, Brace also believed that the very characteristics of the urban process that had disturbed earlier reformers actually provided unique advantages in combating these evils. Twenty years before Brace began his work, Joseph Tuckerman, the Minister at Large in Boston, had taken the position that urban poverty was far worse than being poor in the country. Rural and village poor, he had argued, were an integral part of town and parish. The family's condition and wants were known by their comparatively "opulent" neighbors who would personally attend to their needs. This connection of the rich and the poor was severed by urban growth. Moreover, Tuckerman believed that the anonymity of the city encouraged viciousness. There is in the city a hope "of escape in open shame and crime, and, for those who are inclined to crime, a hope of safety from detection in it; and, as the differences of condition are here more real and sensible, and the sympathies of the classes with each other far weaker, the suffering of virtuous poverty will not only be often far greater, but greater, too, will be the recklessness of vicious poverty."[37]

As early as 1858 Brace began to reassess this traditional position. "Even in our New England villages, it is well known ... that there are families, sometimes two or three generations old, of inveterate paupers." Despite appearances to the contrary, "there is in New York very little of this state of things, outside of the public institutions." In our stable and conservative villages, wicked families tend to remain together, but in the city, with its "incessant change," these families are constantly broken up . . . [and] there is little inherited criminality and pauperism."[38]

Cities also provide another advantage in this matter. The self-respect and personal independence marking village life–more valuable than any amount of charity–nevertheless "tends to keep a wicked or idle family in its present condition." Any individual effort to "improve or educate" an unfortunate family "would be resented or misconstrued." "No machinery of charity" exists in the traditional village "to lift them [the poor] out of the slime." The "natural effect of the best virtues of the rural community" is that an unfortunate family will "really come out much worse than a similar family in the city." With the combination of talent and resources available and the relatively impersonal society of the large town, "there exist machinery and organization through which benevolent and religious persons can approach such families, and their good intentions not be suspected or resented." Further, because of the anonymity of the city, poor persons need not fear that accepting advice will stamp them "in public repute with a bad name."[39] The very qualities of urban life threatening the traditional community could thus be turned to advantage.

Besides its benevolent impersonality, its concentration of resources, and the fluidity of its population, the city was the focus of the American ideology of success. "[In] American life, as compared with European, and city life, as compared with country," Brace observed, "a boundless hope pervades all classes." Even the urban poor feel "the profound forces of American life; the desire of equality, ambition to rise, the sense of self-respect and the passion for education." This spirit, Brace believed, could and should be tapped by the urban philanthropist.[40]

Although the apparent futility of his early work with the broken, defeated, and demoralized men and women at Blackwell's Island and the Five Points Mission persuaded Brace that "no far-reaching and permanent work of reform could succeed among these classes," he was convinced that the "hopeful field" was "evidently among the young." He decided, accordingly, to devote himself "to that

immense class–the *children* of New York." The children of poverty, infinitely more malleable than their parents, might be molded
in the image of middle-class America by drawing them "under the
influence of the moral and fortunate classes."[41]

The first circular issued by the Children's Aid Society in 1853
reveals the mixture of Christian idealism and concern for social
control that motivated Brace and his associates. "As Christian men,"
Brace wrote, "we cannot look upon this multitude of unhappy, de-
serted, and degraded boys and girls without feeling our responsibility to God for them." They have "the same immortality, as the
little ones in our own homes." Equally important, "these boys and
girls, it should be remembered will soon form the great lower class
of our city. They will influence elections; they may shape the policy
of the city; they will assuredly, if unreclaimed, poison society all
around them."[42]

Instead of recommending the construction of more asylums,
which denied the natural workings of family and society, the Children's Aid Society proposed to place children in family settings.
This placing-out system was an alternative to institutionalization.
Although Brace continually complained that the institutional system was unnecessarily expensive,[43] his major objection to it was
that life in reformatory institutions "becomes artificial and un-
natural." Under such an "artificial system," the youth is treated "as
a little machine" and receives no "individual" or "personal influence." Brace condemned any system in which a child is only a
number in a mass, if " 'No. 2 of Cell 426' ... is all that we know of
him." The foremost task of the reformer, he believed, is to discover
a method of helping the young that would "prune dangerous impulses and yet not plant mechanical virtues," that would "use
moral machinery, and yet regard the peculiarities of the individual," that would be "in harmony with the great principles of
political economy and the great impulses of human nature."[44]

While Brace accepted organization and "moral machinery," he
wanted to guard against its assuming "more importance in the eyes
of its organizers than the work itself." Those "who deal with the
poor and semi-criminal are so much inclined to treat them in mass,
or to consider each child as a number or a name, not a person, that

personal influence comes to be forgotten." Child-saving work must seek to preserve, as much as possible, "spontaneous kindness" and "personal influence."[45]

"If we must have an Asylum," Brace thought, it ought to "approach the natural family in its organization." When he visited Germany in 1850–1851, he saw such an asylum in the Rauhe Haus, near Hamburg. This institution operated on the "family" or "cottage" system. The children were grouped into "families" of about twelve who lived together in a cottage. Each cottage was under the charge of a supervisor who acted as "a kind of father." This system seemed to be "the nearest artificial approach to the natural family."[46] Yet even it had limitations. After all, it only imitated the family influence; it was not really a family. Further, its high costs limited the number of children it might reach.[47]

Brace needed a large-scale system for his work in New York, but he was determined that natural relations reminiscent of New England community life be preserved. His solution was the placing-out system. The "large multitude of children" in the city "who are uncared for and ignorant and vagrant" might be placed with western farmers who, always needing labor, would welcome the homeless children into their households and would raise them as part of their own families.[48] The Christian family, "God's reformatory," would surround the child with "continuous, unconscious [influences] . . . no artificial system could ever supply." The placing-out system could be carried out "on a vastly larger scale even than the family system, far more naturally and effectively, and at much less expense to the community." It would secure "individual management for the child" and bring "him under the great natural impulses which train the character most vigorously."[49]

The placing-out system of the Children's Aid Society was an inevitable topic whenever reformers gathered to assess the state of their art. It received its strongest support among philanthropists from the most urbanized eastern states, especially Massachusetts where institutional care was most highly developed.[50] The greatest opposition came from charity leaders in the midwestern states where the children were placed. In his own city of New York, Brace won the praise of the Protestant middle classes, but found spokesmen for the city's Catholic charities hostile to the Children's Aid Society.

Catholic opposition is hardly surprising. The Children's Aid Society was attempting to achieve a consensus on a New England tradition that was fundamentally Protestant and middle class. Many Catholic leaders simply rejected this version of community. The conflict, however, also involved attitudes toward methods of child-saving. Brace was dedicated to bringing an end to institutional child care, and the Catholic Church typically cared for neglected and delinquent children in institutions under the supervision of the religious orders. Catholic charity workers feared that the lack of formal restraints praised by Brace would allow the children to "sink into a moral state worse than that in which they were found in our streets." The organizers of the New York Catholic Protectory, established in 1864, proposed instead a *"reformatory discipline"* that would be "strict, but kind."[51]

Western resistance was phrased in terms of a fear that the Society was flooding the West with urban scum and criminals. Here again, however, the conflict was broader. In a communication to the American Social Science Association Meeting at Saratoga in 1879, Lyman P. Alden, superintendent of the Michigan State Public School for Dependent Children, articulated western objections to the placing-out system. Like most western critics, Alden implied that Brace was unleashing future criminals on the western states. Brace, he said, had done much to commend himself to the people of New York, but "it seems quite improbable that the West, where these children are sent, feels so grateful." Curiously, however, he did not offer any evidence that children placed in Michigan turned out badly (i.e., were arrested). He undoubtedly failed to offer such data because the real issue was not the criminality of the children sent west, but the ideas on child care held by the man sending them.[52]

As reformers in "older" eastern cities grew more confident of the patterns of urban life that had developed, they were ready to return reformation to the community, where they could avail themselves "as much as possible of those remedial agencies which exist in society,—the family, social influences, industrial occupations and the like." In Massachusetts, for example, where institutional care had developed furthest before the Civil War, the *Annual Report* (1865) of the Board of State Charities made a strong and still interesting case against all forms of institutionalization: prisons, reformatories, almshouses, and asylums were all condemned for being ineffective and probably counterproductive.[53]

Samuel Gridley Howe, who may have written the report and who is remembered for his remarkable work with the blind, had begun to question the value of institutionalization even before the war. "What right have we," he reflected in 1857, "to pack off the poor, the old, the blind into asylums? They are of us, our brothers, our sisters–they belong in families; they are deprived of the dearest relations of life in being put away in masses of asylums." Charity leaders in Massachusetts realized the imperfections of ordinary family and community life, but they were confident, nevertheless, that it was in society rather than under the artificial constraints of asylum life that men and women and especially youth could find "activity, life, and a better field for growth, progress and development."[54]

In contrast, men like Alden, faced with the task of building up reformatory systems in newer states, where existing social institutions and patterns of community life seemed particularly fragile and uncertain, turned to the asylum because its orderliness–its mere physical existence–provided a tangible symbol of their effectiveness.[55] Brace's anti-institutional approach was simply inconceivable for these men.

To Brace's argument that a "poor home is better than the best institution," Alden responded sharply: "I *know* this is not so." The average country home "cannot possibly secure" the "training and discipline" required to reform children. In fact, Alden continued, "the majority of even respectable well-to-do families are unfit to train up their own children." While the families Brace selected may embrace "kind enough people . . . they do not understand child-life, how to train and discipline it; and the children placed in such homes are likely, in many cases, to retrograde." He was "very certain that a very much larger percentage of these children would have been saved had they been placed in well regulated industrial institutions" before being placed in families. With their eyes on the apparent disorderliness of family life and the weakness of existing social institutions rather than on the actual behavior of the children sent west, "hard line" educators could not believe that Brace's "soft" methods could possibly be effective.[56]

Opposition from Catholic and western charity leaders, however, never seriously hampered Brace's work. By the time of his death in 1890, the Children's Aid Society had removed approximately 90,000 homeless children from the city and placed them in homes across the country.

Measured by absolute numbers of children sent west, the 1870s marked the peak of the Society's emigration work, but such figures obscure an important change taking place within the organization. As early as 1858 the Trustees noted a growing "difficulty in procuring children for country homes, owing to manufacturing establishments of different kinds having been started" in the city. Two years later, Brace declared that "one great economical cause" is likely to "greatly modify" all future enterprises in behalf of the city's poor children. "We allude to the fact that New York is more and more *becoming a manufacturing city*." The poor, especially women and young girls, are now able to find employment in the city. If this trend toward city employment continues, "a new order of instrumentalities will be necessary for those whose aim it is to raise up the degraded classes of the city."[57]

By assuming that Brace's advocacy of country homes reflected his antiurbanism, historians have failed to notice that an increasing percentage of the Children's Aid Society's budget and energies were directed toward helping children who would reside permanently in the city.[58] Brace observed in 1868 that emigration work had reached its limits; future expansion of the organization's work would move in another direction.[59]

These new programs raised important new problems for Brace's anti-institutional approach to urbanism. No longer able to use the obviously "natural" technique of placing children in Christian families, he had to devise urban institutions that would enhance community and would protect spontaneity and naturalness.

He established a variety of social services to prepare the poor "to meet the struggle for existence." The major emphasis of the new programs was education.[60] Soon after its organization, the Society began establishing industrial schools for the poor children who were not reached by the public school system. These schools were necessary because the public system "breaks down in one direction, and does not reach the classes who most need it." The Society's schools were intended to complement, not to compete with, the public schools. They served those who were "too poor, ragged and necessarily irregular in attendance, to be adapted to the more systematic and respectable places of instruction."[61]

Brace told the teachers in 1865 that the industrial schools had "a *double work* to do." "The first and great influence of the school should be on the habits and morals of the children, and the second on the minds." "Your school," he pointed out, "is an INDUSTRIAL SCHOOL, and is expected to give vagrant, poor, and neglected children, habits of industry, cleanliness, good order and purity." He explained, "They are to be taught to have pleasure in work, to be proud of keeping their hair well brushed, their face and hands clean, and dresses mended; they are to be trained to be punctual and steady; to hang their garments and their hoods in their own places, to move together, and at the word of command; to study quietly and diligently–above all, they should be taught the great trusts of morality." "The main object of the school was not so much to thoroughly educate in books, as to refine and purify the wild children of the street, and to *teach them to work*." Brace was convinced that any street child taught "habits of industry and self-control, neatness and . . . the rudiments of moral and mental education" could easily make an honest living in New York.[62]

With the industrial school, Brace enlisted formal education in the battle against poverty and disorder in the urban community. In his quest for adequate agencies for preserving social order, however, Brace soon recognized that the industrial school did not provide sufficient hold over the poor children during the out-of-school hours. A "lodging-house and all its influences, as well as a school," was needed, "for the former gives a greater control than does a simple Industrial School."[63]

Before long, the industrial school became the center of a cluster of agencies for good in the poorer neighborhoods of the city. An existing free lunch program in the schools was expanded, food and clothing were distributed to the scholars (in a manner that would not pauperize them), mothers' meetings were established so that parents of the children might become "better acquainted with the teacher" and so that Brace and the teachers could instruct the mothers about sanitary conditions and similar topics. The Children's Aid Society responded to the problem of increasing numbers of working mothers by organizing "baby refuges," or what we would call child care centers. These centers, however, were short-lived and never extensive enough to amount to more than a gesture. Brace recognized the lack of wholesome recreational facilities for working youth, and the Children's Aid Society turned the industrial schools into social centers in the evenings. Night schools were also conducted there for working youths. A summer program for the poor children of the tenement districts annually brought from 2,500 to 3,000 tenement children to the Society's summer home at Bath, Long Island, for a week's vacation. The "Sick Children's Fund" provided medical care for poor and neglected children. Other projects were also initiated by the Children's Aid Society to aid permanent urban residents: a Free Sewing School for girls, reading rooms, a model compulsory education law, free kindergartens, circulating school libraries, a model tenement project, cooking and housework lessons, a seaside sanitarium for mothers and sick infants, and "poor people's levees."[64]

Instead of sending the poor out of the city, Brace increasingly strove to devise means of elevating them to respectable places in the urban community. The industrial schools and the allied urban agencies of the Children's Aid Society were to infuse middle-class values into the poorer sections of the city. "Abnormal tendencies" toward evil thus would be "overcome, and latent tendencies to good aroused and developed" by bringing the two ends of society together.[65]

In all of this, Brace was intensely concerned with specifying the relationship between the natural and the artificial in the urban environment. He believed that they could be reconciled within the same institution or social system. He sought to combine the naturalness, spontaneity, and the organic social order of the village community with the formal organizations that were implied by urban industrialism.

Brace's observations on the Object System of teaching, which he introduced into the industrial schools, reveals his propensity to tie spontaneity to an acceptance of the increasingly constraining demands of organizational society. In common with many other mid-century educational leaders, including New York state and city authorities, Brace had high praise for this pedagogy. The Object System stressed the structuring of individual lessons around students' observations of concrete objects presented by the teacher. By emphasizing the senses and usage rather than abstract rules in learning, Object Teaching, according to its proponents, altered formal education to fit children's natural abilities. As Brace put it, the major obstacle in teaching the young was that "children's minds work so much through their senses, while our common systems are so much addressed to their memory and abstract powers."[66]

In contrast to the rigid and mechanical Lancasterian system used by the Free School Society earlier in the century, the Object Teaching System allowed the children a significant amount of freedom within the framework of formal instruction. The "great difficulty" for teachers in the newly emerging school systems, Brace believed, was the "liability of falling into routine–both teachers and scholars going on in a mechanical manner." "To a certain extent, these and other difficulties are obviated" by Object Teaching which, "to a degree, is a substitute for invention in the teacher." The child also had a more active role in a classroom conducted according to the new method. "The principle most insisted on in all this system is, that the child should teach himself, as far as possible."[67] By introducing spontaneity, or its appearance, into instruction, the Object System of teaching eased the transition of children into the formal learning situation of the urban classroom. Ironically, Object Teaching, which offered so many liberating possibilities, was eventually criticized for being as artificial and routinized as what had preceded it.[68]

While praising Object Teaching for its naturalness, Brace could, without any apparent sense of contradiction, simultaneously publicize its advantages in training a modern industrial labor force. After asserting that other systems of teaching left young men "utterly incompetent for using their faculties on practical subjects," Brace declared that the Object System of teaching used in the in-

dustrial schools would produce workers capable of performing the
tasks required in an industrial society.[69]

If Brace's attitude toward Object Teaching begins to suggest his
idea of naturalness as an essential element of urbanism, a close
investigation of his attitudes toward professionalism and large-
scale organization in charity work provides a fuller understanding.
Brace praised the advent of salaried "experts" in charity work, but
he envisioned a role for them quite different than that they perform
in twentieth-century welfare bureaucracies. The modern welfare
professional, whether consciously or not, is a buffer between permanently antagonistic elements of society. Brace, however, based
his thought upon a different concept of community. The philanthropist, according to him, worked toward a lasting reconciliation
within the community. As he wrote in the preface to *The Dangerous Classes of New York*, the book that described his life's work,
his aim had been to "bring the two ends of society nearer together
in human sympathy."[70]

"The great evil of our city life," he believed, is "that classes become so separated. Union Square or the Avenues know as little of
Water Street or Cherry Street as if they were different cities."[71] To
solve this problem of a divided community, it was necessary to
involve more than professional welfare bureaucrats in charity work.
Brace intended to restore relations between the classes through the
use of volunteers, especially at the industrial schools.

The volunteer teachers clearly advanced the organizational goal
of economy and served Brace's educational goals by exerting an unconscious influence for good upon the children, but they also
brought the middle classes into familiar contact with the poor. The
schools, he wrote, "bring a personal influence to bear on the children of poverty and crime, such as nothing else would give," and
"they form a connecting link more and more in our artificial society, necessary, between the lowest poor and the rich, between the
fortunate and the unfortunate." Such a restoration of relations
between the classes would make the city a more humane place to
live, and it would produce a community consensus on middle-class
values.[72]

Yet Brace would not have favored completely volunteer charity–

even were it possible. He considered it right and proper that the bulk of the teaching burden in the industrial schools be handled by salaried teachers.[73] He was unequivocally in favor of organized charity; he had no nostalgic desire to return to the completely informal and voluntaristic charity methods of the village.[74] True, he appreciated the naturalness of social relations in the rural village, but he also saw advantages in the resources, freedom, privacy, and even the impersonality of the city. He hoped to combine the happier aspects of each locale in his charity organization.

He recognized that any charity organized upon a purely volunteer basis would be inadequate because the rather constant needs of the poor require that charity not be "mere holiday work, or a sudden gush of sentiment; but, to be of use, it must be patiently continued, week by week, and month by month, and year by year." Volunteers, who are likely to be irregular in their efforts, can be effective only when "combined with good salaried labor." The Children's Aid Society was structured so that "the fortunate classes in this city, who have felt it a duty of humanity and religion to sacrifice time and means for the benefit of the unfortunate" might work in conjunction with salaried persons who "have become 'experts' in charitable labors." This combination continually brings "to the enterprise a freshness and enthusiasm which nothing else can give," while the "brunt and burden" is carried by one "making his peculiar work a life work and profession."[75]

Instead of relying entirely upon uncertain contributions for funds, Brace proposed that the charity organization's finances be placed on "as sound and rational basis as possible." He had no qualms about abandoning any supposedly traditional American reliance on voluntarism in order to obtain state aid to lay a "solid and permanent basis" for the work of the Children's Aid Society.[76] Yet he was not willing to see a huge public charity replace the combined approach that characterized the Children's Aid Society. He admitted that state charities would have "the advantage of greater solidity and more thorough and expensive machinery, and often more careful organization," but they would lack the "individual enthusiasm" that marked the Children's Aid Society.[77]

The early Charity Organization Society movement, the spearhead of urban philanthropy during the 1880s, retained much of this mid-century romantic spirit.[78] The mixture of metaphors used by Charles S. Fairchild in 1884 to outline the purpose of a Charity Organization Society could also describe Brace's intentions: "Such a society is for cities and large villages, and is designed to be a machine which shall attempt to overcome difficulties caused by the conditions of life in such places,–a machine to restore, in some degree, the natural relations of man to man." Charity Organization leaders like Franklin B. Sanborn and Josephine Shaw Lowell also shared Brace's concern that charity be both organized and individualistic.[79] There is less of a break between Brace's generation of charity workers and the "scientific" philanthropists who founded the Charity Organization Societies than there is between the men and women of the early Charity Organization Societies and the first welfare professionals. Using the mid-century definition of community, the early Charity Organization Society leaders saw their organization as "an artifice to restore the natural relations of men to their fellows, of which life in a city has robbed them." They sought to create a "true commune" by bringing well-to-do volunteers into sympathy with the poor.[80]

These ideas may evoke our sympathies today, but we might remember that Horatio Wood, Brace, and the early leaders of the Charity Organization Society movement also had in common certain assumptions less attractive to modern sensibilities. Their intentions were deeply conservative and their objective was to impose middle-class culture upon the urban poor. Moreover, their reliance upon the volunteer charity workers was founded upon the assumption that middle-class philanthropists were morally superior to the poor they would influence.[81]

Near the end of the century, a new concept of poverty stressing environmental causation and economic exploitation gained wide acceptance. With this view of poverty, the charity workers' presumed moral superiority no longer seemed to justify interference in the lives of the poor. Philanthropists had two alternatives. They could relinquish their sense of superiority and recognize that the poor might have important insights into their own problems, or they could retain their superior authority over the poor by finding a more plausible justification for it than mere class affiliation. The former approach was articulated and pioneered by Jane Addams at Hull House. The latter resulted in the establishment of a professional welfare bureaucracy where the authority of the social worker rested upon presumed scientific knowledge or superior expertise.[82]

Jane Addams realized what Brace and his colleagues must have noticed but were unwilling to admit to themselves. The relation between the charity worker and the poor was not "neighborly." It was, she pointed out, a "clashing of two ethical standards." The life-style that charity workers prescribed for the poor was "incorrigibly bourgeois." Believing that the existing "charitable relation" revealed a "lack of that equality which democracy implies," Addams established a social settlement at Hull House in 1889.[83] She hoped thereby to "give tangible expression to the democratic ideal." Instead of serving as a middle-class outpost in the slum, the social settlement recognized the legitimacy of the cultural values held by the poor. It aimed "to develop whatever of social life its neighborhood may afford." Emptying themselves "of all conceit of opinion and all self-assertion," the residents were "to arouse and interpret the public opinion of their neighborhood." "They must be content to live quietly side by side with their neighbors, until they grow into a sense of relationship and mutual interests."[84] This approach to urban poverty, which has in it the seeds of community organization, offered the possibility of bringing the two ends of society into contact on more equal and democratic terms.[85] However, Jane Addams was not the whole of the charity movement at the turn of the century. The bulk of the movement was diverging toward the professional welfare bureaucracy that would define social work in the twentieth century.

Toward the end of his career, Brace noticed that personal involvement in charity work by the better-off classes was declining.[86] This trend symbolized a larger shift in approaches to social welfare in urban America that Brace only partly perceived. Mid-century community leaders had been relatively open to the problems of the poor, and they had responded to the divisions they saw in urban society by seeking to bridge them. Their definition of community implied an active involvement in social and political affairs. The urban middle classes in the late nineteenth century, however, reacted to the poverty and disorder they saw about them by withdrawing into themselves. They sought to avoid any personal confrontation with the unpleasant lives of the poor people in their midst. Brace noticed manifestations of this in New York, and a recent study of middle-class families in late nineteenth-century Chicago makes the same point: "the history of the community's attitudes toward urban poverty moved from ... open help to a defensive walling in of the middle classes."[87] What we have here is a new conception of community: a view of the community as permanently divided into antagonistic groups. This version of community discourages personal involvement by the better-off classes and provides the background for the professional welfare bureaucrat who serves as a buffer betwen the two groups.

Since this new concept of community made it more difficult for charity organization leaders to recruit volunteers, they hired paid agents. Once this process was begun, it was self-sustaining. In quest of professional recognition, the new social workers were hostile to volunteers. Professionalism and a new organizational ideology eclipsed earlier concerns with the problem of naturalness or organicism in community relations. The professional's major commitment shifted to his function in society. Experts in the welfare bureaucracy, supported by a relatively passive public, increasingly concentrated on providing professional service to a basically anonymous client in a permanently divided society.[88]

These bureaucratic developments reinforced existing class lines instead of dissolving them. They also led to the definition of sympathetic relationships with the poor as unprofessional—as problems of overidentification with the client.[89] Of course, some twentieth-century social workers tried to temper the demands of an organizational society with a concern for community and naturalness in social relations. Yet the delicate balance between community and society that had been maintained during the nineteenth century shifted during the first years of this century. The new equilibrium that was established assumed a less personal and a more abstract conception of community, and it provided the basis for professionalism in social work.

As America's most well-known protoprofessional in urban welfare work during the 1870s and 1880s, Brace was intensely interested in the problem of professionalism. He anticipated his twentieth-century counterpart when he wrote of the inadequacy of inspiration or religion as sole motives for charity workers. He argued the necessity to bolster them with "something of the common inducements of mankind" in the form of adequate salaries, opportunities for promotion, and recognition of their special skills. Yet at other times his distance from the welfare professional of today is striking. Roy Lubove has recently argued that one of the defining characteristics of professional welfare work is its commitment to "function" as opposed to "cause." Brace, however, considered enthusiasm for "good causes" to be essential in a charity worker. If the twentieth-century caseworker often prizes the scientific objectivity of his methods and the clinical detachment with which he approaches his client, Brace insisted that the relationship must always have "a certain generosity and compassion." If the twentieth-century social welfare bureaucrat bows to the idol of business efficiency, Brace warned that "it will not be best to let charity become too much of a business." Brace also anticipated and warned of the dangers of routine in welfare organizations. "Routine may be carried so far as to make the aiding of misery the mere dry working of a machine." He always worried that the Children's Aid Society might become so effectively businesslike that its agents might come "to look on the poor creatures whom we aid, as merely cases–objects of business-charity."[90]

In 1840 an anonymous writer in the *Knickerbocker* magazine expressed a fear that the charity organizations being established in cities to help the poor might turn out to be Frankensteins. "Charity in cities," he wrote, "may rear her monumental piles, and endow them with the munificence of princes. Yet she, too–warm, impulsive, heaven-born Charity–may degenerate into a cold, mechanical, political economy. Her life may be crushed beneath a system." It was this healthy concern for what organizational society could do to the affective side of man that distinguished Brace's "romantic generation" from the "factual generation" who professionalized welfare during the Progressive Era.[91] A concern for community, natural relations, and spontaneity prevented the nineteenth-century

charity movement from rapidly evolving into a modern welfare
bureaucracy. Using the vocabulary of the nineteenth-century literary figures who wrestled with the problem, Brace put his finger
precisely upon this distinguishing characteristic: the charity agent,
he wrote, "must have heart as well as head." [92]

VII.

Cityscape & Landscape in America:
Frederick Law Olmsted

Let us help each other . . . to give our thoughts a
practical turn. . . . Throw your light on the paths in
Politics and Social Improvement and encourage me
to put my foot *down* and *forwards*. There's a
great *work* [that] wants doing in this our generation,
Charley—let's off jacket and go about it.

Frederick Law Olmsted to Charles L. Brace (1847)

I offer a small contribution of individual experience
towards the history of the latter half of the first
century of the American republic,—the period in
which the work of the railroad, the electric telegraph,
the ocean steamship, the Darwinian hypothesis,
and of Universal suffrage began; in which what is
called the temperance reformation and the abolition
of slavery have occurred; in which millions
of people have been concentrating at New York,
Philadelphia, Boston, Baltimore, Cincinnati,
Chicago, St. Louis, and San Francisco, while rural
neighborhoods in New England, Virginia, the
Carolinas and Georgia have been rapidly losing
population and still more rapidly losing various
forms of wealth and worth.

Frederick Law Olmsted (ca. 1877)

The Union of prosaic sense with poetical feeling,
of democratic sympathies with refined and scholarly
tastes, of punctilious respect for facts with tender
hospitality for ideas, has enabled him
[Frederick Law Olmsted] to appreciate and embody,
both in conception and execution of the Park,
the beau-ideal of a people's pleasure ground.

Henry W. Bellows (1861)

IN HERMAN MELVILLE's novel *Pierre* (1852), a country girl who came to New York with Pierre says: "I know nothing of these things, Pierre. But I like not the town. Think'st thou Pierre, the time will ever come when all the earth shall be paved?"[1] Her concern was shared by a whole generation of Americans, many of whom were simultaneously celebrating the rise of American cities. Feeling the multiplicity of the city's stimulation, the artifice of its organization, the complexity and intensity of its demands, the oppressive monotony of its streets and buildings, Americans who were moving from the country into the city longed for the occasional relief provided by the more familiar natural landscape of their rural past.

Some of the strategies developed for bringing the landscape within reach of the urban dweller seem quaintly amusing today: the rural cemeteries that were built on the outskirts of most large cities, or the declaration by the American Art-Union in 1846 that "to the inhabitants of cities . . . a painted landscape is almost essential to preserve a healthy tone to the spirits, lest they forget in the wilderness of bricks which surrounds them the pure delights of nature and a country life."[2] Yet these movements imply an important idea—an idea waiting for someone to articulate it and to broadcast it. During the second half of the nineteenth century, the idea found a spokesman in Frederick Law Olmsted. He understood and explained to urban Americans the possibilities of using the natural landscape creatively in an urban civilization.

Olmsted's work provides an especially fruitful insight into nineteenth-century urbanism because, unlike most planning today, his environmental designs were rooted in a clearly articulated social philosophy. Like his friend Charles Loring Brace, Olmsted looked toward the development of social institutions and physical environments that would strengthen the web of urban community life. While Brace developed philanthropy toward this end, Olmsted hoped to lessen the divisions in urban society by using nature to provide occasional relief from the social antagonisms, nervous tensions, and occupational routine of the city. By bringing nature into the city in the form of parks, Olmsted hoped to raise urban life to a higher level of civilization.

Olmsted's assumption that romantic nature and art might have an elevating effect upon American culture had found expression among earlier American artists and critics. Rejecting or, rather, misunderstanding the radical thrust of the contemporary Transcendental ideal of art as self-fulfillment, the leading spokesmen for American art during the 1840s and 1850s emphasized the usefulness of art, romantic nature, and beauty in refining and stabilizing the disorderly and individualistic society of Jacksonian America.[3]

Andrew Jackson Downing, the most notable of these earlier critics, remarked in 1847 that "one does not need to be much of a philosopher" to perceive "that one of the most striking of our national traits, is the SPIRIT OF UNREST." Admitting that "it is the grand energetic element which leads us to clear vast forests, and settle new States, with a rapidity unparalleled in the world's history," he pointed out that "in another light" this American trait "is by no means so agreeable to the reflective mind." "The *spirit of unrest,* followed into the bosom of society, makes of man a feverish being, in whose Tantalus' cup *repose* is the unattainable drop." Much as he admired the "energy of our people," Downing feared that this active side of the American character was "in some degree the antagonist" of what he valued yet more highly: "the love of order, the obedience to law, the security and repose of society, the love of home." Anything that would keep this energy "within due bounds," without completely stifling it, "may be looked upon as a boon to the nation." And Downing believed that aesthetic taste, as expressed in rural architecture and landscape gardening, would have precisely this influence upon American culture.[4]

Earlier Americans, he admitted, had little time to cultivate taste because the "new world" required a "population full of enterprise and energy to subdue and improve its vast territory." By the 1840s, however, Downing thought he discovered a growing appreciation for "Rural Embellishment." In the older states, where "wealth has accumulated" and where society is more "fixed in its character," a fondness for "those simple and fascinating enjoyments to be found in country life and rural pursuits, is witnessed on every side." Downing was confident that this new feeling toward rural life would temper the "tendency towards constant change, and the restless spirit of emigration, which form part of our national character."[5]

Although many of Olmsted's ideas on the theory and practice of landscape architecture as well as his assumptions about the moral and social influences of rural scenery were anticipated by Downing, there remains an important difference between the two men. Olmsted was a nineteenth-century urban man; Downing was not. Rural architecture and country life, not the city, provided the focus for Downing's work. During the three years preceding his untimely and accidental death in 1852, Downing devoted more attention to the city, particularly his agitation for a park in New York, but he never assumed a truly urban point of view. Had he lived longer he might have become an urban man. In fact, however, Downing, who lived in a romantic villa at Newburgh, on the Hudson River, remained essentially a rural gentleman.

Downing's major interest was in the improvement of country residences. His picturesque aesthetic stressed the essential harmony of domestic architecture: the rural structure blending comfortably into its natural setting.[6] He could not accommodate the whiteness and the straight lines of the Greek temple to this vision, and he is remembered in the history of architecture for his opposition to the Greek revival style in domestic architecture.[7] The formal order of classicism also disturbed him because it seemed to symbolize the power of the city and man's dominance over nature. He translated this antiurban bias and distrust of progress into an aesthetic choice for Gothic architecture and rural scenery. He hoped that the cultivation of romantic taste in rural architecture would temper the aggressiveness and acquisitiveness that pervaded American society. A fitting and tasteful Gothic cottage or villa adapted to its natural setting, according to Downing, was a "powerful means of civilization." The "happiest social and moral development of our people" might be found in country houses located amid the "peace of sylvan scenes, surrounded by the perennial freshness of nature, enriched without and within by the objects of universal beauty and interest."[8]

Downing's aesthetic vision surpassed Jefferson's in its greater sensitivity to the relationships of the romantic sensibility, landscape art, and urbanization, but his ideas remained, nevertheless, within the framework of the Jeffersonian middle landscape ideal. Avoiding the clear and direct confrontation of cityscape and landscape represented by Justice Story's interpretation of Mount Auburn

Cemetery and by Olmsted's later urban park designs, Downing's aesthetic theory, even in his park writings, celebrated the older ideal of a "harmonious union" of nature and art within an essentially rural context.[9]

Olmsted, who shared Downing's concern for "taste" and for a less individualistic and disorderly society, went beyond his predecessor by assuming an urban perspective. In his innumerable reports and in his designs for dozens of parks, suburbs, college campuses, and public buildings, he combined his commitment to the natural landscape with an acceptance, even an embrace, of the modern city. While Downing's observations on landscape and society in America hardly suggest the industrial development that transformed nineteenth-century urban life, the industrial city, with its dirt and noise, extreme crowding, class and ethnic divisions, extensive economic organizations, occupational routine, and physical chaos, is the obvious focal point for Olmsted's work.

Frederick Law Olmsted was born at Hartford, Connecticut, on April 26, 1822. He later wrote that his "mother died while I was so young that I have but a tradition of memory rather than the faintest recollection of her." He remembered that his father, a prosperous merchant, had little inclination or ability to give oral instruction, but that he was highly sensitive to natural beauty. "I see," Olmsted recalled, "that the unpremeditated and insensible influence which came to me from him was probably the strongest element in my training."[10]

From Horace Bushnell, whose sermons he attended in Hartford, Olmsted, like Brace, learned of the importance of nonverbal influences in the development of character. Bushnell's intellectual style also provided Olmsted with an example of a man seeking to accommodate growth and change to a romantic perspective.[11] Significantly, Olmsted and Bushnell later collaborated in planning what is now Bushnell Park in Hartford.[12]

After receiving his early education in the homes of a series of ministers, Olmsted entered Yale in 1836. Giving eye troubles as his reason, he quit school before the year was out. His father's wealth and patience allowed Frederick the luxury of many false starts and mistakes before he found his true career, and he spent the next thirty years drifting from one occupation to another until he finally made park and city planning his profession.

His desultory preparation for a career began with the study of engineering with F. A. Barton of Andover, Massachusetts. Olmsted later described the experience in an autobiographical fragment: "I was nominally the pupil of a topographical engineer but really for the most part given over to a decently restrained vagabond life."[13] After unhappy experiences clerking in a New York mercantile house and as a sailor, Olmsted decided to become a farmer. He initially studied farming with an uncle, but soon placed himself under the instruction of George Geddes, a prominent scientific farmer in upstate New York. In January 1847 his father set him up on his own farm at Guilford, Connecticut. Unfortunately, the farm did not prosper, and after only one season Frederick went broke. A year later, the elder Olmsted purchased another farm for his son, this one on Staten Island. Here Olmsted settled down to a life of gentleman farmer and literary man. He contributed to Andrew Jackson Downing's magazine, *Horticulturist*, and, after a trip to Europe with his brother and Charles Loring Brace, he published his first book, *Walks and Talks of an American Farmer in England* (1852). With the exception of the curious fact that nearly one-third of a book ostensibly on English agricultural life was devoted to urban topics, there was no suggestion during these years that by the outbreak of the Civil War Olmsted would be committed to an urban-industrial civilization in America.

Olmsted undoubtedly agreed when Downing in 1847 celebrated "cultivators of the soil" as the "great industrial class in this country." He clearly revealed his agrarian preferences when he advised his brother John, who had become ill at Yale in 1845, to quit school and to become a farmer. There is no sense in wrecking your health at school "merely for a bit of sheep's skin." The "rural pursuits" of a scientific farmer would do more than college "to elevate and enlarge" the mind. Moreover, "the objects of a farmer . . . are such as to relieve him from the annoyances which the envy and opposition of rivals, constantly inflict in most other occupations. . . . For my part I believe that our farmers are, and have cause to be, the most contented men in the world."[14] In 1845 farming appealed to Olmsted as a way of avoiding the disturbing competition that increasingly marked American society; later he would see parks, suburbs, and genuine urbanity as stabilizing forces that might encourage the development of a noncompetitive, organic urban community.

Like so many young men of his generation, Olmsted expressed a desire to "make myself useful in the world, to make others happy, to help to advance the condition of Society," but there is no indication that during the 1840s he saw future progress in any way linked to life in the nation's cities. In fact, he expected that it would be as a "Country Squire in Old Connecticut" that he might help "as far as I could [to foster] in the popular mind generosity, charity, taste, and etc."[15]

No one event, as Albert Fein has pointed out, can fully explain Olmsted's shift of interest from the farm to the city. The most obvious influence was the transformation of the American landscape itself, but other more personal causes were also at work: his inability to make the Staten Island farm pay; the influence of Andrew Jackson Downing, who was turning his attention to urban parks; and his friendship with Charles Loring Brace, who was beginning his work in urban philanthropy. Most significant of all, however, may have been his journeys to the American South between 1853 and 1857.[16]

Six months before setting out on his first southern journey, Olmsted had visited the utopian North American Phalanx, near Red Bank, New Jersey. Although he was much impressed with the unselfishness and cooperation he found in this Fourierist community established by Albert Brisbane in 1843, he thought that educational opportunities, in the broadest sense, were too limited there. Describing the visit in a letter to Brace, Olmsted expressed his first doubts about the superiority of rural life.[17] In the rural (and slave) South, these doubts ripened into a firm conviction that the city, not the country, offered the greatest possibilities for social democracy.

The idea of a southern tour emerged from Olmsted's debates with Brace over slavery. Brace was an abolitionist; Olmsted was not, although he disliked slavery. The two thought that their recurring argument might be settled if Olmsted went to the South and judged conditions firsthand. Brace broached the project to his friend Henry J. Raymond, editor of the *New York Times*. Raymond, who had been impressed with Olmsted's book on England

and who shared Olmsted's Free Soil political opinions, engaged him as a special correspondent.[18]

Olmsted's reports to the *Times* were the most widely read of all such reports. They were later collected into three books that remain unsurpassed in their description of social and economic conditions in the South on the eve of the Civil War.[19] Their interest for us, however, is that they reveal as much about Olmsted and northern society as they do of the slave system. They amount to a justification of the free labor system of the urban-industrial North against the slave system and its defenders.

Olmsted judged the South against essentially urban and industrial standards: the cities were small, inferior, and dirty; lyceums, public libraries, art galleries, and parks were lacking; industrial development lagged.[20] He saw the issue as a conflict between two opposing social systems, and he was too committed to the northern one to approach the South in any other manner.[21]

The use of slave labor was not condemned as a sin by Olmsted; he presented, instead, a basically economic argument, which may account for the tremendous influence of his writings in the North. Only ten days after leaving New York for the South, Olmsted wrote to Brace: "I shall be able to show conclusively I think that free labor is cheaper than slave."[22] His reasons reveal a sophisticated appreciation of the role of interest and spontaneous activity in releasing the energies of labor in modern economies and societies.

In common with the diverse group of men who soon came together to form the Republican party, Olmsted believed that the spontaneous interest of the worker was a more effective stimulus to work than any artificially imposed regimen. Herein lay the superiority of the free labor system of the industrial North. Comparing South and North, he wrote: work men "mechanically, under a task-master, so that they shall have no occasion to use discretion, except to avoid the imposition of additional labor, or other punishment; deny them, as much as possible, the means of enlarged information, and high mental culture—and what can be expected of them." Inevitably, "their ingenuity, enterprise, and skill will be paralyzed." A country with such a labor system can never compare favorably "with countries adjoining, in which a more simple, natural, and healthy system of labor prevails." "As a general rule,"

Olmsted concluded, a man will "always work harder, more skill-fully, and with more exercise of discretion, for himself than for any one else; especially so if his work for another is not wholly volun-tary and his task [not] self-imposed."[23] This concern for what he considered natural impulses in the stimulation of economic activity would reappear later as an important part of his rationale for public parks.

If his opposition to slavery as a form of labor was basically eco-nomic, his condemnation of it as the foundation of a social system was based upon his moral commitment to social democracy—a commitment deepened by what he saw in the South. Writing in the third person, he declared in the preface to *A Journey in the Sea-board Slave States* that "as a democrat he went to study the South —its institutions, and its people; more than ever a democrat, he has returned from this labor."[24] Olmsted deplored the South's rejection of Jeffersonian democracy in favor of an aristocratic cavalier myth. His southern experiences enabled him to see through this myth cultivated so earnestly by southern leaders and accepted by many in the North. He reported that he looked in vain for the southern gentleman celebrated in the myth: "The southern gentleman, as we ordinarily conceive him to be, is as rare a phenomenon in the South at the present day as is the old squire of Geoffrey Crayon in modern England."[25]

Yet Olmsted was painfully aware that neither had the dem-ocratic North, plagued by its "love of money," produced many gentlemen. In one of his last dispatches to the *New York Times*, Olmsted posed and answered the question of whether an inference "unfavorable to Democratic Institutions" should be drawn from this fact. "I think not. Without regard to the future, and to what we may yet become under Democracy, the condition and character of our people *as a whole*, to the best of my judgment, is better . . . than that of the people, *including all classes*, of any other nation. Very much more so than those of the South."[26]

In spite of the widespread opportunities for upward social mo-bility that Olmsted assumed were present in the North, he could not deny that in New York and some other large northern cities "we seem [to be] taking some pains to form a permanent lower class."[27] Writing to Brace from the South, Olmsted admitted that the existence of "rowdyism" and "ruffianism" among the common people of the North made him "very melancholy." He saw two choices. He could either accept the southern critique of urban industrialism and become an "Aristocrat," or become "more of a Democrat than I have been – a Socialist Democrat."

Believing that "government should have in view the encouragement of a democratic condition of society as well as of government," he chose social democracy. Convinced that "the poor & wicked need more than to be let alone," Olmsted proposed the development of social and political institutions "that shall more directly *assist* the poor and degraded to elevate themselves." Doubting that "our state of society is sufficiently Democratic . . . or likely to be by mere *laisser allez*," Olmsted urged that "our educational principle . . . be enlarged and made to include more than these miserable common schools." What the poor need is "an education to refinement and taste and the mental & moral capital of gentlemen." The letter was intended to encourage Brace to continue his philanthropic work with the poor children of New York, but Olmsted's concluding remarks were broad enough to explain his own later career as a city planner: "Well the moral of this damndly long letter," he wrote, is "Go ahead with the Children's Aid and get up parks, gardens, music, dancing schools, reunions which will be so attractive as to force into contact the good & bad, the gentlemanly and the rowdy."[28] Ironically, it was in the rural South that Olmsted arrived at the theory of urban democracy that guided his later career in northern cities.

The prospective country squire was becoming a nineteenth-century urban man. During the Civil War, Olmsted decided that the future lay with the city. "There can be no doubt," he told the American Social Science Association in 1870, "that, in all modern civilization, as in that of the ancients, there is a strong drift townward." It would seem, he thought, "more rational to prepare for a continued rising of the townward flood than to count upon its subsidence." Those who looked upon this urban trend as a great evil received a sharp challenge from Olmsted: "To avoid prolonged discussion of the question thus suggested I will refer but briefly to the intimate connection which is evident between the growth of towns and the dying out of slavery and feudal customs, of priest-craft and government by divine right, the multiplication of books, newspapers, schools, and other means of popular education and the adoption of improved methods of communication, transportation, and of various labor-saving inventions."[29]

Olmsted's own life, as he himself recognized, expressed the trans-formation that was occurring in America during his lifetime. If his own interests shifted from the country to the city, he pointed out in an autobiographical fragment that this represented one indi-vidual's experience within a larger social movement. "Millions of people," he wrote, "have been concentrating at New York, Phila-delphia, Boston, Baltimore, Cincinnati, Chicago, St. Louis, and San Francisco, while rural neighborhoods in New England, Virginia, the Carolinas and Georgia have been rapidly losing population and ... wealth and worth."[30]

This process of depopulation left rural culture impoverished. In common with most urban intellectuals, especially those who took the New York *Nation* as their standard, Olmsted, who was instru-mental in founding the magazine, hoped that the agricultural col-leges to be established by the Morrill Act might serve as vehicles, not unlike the railroads, for bringing urban culture to the country-side.[31] Although he saw some indications that the "conveniences and habits of towns-people" were being extended to rural districts, Olmsted realized that American cities "are likely to be still more attractive to population in the future," particularly to women. "Is it astonishing?" Olmsted thought not: "Compare advantages in respect simply to schools, libraries, music, and the fine arts." Even "the greatest wealth can hardly command as much of these in the country as the poorest work-girl is offered ... in Boston at the mere cost of a walk for a short distance over a good, firm, clean pathway, lighted at night and made interesting to her by shop fronts and the variety of people passing."[32] Yet for all the advantages gained through "the growth of towns and the spread of town ways of liv-ing," Olmsted perceived "some grave drawbacks."[33]

His analysis of urban defects carries him far beyond Thomas Jefferson and places him alongside modern urban critics. He denied the assumption held in the past that the "larger the population of a town should be allowed to become, the greater would be the inconvenience and danger to which all who ventured to live in it would necessarily be subject." He claimed that in comparison with the smaller towns of earlier times, in the great cities of the nineteenth century the chance of living to old age is greater, epidemics less frequent and more controllable, fires less common, ruffians much better held in check, mobs less frequently formed, and "there is a smaller proportion of the population given over to vice and crime and a vastly larger proportion of well-educated, orderly, industrious and well-to-do citizens."[34]

Modern urban life, however, imposed psychological burdens that particularly concerned Olmsted: what "we talk of . . . under the name of vital exhaustion, nervous irritation and constitutional depression; when we speak of tendencies, through excessive materialism, to loss of faith and lowness of spirit, by which life is made, to some, questionably worth the living." Although he believed that the middle classes were particularly affected by this problem, he saw symptoms of it in all classes.[35] The fundamental defect of the American city, in Olmsted's view, was its failure to encourage the happiness of urban populations.

The social, economic, and technological forces that had created the modern city could be used to solve its problems. All that was necessary, according to Olmsted, was to redirect them. Historically they had been pointed toward selfishly individualistic economic goals. Olmsted insisted that in the future these city-building forces must be directed, on a metropolitan scale, toward social, even psychological, needs, instead of purely economic ones.[36] The old theory asserting that it is "the best government which governs least" must be abandoned for a more positive understanding of government. "It is the main duty of government, if it is not the sole duty of government, to provide means of protection for all its citizens in the pursuit of happiness against the obstacles, otherwise insurmountable, which the selfishness of individuals or combinations of individuals is liable to interpose to that pursuit."[37]

Specifically, Olmsted urged the development of large urban parks and suburban neighborhoods. Parks and suburbs historically have served the needs of the middle classes more than the poor, but Olmsted's intention was to provide all classes with relief from the less happy aspects of urban life. Parks, especially, should bring various classes into familiar contact, into a community. The city park, for Olmsted, symbolized the possibilities of democratic urban life.[38]

It seemed particularly important to have parks and suburbs connected with American cities because a large proportion of the successful men there were born in the country. "A country boy receives a common school education, exhibits ability and at a comparatively early age finds himself engaged in business in a provincial town; as his experience and capacity increase he seeks enlarged opportunities for the exercise of his powers and . . . ultimately finds himself drawn by an irresistible magnetic force to the commercial cities; . . . and the sharp country boy becomes the keen city man." Yet, Olmsted asserted, he finds city life without parks and suburban residences unpleasant. "Trees and grass are . . . wrought into the very texture and fibre of his constitution and without being aware of it he feels day by day that his life needs a suggestion of the old country flavor to make it palatable as well as profitable." Olmsted hastened to add that "we do not . . . mean to argue that the tastes to which we have referred are limited solely to citizens whose early life has been passed in the country," but they present an especially common and understandable case.[39]

These statements recall Thoreau's famous reminder that "our ancestors were savages" and that "in Wildness is the preservation of the World." More importantly, these nineteenth-century assumptions about man's deep ties to nature, based upon nothing but casual observation, common sense, and feeling, are now being recognized in environmental research. If it is clear that man's cultural development has allowed him to adapt to urban life, some recent research suggests that it is neither wise nor possible to ignore the evolutionary past which ties man to nature.[40]

The gridiron plan devised for New York in 1811 reflected the economic and speculative basis of planning detested by Olmsted. The three commissioners appointed to devise a plan for the city rejected any "supposed improvements" which may "embellish" a plan. They preferred, in their words, "rectilinear and rectangular streets" because "strait sided, and right angled houses are the most cheap to build, and the most convenient to live in." The commissioners also calmly dismissed proposals for reserving substantial tracts of land for public parks: "It may, to many, be a matter of surprise," they wrote, "that so few vacant places have been left, and those so small, for the benefit of fresh air, and consequent preservation of health." But the "large arms of the sea which embrace Manhattan Island" make its situation exceptionally healthy. Furthermore, when from the same cause the "convenience of commerce" is "peculiarly felicitous" and "the price of land is so uncommonly great, it seemed proper to admit principles of economy to greater influence than might, under circumstances of a different kind, have consisted with the dictates of prudence and the sense of duty."[41]

This apology was generally accepted during the following decades. Thus the total area of pleasure grounds open to the public at mid-century, when urban development had already proceeded beyond Thirty-Fourth Street, did not exceed one hundred acres. The largest single park, the Battery, contained only twenty-one.[42] In the midst of the rapid growth generated by the Erie Canal and the advent of industrial production in the city, however, New Yorkers began to reconsider. William Cullen Bryant and Andrew Jackson Downing gave voice to a movement for a New York Park that culminated with the passage of a law in the state legislature in July 1853. The city was authorized by it to take the present site of Central Park.[43]

Once land for the park was acquired, topographical surveys were carried out under the direction of Egbert L. Viele. Viele, who had been trained at West Point, served in the Mexican War before resigning his commission in 1853 to open an office in New York as a civil engineer. Three years later, he was appointed chief engineer of the projected park.

Olmsted's long association with Central Park began in 1857, when he was appointed Viele's assistant. When he applied for the job, he had no intention of making park and city planning a career. He was more interested in the salary than anything else. On first learning of the job, he wrote to his brother that he would try to get it: "What else can I do for a living?"[44]

Like so many men who forged new careers in a changing America, Olmsted had been unable to find a satisfactory occupation among the traditional careers available to his generation. He was thirty-seven years old in 1857. Unable to make a living out of his farm or his writing, he was still financially dependent upon his father. Not long before he applied for the Central Park job, he had written to Parke Godwin: "I know . . . that I have no talent at all for business." He feared that he had "no capacity to earn a decent living for even a single man."[45] The Central Park position did not immediately settle Olmsted's problem of vocation. When the Civil War broke out, he resigned from the park to serve as general secretary of the United States Sanitary Commission. Two years later, emotionally and physically exhausted, he left the Sanitary Commission in order to manage a mining estate in Mariposa, California. In 1864, while Olmsted was in California, Horace Bushnell, in a prescient essay, called for the creation of "a new profession, . . . a city-planning profession." Apparently unaware of his Hartford pastor's proposal, Olmsted, now forty-three years old, returned to New York in 1865 determined to make park and city planning his life's work.[46]

Olmsted's first effort in environmental design was a plan for laying out Central Park. In 1858 Calvert Vaux, a former partner of the late Andrew Jackson Downing, invited Olmsted to collaborate with him in preparing an entry for the competition sponsored by the commissioners of the park. This marked the beginning of a long and fruitful partnership. That much of Olmsted's work was done in collaboration with Vaux poses a problem of credit. Vaux was a talented architect; his credits include the Metropolitan Museum of Art and the Museum of Natural History in New York. He also authored a minor architectural classic, *Villas and Cottages* (1857). Yet he never received the credit he deserved, or at least he thought he deserved, as a landscape architect. Olmsted, who took administrative responsibility for their work and who participated more fully in the general cultural life of the nation, became the more prominent public and historical figure. Thus overshadowed by his partner, Vaux never established a separate identity as a landscape architect. Whenever the opportunity arose, however, Olmsted insisted that Vaux get his full share of credit for their joint works.[47]

Their design for Central Park, signed "Greensward," won the competition, and Olmsted was appointed architect-in-chief to supervise construction according to the plan. The "Greensward" plan contained the fundamental principles that Olmsted would repeat and elaborate upon for forty years as America's foremost landscape architect and city planner. The "highest ideal that can be aimed for in a park," Olmsted and Vaux wrote, is a "most decided contrast to the confined and formal lines of the city." This simple idea, implicit, as Olmsted often acknowledged, in the rural cemetery movement, became the basis of a sophisticated approach to environmental design.[48]

Olmsted's parks were designed explicitly for urban dwellers; they were to be "suitable for the distinctly rural recreation of people, as a relief and counterpoise to the urban conditions of their ordinary life." The park idea, however, "pointed to something more than mere exemption from urban conditions, namely to the formation of an opposite class of conditions; conditions remedial of the influences of urban conditions." The "feeling of relief experienced by those entering" a park ought to generate *"a sense of enlarged freedom."* The end sought was ultimately psychological: "The main object and justification [of a park] is simply to produce a certain influence in the minds of people and through this to make life in the city healthier and happier."[49]

In Olmsted's view, the park meant life, not death for the American city. Considering that the park movement "has occurred simultaneously with a great enlargement of towns and development of urban habits, is it not reasonable," Olmsted asked, "to regard it as a self-preserving instinct of civilization?"[50]

Mid-century New York, the city Olmsted knew best, imposed troubling burdens upon its citizens. In place of the almost casual pace that had characterized economic affairs and other dimensions of life in the eighteenth-century mercantile city, New York had developed a "severely workful" atmosphere, to borrow a phrase from Dickens's description of Coketown. This shift was associated with social and economic change. After about 1850, developments in transportation and technology, the availability of cheap, mostly immigrant, labor, and economies of scale stimulated the location of industrial production there. The city had also become the financial and administrative hub of a rapidly growing national economy. These industrial and organizational developments fragmented older forms of community that had nourished a relaxed pattern of life. Now, in an environment of increased social antagonisms and tensions, restraint and continuous exertion seemed essential. Businessmen, professionals, and clerks found themselves involved in extensive and highly organized economic institutions, where they were often occupied with routine work. The working class had to perform monotonous tasks in larger and more coercive industrial work groups. The resulting personal stress demanded relief.

Men and women were losing the sense of sociability and neighborliness that Olmsted remembered from his New England boyhood.[51] Nineteenth-century urban life seemed to encourage antisocial attitudes. Whenever we walk through the crowded streets of the city, Olmsted explained, "to merely avoid collision with those we meet and pass upon the sidewalks we have constantly to watch, to foresee, and to guard against their movements." We become adversaries–calculating strength and intentions. "Our minds are thus brought into close dealings with other minds without any friendly flowing toward them, but rather a drawing from them." "People from the country," he pointed out, are immediately "conscious of the effect on their nerves and minds" of this "street contact." The pursuit of business in the city "has the same tendency–a tendency to regard others in a hard if not always hardening way." Such behavior, Olmsted felt, not only is detrimental to the development of common feelings but also can cause much individual suffering. "It is upon our opportunities of relief from it . . . that not only our comfort in town life, but our ability to maintain a temperate, good-natured, and healthy state of mind depends."[52]

The essential value of a park in urban society is to provide "the greatest possible contrast with the restraining and confining conditions of the town, those conditions which compel us to walk circumspectly, watchfully, jealously, which compel us to look closely upon others without sympathy." Park scenery, according to Olmsted, offered an "opportunity for people to come together for the single purpose of enjoyment, unembarrassed by the limitations with which they are surrounded at home, or in the pursuit of their daily avocations."[53]

Olmsted believed that ensuring the mental and physical health of urban populations should in itself justify expenditures on parks. A city park, however, had a secondary but not unimportant economic value. Olmsted explained to cost-conscious city governments that parks inevitably resulted in an increase of material wealth in the city. "And the reason is obvious: all wealth is the result of labor," and unless some provision is made for the recuperation of the force expended in labor, "the power of each individual to add to the wealth of the community is, as a necessary consequence, also soon lost." The process of recuperation requires "the unbending of the faculties which have been tasked, and this *unbending* of the faculties we find is impossible, except by the occupation of the imagination with objects and reflections of a quite different character from those which are associated with their bent condition. . . . And this is what is found by townspeople in a park."[54] Businessmen, particularly, appreciated the opportunity of relief afforded by the rural scenery of a public park. The community, in turn, benefited because active men were able to remain in business longer and with more regularity. Olmsted also pointed out that a public park might pay for itself by drawing money into the city and by raising the value of the land adjoining it. Although Olmsted rarely resorted to this land-value argument himself, others did. In particular, Horace W. S. Cleveland, an important Midwestern landscape architect who had worked under Olmsted in the 1860s, effectively urged this lesson of Central Park upon the civic leaders of Minneapolis in persuading them to develop that city's remarkable park system.[55]

Realizing that American urban populations were highly mobile, Olmsted believed that a public park might provide a valuable stabilizing influence. When he prepared a park and city planning proposal for San Francisco in 1865, Olmsted pointed out that in comparing the city directories for 1861 and 1862 he discovered that of 5,500 merchants and tradesmen of the "more substantial class" in the city in 1861, only 3,400 remained in 1862. Of "small dealers" there in 1861, only 60 percent were in the city a year later. He was unable to determine how many of these changes in the directory listings must be attributed to movement out of the city. However, he remarked upon "the manner of life of the large class which is so ready for change," and he observed that "its interest in the permanent improvement of the city, differs but little from that of strangers or mere sojourners."[56] Under such conditions, how would the city's population develop a civic identity? He explained to the city government that the controlling purpose in establishing a pleasure ground in San Francisco is to "offer inducements to men of wealth to remain, and to all citizens to pursue commerce less constantly, to acquire habits of living healthily and happy from day to day, and of regarding San Francisco as their home for life."[57]

Mid-century cultural leaders considered the nation's most urgent social need to be the development of institutions in the cities that brought together all social classes. Brace spoke for this ideal through the style of charity organization he developed; Olmsted hoped that parks also might serve to bring the two ends of society into communication. Olmsted was happy to report to the American Social Science Association in 1870 that in Central Park or in Brooklyn's Prospect Park "you may . . . often see vast numbers of persons brought closely together, poor and rich, young and old, Jew and Gentile. I have seen a hundred thousand thus congregated . . . [and] I have looked studiously but vainly among them for a single face completely unsympathetic with the prevailing expression of good nature and light-heartedness." Echoing the aspirations that Andrew Jackson Downing had expressed for a New York park twenty years earlier, Olmsted and his generation hoped that parks might provide an opportunity in the modern city for all classes to come together in a democratic, but refined, spirit.[58]

This picture of Central Park may have provided an appealing image for Olmsted's audience, but Seymour Mandelbaum's recent criticism of it seems just. Olmsted's united community was in fact limited. Since movement was difficult and costly, Central Park was primarily a park for the more fortunate members of society. Mandelbaum errs, however, when he goes on to accuse Olmsted of ignoring the possibilities of smaller neighborhood centers in the denser parts of the city.[59] In the same address in which he presented Central Park as a symbol of community, Olmsted outlined the possibilities of a complete park system that would include not only large parks like Central Park, but also "small grounds so distributed through a large town that some one of them could be easily reached by a short walk from every house."[60] During the 1870s, Olmsted made modest efforts to implement this proposal in New York, and in 1895, in the last article he ever published, he repeated his call for a complete park system.[61]

Central Park itself was intended to be of especial value to the poor. Granted that the park was more accessible to the upper half of society, the fact remains that many of the less fortunate classes took advantage of its pleasures. "One great purpose" of the park, Olmsted wrote in 1858, is "to supply the hundreds of thousands of tired workers, who have no opportunity to spend their summers in the country, a specimen of God's handiwork that shall be to them, inexpensively, what a month or two in the White Mountains or the Adirondacks is, at great cost, to those in easier circumstances."[62] This genuine sympathy for the plight of the workingman, however, reflects only one side of Olmsted's understanding of social democracy. He hoped that the park would bring happiness and joy to the lives of the urban masses, but, like his friend Brace, Olmsted combined a sincere feeling for the less fortunate with a somewhat manipulative concern for raising them up to middle-class standards.

Society, he thought, should accept the leadership of the best men. As communities matured, a class of persons emerged as leaders. These men "have had the opportunity of educating their tastes in constructive activity" and have had sufficient leisure to "acquire contemplative habits of mind." "Many public interests fall to the care of their class, and they come, sometimes unconsciously to themselves, and without distinct recognition by others, to be the leaders of public opinion in all fields of common interest" where matters of taste are involved. "By their example, and by quiet persuasion in ordinary social intercourse, they direct the action of many men of greater energy and practical ability, but of less mature taste than themselves."[63] The resulting democratic community envisioned by Olmsted was settled, organic, and surprisingly hierarchical. If we see contradictions within such a vision of social democracy, Olmsted's generation saw no difficulty in recommending that Central Park, their symbol of the democratic community, be surrounded by elegant private villas that would exert an elevating influence upon the masses who visited the park.[64]

This conception of the democratic community owed much to the experience of European travel. If Jefferson had been repelled by European cities, mid-century Americans traveling to the Old World reacted quite differently. The great cities of Europe seemed more orderly than their own. They attributed this apparent stability to the refining effect of parks and art upon the mass of the urban population. As a result, American urban reformers became extremely conscious of the possibilities of exerting a beneficent moral influence upon the population of their cities by manipulating the physical environment. The parks, cemeteries, museums, and monuments they promoted in American cities were intended, in the words of Andrew Jackson Downing, to raise "up the working-man to the same level of enjoyment with the man of leisure and accomplishment."[65] By 1870 Olmsted was ready to assess the effect of Central Park in improving the character of New York's population: "No one who has closely observed the conduct of the people who visit the Park, can doubt that it exercises a distinctly harmonizing and refining influence upon the most unfortunate and lawless classes of the city,—an influence favorable to courtesy, self-control, and temperance."[66]

This faith in the moral and social influence of civic beauty derived from a particular aesthetic theory. Olmsted, Downing, and many other mid-century critics assumed that men could agree on the beautiful. Taste, or men's capacity for perceiving beauty, could be cultivated. Moreover, beauty, truth, and morality were equated. This aesthetic assumption placed art and art criticism in the realm of moral education. A pedagogic view of art resulted.[67] Believing that "the most important part of education is not that given by the schoolmaster," Olmsted was convinced, therefore, that the moral and social influences of parks and civic beauty were crucially important in the formation of the national character.[68]

Repulsed by the "brutal wastefulness of wealth" in America, he envisioned an urban civilization that recognized an essential community of interest and sympathy among all its citizens. For Olmsted, this social ideal implied free yet refined social intercourse and a "state of mind" susceptible to the "charm of scenery." Parks, he hoped, would exert a "manifestly civilizing effect" in this direction.[69] Such an influence seemed especially valuable for the "steady, industrious, thrifty men with families, who are generally gaining ground and getting on in the world. . . . This class is, indeed, to be more considered than any other, not because merely of its relation

East Chelmsford (Lowell) in 1825

Lowell in 1833

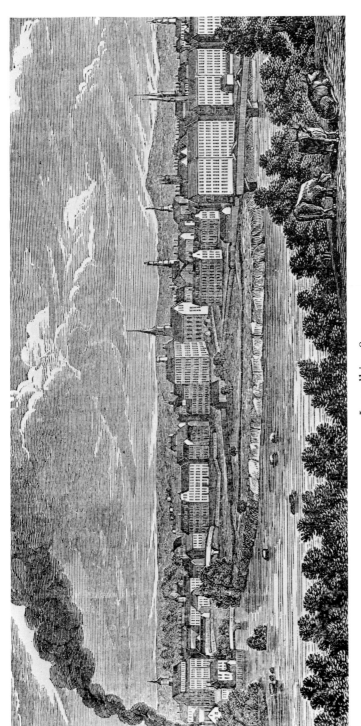

Lowell in 1839

Lowell in 1845

to all profitable production, . . . but because out of it are constantly arising the men upon the soundness of whose judgment and the healthy development of whose faculties the destiny of the whole community is pretty sure to be sooner or later mainly dependent."[70]

The "special restraints" and "exertions . . . necessary to satisfactory success in the honorable pursuit of any ordinary calling" in nineteenth-century American cities had become so great, in Olmsted's opinion, that a high level of civilization was impossible if they were "long continued without relief." Given this situation, "civilization can only advance . . . by processes which admit of a division of life into two parts": one devoted to "some service of general commerce—it may be that of a banker, lawyer, a carpenter or a cabman—the other occupied in such a manner as will relieve the effect of the special activities, strains and restraints of the first." Without this division and the balance it allows, the scope of the human personality would be unduly narrowed. Olmsted praised parks for their role in preserving this equilibrium. No less important, however, were suburbs. Suburban living, he noted toward the end of his career, represented "a long-growing and rapidly augmenting tendency of civilization to separate and greatly distinguish business premises from domestic premises,"—the one being "closely and compactly built," the other "picturesque, sylvan and rural."[71]

Olmsted himself left New York in 1881 to take up residence in Brookline, a Boston suburb. To his friend Brace he wrote: "I enjoy this suburban country beyond expression." This move marks Olmsted's participation in a trend that he had been praising since he prepared suburban plans for Berkeley, California, in 1866, and for Riverside, near Chicago, two years later.[72] He predicted in the Riverside plan that the compact part of American cities would in the future be inhabited only by those who were obliged to live there while "the more intelligent and more fortunate classes" will seek the "special charms and substantial advantages of rural life" in their homes, without any "sacrifices of urban convenience."[73]

"Suburban neighborhoods" seemed to provide the best possibilities for taking advantage of the benefits of modern civilization. The development of suburbs, according to Olmsted, was not an antiurban movement based upon an American agrarian ideology.

Beyond making the obvious point that the tendency to "separate domestic from commercial life" was a worldwide movement and not simply American, Olmsted argued that it was perfectly sensible that large towns should be marked by movement "in two opposite directions—one to concentration for business and social purposes, the other to dispersion for domestic purposes." Just as a house must have different rooms and passages for its various functions, so must "a metropolis be specially adapted at different points to different ends."[74]

Today's urban critics are increasingly attracted to the concept of an urban village. Olmsted, who once wrote that "Vil-urban might be a better word" for his ideal, shared with these critics a belief that urban life can be satisfying only if lived in small communities within the larger metropolis. However, his suburban idea lacks the sense of functional completeness, especially in respect to the economy, implied by the urban village concept.[75]

Olmsted believed that "beyond a certain point, density of residence is incompatible with a high degree of cleanliness or a high degree of health, comfort and civilization." He immediately recognized, however, that the same modern developments in transportation and communication that were creating great cities expanded the possibilities of urban life by facilitating the development of small residential neighborhoods within the larger metropolis. This technology made it possible to combine "the conditions of health and of ruralist beauty of a loosely built New England village with a certain degree of the material and social advantages of a Town."[76]

Since the suburban idea today evokes for many the image of suburban sprawl at Los Angeles, I should establish briefly the difference between Olmsted's original idea and what it has become in mid twentieth-century America. Unlike the case of Los Angeles, a fragmented metropolis that has been referred to as seven (or seventy) suburbs in search of a city, the suburbs envisioned by Olmsted were clearly and essentially linked to the urban center.[77] He insisted that suburbs be near the central commercial district and be considered "an integral element of the attractions of the city." Yet they must remain "wholly untownlike" in their general character.[78] Cityscape and landscape remained distinct. This relationship distinguished romantic suburbs from modern American suburbs that, in the words of John Burchard and Albert Bush-Brown, have "succeeded in averaging down both the city and the village."[79] Instead of forming endless and look-alike residential tracts, Olmsted's suburbs were planned as "a series of neighborhoods of a peculiar character." The sense of differentiated communal life that these neighborhoods displayed marks them off from present-day suburbs.[80]

While allowing "for the enjoyment of the essential, intellectual, artistic and social privileges which specially pertain to a metropolitan condition of society," the suburb, like the park, was intended to alleviate the hardening influences of city life. But a suburb, for Olmsted, was not exactly like a park. The "essential qualification of a park is range" with its suggestion of free movement. In the suburb, however, "all that favors movement should be subordinated" to the theme of "domesticity" and the "idea of habitation."[81] The suburb was to provide a setting for domestic life free of the commotion, crowding, and physical chaos that characterized the central portion of the industrial city.

Within the suburb itself, two general considerations were central to Olmsted's theory: "first, that of the domiciliation of men by families, each family being well provided for in regard to its domestic in-door and out-door private life; second, that of the harmonious association and co-operation of men in a community, and the intimate relationship and constant intercourse, and interdependence between families." The twentieth-century suburb seems to have achieved greater success in attaining the former than the latter goal, but Olmsted insisted that "each has its charm, and the charm of both should be aided and acknowledged by all means in the general plan of every suburb." As if he had a premonition that the privatist aspect of suburban living might someday dominate the communal, Olmsted emphasized that "families dwelling within a suburb enjoy much in common, and all the more enjoy it because it is in common." That the very things they held in common—religious, social, economic, and ethnic backgrounds—excluded many Americans from their community, should not blind us to Olmsted's ideal. His goal, lost in today's equally homogeneous suburbs, was to have a residential district manifest its sense of community "in the completeness, and choiceness, and beauty of the

means they possess of coming together, of being together, and especially of recreating and enjoying them[selves] together on common
grounds, and under common shades."[82]

The suburb should be designed to stimulate sociability. The private house and private family should not be entirely self-sufficient
because this would cut off avenues of sympathy with fellow members of the community. For instance, Olmsted believed that it was
not necessary for every house to "command fine distant or general
views, it is rather better that standpoints for these should be possessed by each family in common with others, at some little distance from the house, so as to afford inducement and occasion for
going more out from it, and for realizing and keeping up acquaint-
ances by the eye at least, with the community." These must be
"points in the neighborhood at which there are scenes" interesting
enough to attract members of the community to them as "social
rendez-vous of the neighborhood."[83]

If the suburban neighborhood is to be the focus of an open community life, it must be differentiated from the general landscape
and from the urban center to which it is linked. "In other words,
a neighborhood being desirable, the existence of a neighborhood
should be obvious, and for this reason the scenery which marks the
neighborhood should be readily distinguishable."[84] Under such
conditions, residents could develop a sense of belonging. Although
Olmsted's thought was dominated by the image of Central Park
as a symbol of social unity, he encouraged the development of
suburban neighborhoods and downtown public squares as the foci
of communal life because he recognized that in the course of their
daily lives men do not usually leap to a vision of the whole city as
a single, united community.

Like his friend Brace, Olmsted was concerned with the problem
of community and the relationship between the natural and the
artificial in the city. While Brace worked out a means of preserving
a degree of naturalness and spontaneity in the large-scale organizations apparently necessary in urban society, Olmsted, in Lewis
Mumford's phrase, "naturalized the city."[85] Olmsted believed that
by using landscape art imaginatively he could create an urban environment that would encourage a gratifying naturalness in social

relations and would preserve a welcome sense of psychic freedom for urban dwellers hemmed in by large buildings, dirty factories, and social routine. He tried to civilize American urban life by using landscape and cityscape as counterpoises.

Toward the end of the century, Olmsted found it increasingly difficult to explain the idea of using cityscape and landscape in this manner.[86] This idea, so obvious fifty years before, lost its relevance for a generation of urban leaders who relied upon machine metaphors to define the good society and who declared an end to the distinction between city and country.[87] If we recall that Olmsted's work was not rediscovered by Lewis Mumford until about 1930, the degree to which the nineteenth-century tradition was obliterated during the Progressive Era becomes apparent. The greatest irony occurred during the 1920s when Olmsted's son, himself a leading planner, used the overpass, invented by his father to preserve the natural landscape at Central Park, to begin the obliteration of the landscape at Los Angeles.[88]

Olmsted's experience as landscape architect for the World's Columbian Exposition, held in Chicago in 1893, illustrates the decline of the nineteenth-century version of urbanism for which he was a major spokesman. As the nation's foremost landscape architect, he was involved in the project's planning from the beginning. In fact, it was at his suggestion that Jackson Park was selected as the site for the Exposition.[89] Yet Olmsted was never fully satisfied with the famous "White City" that grew up on the site and so captivated Americans as to become the stimulus for a city planning movement during the Progressive Era.[90] He had two objections. One was his disappointment that the Exposition did not appear as a "frankly temporary" pageant.[91] His second objection points directly to the central issue of nineteenth-century urbanism–the relationship between landscape and cityscape in city planning.

Olmsted, as he had done with clients for nearly forty years, urged the builders of the Exposition to strive in their general plan for a combination of "architecture and landscape." He hoped that a lagoon with a wooded island, which lay just to the north of the main plaza, would be used by the builders to counterbalance the dominant architectural effects of the Exposition. Daniel Burnham, chief of construction and destined to be America's leading city planner during the Progressive Era, did not, however, want the wooded island to be wasted. He proposed putting a music hall there. Olmsted replied that "it would be a great misfortune to have a music hall, or any occasion for drawing crowds to the Island." He argued that nothing possibly done on the island "will be worth nearly as much as to have it so treated as to coax the imagination to see in it a place of relief from all the splendor and glory and noise and human multitudinous of the great surrounding Babylon."[92] Just before the Exposition opened to the public, Olmsted repeated his "fear" that with the "great towering masses of white, glistening in the clear, hot Summer sunlight of Chicago" some "dark green foliage" is necessary for "relief." Visiting the Exposition after it opened, Olmsted thought he saw in the faces of the crowds the same "businesslike, common, dull, anxious and care-worn" expressions that had led him to urge building public parks in the nineteenth-century city.[93]

In a report to the American Institute of Architects, Olmsted explained his unhappiness with this aspect of the Exposition, and, in effect, provided the obituary for the version of urbanism represented in his long career. He pointed out that "it was our original intention" to have the wooded island "occupying a central position." Characterized "by calmness and naturalness," it would "serve as a foil to the artificial grandeur and sumptuousness of the other parts of the scenery." But "after a time demands came for the use of the island for a great variety of purposes, and at length we became convinced that it would be impossible to successfully resist these demands." He considered it fortunate that in the end only a temple and a Japanese garden were placed on the island. "Nevertheless, we consider that these introductions have much injured the island for the purpose which in our primary design it was to serve. If they could have been avoided, I am sure that the Exposition would have made a much more agreeable general impression."[94]

But Chicago in 1893 was not the New York that had applauded his "Greensward" plan in 1858. No one at Chicago missed the natural scenery: people were too busy joining Henry Adams in the Machinery Building to study the dynamo. Moreover, as Peter Schmitt has recently shown, Americans at the turn of the century began to have difficulty distinguishing between natural landscape parks and Japanese or any other kind of gardens.[95] Olmsted must have nodded a sad assent when he received a letter in June 1893 from Horace W. S. Cleveland, another elder statesman among landscape architects, complaining that Americans do not understand what a park is: they seem to think of parks as "mere places of amusement to attract crowds by spectacular exhibitions."[96]

The transformation of the park ideal into gardens and exhibitions marks the death of the tradition for which Olmsted spoke. That tradition represented an attempt to harmonize the economic and cultural possibilities of urban living with a somewhat idealized heritage of New England town life that emphasized the ideas of organic social relations, community, and natural beauty. It was not really recognized at the time, but when Americans transformed Olmsted's park ideal they lost touch with this older heritage. And when urban leaders during the Progressive Era abandoned the concerns of Olmsted and Brace in favor of monumental city planning and the bureaucratic ideal of the "city efficient," something very important, something worth recovering, was lost.[97]

The urban tradition for which Olmsted and Brace spoke seems to point toward the possibility of expanding the area of freedom and spontaneity within the general framework of our urban and organizational society. American urban culture might have been enriched had the Progressives been more sensitive to these issues. Their failure to appreciate, to expand, and develop this nineteenth-century urban vision is regrettable. Admittedly, the urban ideas articulated by Olmsted and Brace are elitist in their assumptions and sometimes appear to use spontaneity merely to strengthen urban and organizational developments. Yet a more democratic and humanistic expression of these ideas, a version suggested, for instance, by Jane Addams, implies meaningful interactions among men and women within a natural as opposed to a functional context. Spontaneity and naturalness, central to the nineteenth-century urban vision, could thus contribute to the recovery of wholeness in human relationships within our presently distraught urban civilization.

Epilogue

The urban ideas of Charles Loring Brace and Frederick Law Olmsted possessed an impressive cultural resonance during the middle of the nineteenth century. They responded to the widespread concern for preserving a balance between nature and art, spontaneity and organization, romantic and utilitarian points of view. Toward the end of their long lives, however, Brace and Olmsted sensed, quite correctly, that this resonance had weakened, leaving them as outsiders. American cultural imperatives found a different equilibrium. In the emerging organizational society, community had lost its personal meaning. And nature had become less accessible, less tangible, less important to urban Americans.

The institutional antecedents of this cultural transformation are various. Anticipations of the modern bureaucratic style abound in antebellum America: the Jacksonian party system, the emerging school systems, organized philanthropy, and the professions.[1] The Civil War accelerated the impulse toward centralization and bureaucratization.[2] One of the most compelling interpretations of this cultural transformation focuses upon the United States Sanitary Commission in order to illustrate the importance of the crisis of union in reshaping American values.[3] The conservative elite who organized the Sanitary Commission hoped it would teach Americans, soldiers and civilians alike, the value of authority and discipline and would warn them of the dangers of spontaneity. The commission, in this interpretation, is both a cause and a symbol of an increasing acceptance of large, impersonal, elite-dominated organizations in American life.

The extraordinary cultural impact of the Civil War cannot be denied. My point in this study, however, is that the city played a crucial role in these intellectual and institutional changes and that the mid-century resolution stands in sharp contrast to the modern bureaucratic style. The Sanitary Commission itself provides an example.

The Reverend Henry W. Bellows, the president of the commission and its driving force, acknowledged after the war that the social philosophy of the organization owed much to recent developments in urban philanthropy. When Charles Stillé, librarian of Yale College and a commission member, set out in 1865 to write a history of the Sanitary Commission, he asked Bellows for an account of its origins. Bellows replied that before the war he had been studying various "questions in Social Science, the sources of poverty, drunkenness & crime, & the means of dealing with them." His preparations for a series of lectures in New York and at Boston's Lowell Institute brought him "into mental contact with the noble Englishmen who for twenty years past have been battling so courageously for Sanitary Reform in Cities & towns in Great Britain."

His subsequent public discussions of poverty "led the few friends of Sanitary Reform in the City of New York . . . to solicit my aid & co-operation in their movements." So far as these men can be identified, they represent a particular point of view within mid-century reform circles. They were connected with the moralistic and highly structured New York Association for Improving the Condition of the Poor and, to a lesser extent, the New York House of Refuge.[4] Bellows's ideas on urban reform were formed during his association with these conservative reformers.

On the eve of the Civil War, he recalled, "I had fairly arrived at very strong & clear convictions on the subject of the preventable character of most social evils & sicknesses–& I had a deep persuasion that poverty . . . in a country like ours, was a *spiritual* disorder, to be treated far more with moral tonics than with practical relief." The elimination of poverty could be achieved, he thought, "by equal laws, by general religious education, by encouraging self-respect & self reliance & by withholding careless relief."

Bellows had reached these conclusions before the attack on Fort Sumter. And when the outbreak of war "aroused the men of the nation to arms, & called the women to the consideration of what they could do to cheer, comfort & protect their brothers in the camp & field,–the necessarily crude character of the spontaneous beneficence that showed itself–at once attracted my attention." "Without distinct notions of what was needed," he feared that the "excitement" raging in the "Churches, & Schools & Women" might do "as much harm as good." With this concern, he set out to organize the Sanitary Commission.[5]

Beside the question of urban origins, however, there remains the issue of whether the Sanitary Commission implies the emergence, as early as 1861, of the modern bureaucratic style as the predominant orientation of American culture. Had the drive for administrative rationalization, efficiency, and professionalism already shattered the complex urban vision of Olmsted and Brace? What of the mid-century concern for preserving nature, spontaneity, and community?

It is possible to address these questions directly because Bellows, "having acquired a great respect for his organizing powers in watching his operations & discipline at the Central Park," selected Olmsted to serve as general secretary of the Sanitary Commission.[6] In this position, it must be acknowledged, Olmsted assumed a more hard-headed approach to philanthropy than his friend Brace. He phrased his concern about the dangers of individual and uncoordinated benevolence in stronger terms than Brace would have used. He also accepted the commission's policy of using paid agents instead of volunteers in relief work. When Brace volunteered his services, Olmsted replied that he had found "mercenaries" to be "better than gratuitous volunteers." "Consequently," he told Brace, "in the way of business, I don't want you; for any man without a clearly defined function about the army is a nuisance."[7] Moreover, like the more conservative Bellows, Olmsted defined the commission as an organization directing the nation's "emotional energies into channels of wholesale activity," thereby "forestalling and neutralizing unwholesome excitations of feeling."[8]

Are we, in effect, describing the bureaucratic mentality that I have already argued belongs to a later period in our history? I think not. Olmsted can be characterized as a one-dimensional twentieth-century bureaucrat only if we forget the full complexity of the man. We have already seen that nature, spontaneity, and the encouragement of democratic sympathies were key elements of Olmsted's social philosophy before and after the war. Lewis Mumford, writing in a different context, reflects upon the "tendency in every culture to reduce the complicated order that serves life, an order that penetrates many different levels of experience, that includes 'material' and 'spiritual' attributes, to a single uniform system."[9] It would require a similarly reductive analytical approach to ignore the very combination of romantic and utilitarian impulses that explains the greatness of Olmsted's achievement.

Olmsted contained in himself the dilemmas at the core of the emerging urban culture. Even Bellows perceived the union of opposites that accounts for the cultural resonance of Olmsted's style at mid-century. The complexity of Olmsted's character and thought, Bellows wrote, exemplifies "the union of prosaic sense with poetical feeling, of democratic sympathies with refined and scholarly tastes, of punctilious respect for facts with tender hospitality for ideas."[10] Olmsted himself insisted that the planner needed artistic vision as well as ability in "matters of organization & discipline." "At the bottom of the most important function of my office" as superintendent of Central Park, he told the Board of Commissioners, "is a natural, spontaneous, individual action of the imagination—of *creative fancy*."[11]

The bureaucratic mentality emerged a generation later. It was the product of intellectual as well as institutional changes.[12] While economic and technological developments stimulated the growth of large organizations, American social thought faltered. By the 1890s, Darwinism and industrial strife had eroded the moral certitude beneath traditional culture and the assumptions about the fundamental harmony of the social order. Spontaneity and the organic community, therefore, became problematical for American social thinkers. The apparent disintegration of the collective social ethic produced a crisis in confidence that translated the earlier concern for social order into a quest for control. Nature, moreover, was divested of its power to inspire.

While the passing of traditional culture offered the possibility of liberating thought and imagination, its more general effect was the enhancement of bureaucratic ideas. With traditional ideals collapsing and European decadence becoming unacceptable even to such a pessimist as Brooks Adams, American social thinkers embraced activism. Social vision and moral commitment were abandoned in favor of administrative energy and bureaucratic adjustment.

The complex commitments contained in the urban vision of Brace and Olmsted were drastically simplified. The attempt to preserve community, spontaneity, and natural beauty in an urban and organizational society was abandoned in the Progressive Era. Progressive reformers, in the words of Robert Wiebe, persuaded themselves "that every man, properly educated, would desire a functional, efficient society."[13] The Progressive impulse toward "rationalization"[14] meant the replacement of traditional forms of life, emotion, and social vision by an instrumental, systematic, and practical style of thought and activity. Whatever its material benefits, "this philosophy of intelligent control," as Randolph Bourne called it, has never been fully satisfactory. The disturbing question that he posed in 1917 still haunts the American mind: "Is there something in these realistic attitudes," he asked, "that works actually against poetic vision, against concern for the quality of life as above the machinery of life?"[15]

This gnawing doubt probably accounts for the increasing numbers of historians who are probing nineteenth-century history in search of the roots of modern American social institutions and for the origins of the contemporary bureaucratic mind. This scholarly purpose has already illuminated much of our cultural history; it promises to be fruitful in the future.[16] But it also implies an important problem. Because it assumes the direction of nineteenth-century history toward our own present, it invites distortion of nineteenth-century culture. It also communicates an unwarranted sense of historical inevitability. There is a danger of dismissing those parts of nineteenth-century culture that seem incompatible with a trend toward rationalization as simply manifestations of "cultural lag" or of "popular romanticism." These apparent anomalies may, however, imply important historical alternatives to the dominant direction of American cultural development.

If the study of history can sensitize us to the burden of the past, it can also release us from myths of historical inevitability. The commitment of Brace, Olmsted, and many of their contemporaries to art *and* nature, spontaneity *and* structure, community *and* organization, science *and* sentiment deserves the serious consideration of historians. Far from representing "cultural lag," Brace's Children's Aid Society, with its anti-institutional animus, was a considered response to earlier and extreme efforts to rationalize social institutions. Likewise, rural cemeteries and Olmsted's Central Park represent far more than agrarian nostalgia. They were serious efforts to preserve nature and spontaneity in an increasingly artificial and rationally organized environment.

The cases of Olmsted, Brace, and many of their contemporaries suggest that the trend from "boundlessness to consolidation," to borrow John Higham's recent phrase, was not without important complexities.[17] If viewed with antebellum eyes rather than from a post-Progressive point of view, these complexities suggest the contingencies, the possibilities, woven into the fabric of American history.

This mid-century urban vision represents a lost heritage. When American intellectuals were confident that the fundamental social problems facing the United States required centralization, professional expertise, "science," and federal planning, the romantic impulse in mid-century social thought evoked little sympathy. The continued presence of these social problems, in an era of unprecedented centralization, bureaucratization, and scientism, however, has shaken the confidence of many. The complex urban vision of Brace and Olmsted now finds a more sympathetic understanding. Their concern for community, nature, and spontaneity attracts our sympathies because these qualities are so notably deficient in twentieth-century urban culture.

But nostalgia must not obscure the limitations of the mid-century urban vision. We cannot forget the elitist assumptions of the nineteenth-century urbanists we have discussed. Although they deserve full credit for their efforts to improve the conditions of life in American cities, we must acknowledge the narrowness of their conception of social democracy. Can we casually accept their willingness to manipulate less powerful members of the community and their attempt to impose a middle class life-style upon the poor?

When we consider their time and place, there is no point in faulting nineteenth-century urbanists: democracy means something different today. The challenge of twentieth-century urbanism is to recover their humane concern for nature and community within a fuller definition of democracy and culture.

Appendix A. Business in Lowell

The size of the bourgeoisie in Lowell may be judged, in part, by the variety of goods and services available there. What follows is a selected list of goods and services offered in Lowell according to the *Lowell City Directory for 1851.* The number in parentheses indicates the number of businesses offering the particular product or service. (This number includes an undetermined amount of overlap, especially in reference to retail goods.)

Agricultural tools, retailers (3)
Apothecaries (21)
Architects (2)
Auctioneers (4)
Bakers (8)
Baths (2)
Bedstead Manufactory (1)
Beer Manufactory (1)
Bell Hangers (2)
Belt and Roll Manufactory (1)
Blacksmith (15)
Boat Builder (1)
Bonnet bleachery (3)
Bonnets and Millinery goods (1)
Book binders (2)
Booksellers and stationers (11)
Boot and shoe makers (6)
Boots, shoes, and rubbers (45)
Bowling saloons (3)
Box makers (2)
Brass founder (1)
Brewer (1)
Broker (2)
Brush manufacturer (1)
Bung manufacturer (1)
Cabinet maker (1)
Camphene (2)
Cap makers (2)

Card manufacturer (1)
Carpenters and builders (27)
Carpetings (4)
Carpet manufacturer (4)
Carriage manufacturer (4)
China glass (6)
Cigar manufacturer (3)
Clock repairer (1)
Clothing stores (26)
Coal and wood (6)
Coffee grinder (1)
Coffin warehouses (3)
Commission merchant (1)
Confectionary (12)
Coopers (2)
Currier (1)
Cutlery (1)
Daguerrian artists (6)
Dentists (12)
Doors, blinds, sashes (4)
Dressmakers (33)
Dry Goods (29)
Dyers (4)
Engineers (6)
Engravers and designer (1)
Fancy goods (3)
File cutter (1)
Flour and grain (5)

Furniture (5)
Furs (3)
Gardeners (2)
Gas engineers (2)
Grave stones (3)
Grist mills (2)
Gunsmith (1)
Hairdressers (15)
Hardware (4)
Harness makers (5)
Ice dealers (2)
Ink and blacking (2)
Intelligence offices (2)
Iron dealer (1)
Jewelry and watches (14)
Kitchen furnishings (1)
Lamps and burning fuel (1)
Leather dealers (2)
Leeches (1)
Libraries (3)
Livery stables (13)
Lock manufactories (2)
Looking glasses (2)
Loom harnesses (3)
Loom picker manufacturer (1)
Lumber (7)
Machine shops (6)
Masons (11)
Millinery goods (29)
Music stores (4)
Nurses (28)
Painters (coach) (2)
Painters (house) (15)
Painters (signs, etc.) (6)
Paper makers (2)
Paper hanging (9)
Periodical depots (3)
Piano fortes (2)
Plan makers (3)

Plumber (1)
Powder manufactory (1)
Print block maker (1)
Printers (9)
Provisions (27)
Public houses (8)
Pump makers (2)
Real estate agents (2)
Reed manufacturer (2)
Restorators and oyster saloons (16)
Roll coverer (1)
Rope maker (1)
Saw filers (2)
Sawing (3)
Scale makers (1)
Screw bolt manufacturer (1)
Shuttle manufacturer (1)
Stamp and stencil cutters (2)
Stocking yarn manufacturer (1)
Stone cutters (3)
Stoves (8)
Tailoresses (6)
Teachers (private) (2)
Teachers of dancing (1)
Teachers of music (3)
Teachers of penmanship (3)
Telegraph office (1)
Tin plate and sheet iron (9)
Trunk manufacturer (9)
Umbrellas (2)
Undertakers (4)
Variety stores (56)
Varnish manufacturer (1)
Veterinary surgeon (1)
Wadding manufacturer (1)
Wines and liquour (2)
Wire worker (1)
Wood turner (1)

Appendix B. Geographical Origin of Operatives: Percentage Distribution in the Hamilton Manufacturing Company

Year	U.S. %	Irish %	Total Foreign %
July 1, 1830– Dec. 31, 1830 (1,176 persons)	96.26	2.64	3.74
Jan. 20, 1835– Dec. 4, 1836 (1,213 persons)	96.21	2.64	3.79
Oct. 2, 1839– Apr. 23, 1845 (516 persons)	94.96	3.10	5.04
Oct. 8, 1844– Apr. 27, 1846 (686 persons)	92.13	5.68	7.87
Mar. 28, 1848– Oct. 18, 1850 (669 persons)	68.16	24.36	31.84
June, 1854– June 14, 1856 (790 persons)	47.47	42.78	52.53
May 27, 1858– Nov. 27, 1860 (811 persons)	41.80	44.14	58.20
Oct., 1865– April, 1867 (700 persons)	51.00	26.14	49.00
Oct., 1870– Mar., 1873 (818 persons)	43.52	28.25	56.48
May, 1873– Nov., 1876 (767 persons)	47.07	27.51	52.93

SOURCE: Robert G. Layer, *Earnings of Cotton Mill Operatives, 1825–1914* (Cambridge: Committee on Research in Economic History, Inc., 1955), pp. 70–71.

Notes

I. Introduction: The Challenge of the City

Headquotes are from David Ramsay, *The History of the American Revolution*, 2 vols. (Dublin: William Jones, 1793), 2: 635–36; and Frederick Law Olmsted, "The Beginning of Central Park: A Fragment of Autobiography," reprinted in *Landscape into Cityscape: Frederick Law Olmsted's Plans for a Greater New York City*, ed. Albert Fein (Ithaca, N.Y.: Cornell University Press, 1967), p. 52.

1. Henry Adams, *The United States in 1800* (Ithaca, N.Y.: Cornell University Press, 1963), p. 12.

2. Bureau of the Census, *Historical Statistics of the United States, 1789–1945* (Washington: Government Printing Office, 1949), p. 29.

3. Thomas Jefferson, *Notes on the State of Virginia*, ed. Thomas P. Abernethy (New York: Harper Torchbook, 1964), p. 157; Alexander Hamilton, *The Papers of Alexander Hamilton*, ed. Harold C. Syrett (New York: Columbia University Press, 1961–), 10: 236.

4. Washington is quoted in Charles A. Beard and Mary R. Beard, *The Rise of American Civilization*, 2 vols. in one (New York: Macmillan, 1930), 1: 543; Benjamin Franklin to [?] [1783], *The Writings of Benjamin Franklin*, ed. Albert H. Smyth, 10 vols. (New York: Macmillan, 1905–1907), 9: 149–50; Benjamin Franklin to Dr. Joshua Babcock, London, January 13, 1772, ibid., 5: 361; Benjamin Franklin, "The Internal State of America: Being a True Description of the Interest and Policy of that Vast Continent [1784]," ibid., 10: 117; Benjamin Franklin to Jonathan Shipley, Philadelphia, February 24, 1786, ibid., 9: 491; Benjamin Franklin, "Consolation for America, or remarks on her real situation, interests and policy," *American Museum* 1 (January 1787): 5; Benjamin Rush to Elias Boudinot [?], Philadelphia, July 9, 1788, *Letters of Benjamin Rush*, ed. L. H. Butterfield, 2 vols. (Princeton, N.J.: Princeton University Press, 1951), 1: 472; Tench Coxe, *A View of the United States of America . . .* (Philadelphia: Hall and Wrigley & Merriman, 1794), pp. 7, 6; [George Logan], *Letters Addressed to the Yeomanry of the United States . . .* (Philadelphia: Eleazer Oswald, 1791), p. 9; and John Adams, *Diary and Autobiography of John Adams*, ed. L. H. Butterfield, 4 vols. (New York: Atheneum, 1964), 1: 247.

5. I am indebted for this insight to Irving Kristol, "Urban Civilization and Its Discontents," *Commentary* 50 (July 1970): 29–35, though I cannot accept the general conclusions of his argument.

6. Clinton Rossiter, *The First American Revolution* (New York: Harvest Book, 1956), p. 232.

7. Jefferson, *Notes on the State of Virginia*, p. 158.

8. Chester Eisinger, "The Freehold Concept in Eighteenth Century American Letters," *William and Mary Quarterly* 4 (January 1947): 47.

9. Thomas Jefferson to John Adams, Monticello, February 28, 1796, *The Adams-*

Jefferson Letters, ed. Lester J. Cappon, 2 vols. (Chapel Hill: University of North Carolina Press, 1959), 1: 260; and Thomas Jefferson to John Adams, Monticello, October 28, 1813, ibid., 2: 391.

10. Adrienne Koch and William Peden, eds., *The Selected Writings of John and John Quincy Adams* (New York: Alfred A. Knopf, 1946), p. 105.

11. Jefferson, *Notes on the State of Virginia*, p. 157. For Madison's views on this point, see James Madison, "Republican Distribution of Citizens," in *Writings of James Madison*, ed. Gaillard Hunt, 9 vols. (New York: G. P. Putnam's Sons, 1900–1910), 6: 96–98.

12. David Howell to Jonathan Arnold, Annapolis, February 21, 1784, in William R. Staples, *Rhode Island in the Continental Congress* (Providence: Providence Press Company, 1870), p. 479; U.S., Congress, House, *Debates and Proceedings in Congress of the United States*, 11th Cong., 2d sess. (April 18, 1810), p. 1906. For the Federalist credentials of Howell and Key, see David H. Fischer, *The Revolution of American Conservatism: The Federalist Party in the Era of Jeffersonian Democracy* (New York: Harper & Row, 1965), pp. 279–80, 363.

13. Russell B. Nye, *The Cultural Life of the New Nation* (New York: Harper Torchbook, 1960), p. 126 (Cabot quote); and Samuel Eliot Morison, *Harrison Gray Otis: The Urbane Federalist, 1765–1848* (Boston: Houghton Mifflin, 1969), esp. pp. 125, 201, 512.

14. Nye, *The Cultural Life of the New Nation*, p. 120; and James M. Banner, Jr., *To the Hartford Convention: The Federalists and the Origins of Party Politics in Massachusetts, 1789–1815* (New York: Alfred A. Knopf, 1970), pp. 28, 110–15.

15. Linda Kerber, *Federalists in Dissent: Imagery and Ideology in Jeffersonian America* (Ithaca, N.Y.: Cornell University Press, 1970), p. 185. See also Fischer, *The Revolution in American Conservatism*, pp. 172–73.

16. Marvin Meyers, *The Jacksonian Persuasion* (New York: Vintage Book, 1960), pp. 239–40.

17. Benjamin Franklin to Benjamin Vaughan, Passy, July 26, 1784, *Writings*, ed. Smyth, 9: 245–46. See also Franklin, "Consolation for America," pp. 5–8; and Benjamin Franklin, "The Internal State of America; Being a True Description of the Interest and Policy of that Vast Continent [1784]," *Writings*, ed. Smyth, 10: 121–22.

18. Thomas Jefferson to Mr. Pictet, Washington, February 5, 1803, *The Writings of Thomas Jefferson*, ed. Albert Ellery Bergh, 20 vols. (Washington, D.C.: Thomas Jefferson Memorial Association, 1907), 10: 356. See also Thomas Jefferson to George Mason, Philadelphia, February 4, 1791, *The Works of Thomas Jefferson*, ed. Paul L. Ford, 12 vols. (New York: G. P. Putnam's Sons, 1904–1905), 6: 186; Thomas Jefferson, "Notes on Prof. Ebeling's Letter of July 30, 1795," ibid., 8: 210; Thomas Jefferson, "Answers to First Queries of Jean Nicholas Démeunier [1786]," *The Papers of Thomas Jefferson*, ed. Julian P. Boyd (Princeton, N.J.: Princeton University Press, 1950–), 10: 16.

19. Thomas Barnard, *A Sermon Preached in Boston, New-England, Before the Society for Encouraging Industry, and Employing the Poor, September 20, 1758* (Boston: Kneeland, 1758), p. 19. This specific metaphor dates back at least to 1654. See J. Franklin Jameson, ed., *Johnson's Wonder-Working Providence* [1654] (New York: Barnes & Noble, 1937), p. 108.

20. Leo Marx's book *The Machine in the Garden* (New York: Oxford University Press, 1964) is an extended essay in definition of this term.

21. See Howard Mumford Jones, *O Strange New World: American Culture: The Formative Years* (New York: Viking Press, 1964), chapts. 1–5.

22. An important but neglected study of the idea of civilization in the thought of the founding fathers is Charles A. Beard and Mary R. Beard, *The American Spirit: A Study of the Idea of Civilization in the United States* (New York: Macmillan, 1942), chapt. 4.

23. Richard Price, *Observations on the Importance of the American Revolution* (Dublin: L. White, 1785), p. 69.

24. John William Ward, *Andrew Jackson: Symbol for an Age* (New York: Oxford University Press, 1962), pp. 33, 36.

25. Bureau of Census, *Historical Statistics of the United States, 1789–1945*, p. 29.

26. The phrase *nature's nation* is taken from Perry Miller, *Nature's Nation* (Cambridge: Harvard University Press, 1967).

27. Thomas Cole to Luman Reed, Catskill, September 18, 1833, in Louis Legrand Noble, *The Life and Works of Thomas Cole*, ed. Elliot S. Vessell (Cambridge: Harvard University Press, 1964), pp. 129–31.

28. Letter reprinted in ibid., p. 167.

29. Perry Miller, "Nature and the National Ego," in *Errand into the Wilderness* (New York: Harper Torchbook, 1964), p. 215.

30. Darkness and Gothic architecture were associated with nature and whiteness and classical architecture with artificiality in nineteenth-century American aesthetic thought. (See Roger B. Stein, *John Ruskin and Aesthetic Thought in America, 1840–1900* [Cambridge: Harvard University Press, 1967], p. 48.)

31. [M. D. Bacon,] "Great Cities," *Putnam's Monthly Magazine* 5 (March 1855): 254. This article has been attributed to Bacon by Albert Fein in his "The American City: The Ideal and the Real," in *The Rise of an American Architecture*, ed. Edgar Kaufmann, Jr. (New York: Praeger, 1970), p. 106.

32. Charles S. Fairchild, "Objects of Charity Organization," National Conference of Charities and Correction, *Proceedings* 11 (1884): 65. See also William A. Scott, *A Lecture on the Influence of Great Cities* (San Francisco: Whitton, Town & Co., 1854), pp. 5–6; [Isaac C. Kendall,] *The Growth of New York* (New York: George W. Wood, 1865), pp. 5–6; and Samuel Eliot, *The Functions of a City: An Oration before the City Authorities of Boston on the Fourth of July, 1868* (Boston: Alfred Mudge & Son, 1868), p. 8.

33. Alexis de Tocqueville, *Democracy in America*, ed. Phillips Bradley (New York: Vintage Books, 1945), 1: 299–300. Many Americans during the 1830s held the same opinion. See, for example, Charles A. Goodrich, *A History of the United States of America*, rev. ed. (Hartford, Conn.: H. F. Sumner & Co., 1833), pp. 522–23; G., "American Society," *Knickerbocker* 8 (August 1836): 210–13; and Ward, *Andrew Jackson*, passim.

34. Samuel Miller, *The Difficulties and Temptations Which Attend Preaching of the Gospel in Great Cities* (Baltimore: J. Robinson, 1820), p. 32. The background of this sermon is significant; it is explained in Wilson Smith, "John Locke in the Great Unitarian Controversy," in *Freedom and Reform: Essays in Honor of Henry*

Steele Commager, ed. Harold M. Hyman and Leonard W. Levy (New York: Harper & Row, 1967), pp. 78–100.

35. Orville Dewey, *A Sermon . . . on the Moral Importance of Cities, and the Moral Means for their Reformation* (New York: David Felt & Co., 1836), pp. 5, 15.

36. Edward Lathrop, *Metropolitan Influence: Cities in Their Relation to the World's Evangelization* (New York: Lewis Colby, 1851), pp. 18–22, 9. See also Albert Barnes, *Sermons on Revivals* (New York: John S. Taylor and Co., 1841).

37. Richard Storrs, Jr., *A Plea for the Preaching of Christ in Cities* (New York: Published by the Association [YMCA], 1864), pp. 9, 14. See also John Todd, *The Moral Influence, Dangers and Duties, Connected with Great Cities* (Northampton: J. H. Butler, 1841), pp. 10–13, 95–96; and Barnes, *Sermons on Revivals*, pp. 84–94, 181–85.

38. Some of the more important discussions by easterners are Henry P. Tappan, *The Growth of Cities: A Discourse Delivered before the New York Geographical Society* (New York: R. Craighead, 1855); Samuel Osgood, *New York in the Nineteenth Century* (New York: Printed for the [New York Historical] Society, 1867); Henry W. Bellows, "The Townward Tendency," *City* 1 (January 1872): 36–40; "The Townward Tendency," *Every Saturday* 3 (October 21, 1871): 402; "The Future of Great Cities," *Nation* 2 (February 22, 1866): 232; "City and Country," ibid., 5 (September 26, 1867): 256–57; Leonard Kip, "The Building of Our Cities," *Hours at Home* 11 (July 1870): 206–12; O. Vandenburg, "The City of New York Ten Years Hence," ibid., 7 (August 1868): 350–59; and [Kendall,] *The Growth of New York*.

39. George Tucker, *Progress of the United States in Population and Wealth* (New York: Press of Hunt's Merchant's Magazine, 1843), p. 127; Scott, *A Lecture on the Influence of Great Cities*, p. 6.

40. James Fenimore Cooper, *New York*, ed. Dixon Ryan Fox (New York: William Farquhar Payson, 1930), pp. 56–57. For a full discussion of Cooper's accommodation to the city, see Thomas Bender, "James Fenimore Cooper and the City," *New York History* 51 (April 1970): 287–305.

41. Richard Hildreth, *Despotism in America: An Inquiry into . . . the Slave-Holding System in the United States* (Boston: John P. Jewett and Company, 1854), pp. 138–39; Francis Bowen, *American Political Economy* (New York: Charles Scribner's, Sons, 1870), p. 79.

42. [Bacon,] "Great Cities," p. 256. See also Tappan, *The Growth of Cities*, pp. 7–9, 15, 17–18, 25–26; "City and Country," pp. 256–57; and Review of *Life in Prairie Land*, by Mrs. Eliza Farnham, in the *Literary World* 1 (July 17, 1847): 557–59.

43. Merrill D. Peterson, *The Jeffersonian Image in the American Mind* (New York: Oxford University Press, 1960), p. 209. On the relationship of urbanization, centralization, and war, see John Higham, *From Boundlessness to Consolidation: The Transformation of American Culture, 1848–1860* (Ann Arbor, Mich.: William L. Clements Library, 1969); and George M. Frederickson, *The Inner Civil War: Northern Intellectuals and the Crisis of the Union* (New York: Harper Torchbook, 1968).

44. Ebenezer Platt Rogers, *The Glory of New York: A Discourse Delivered in*

the South Reformed Church on Thanksgiving Day . . . (New York: United States Publishing Company, 1874), p. 5.

45. Henry W. Bellows, "Cities and Parks: With Special Reference to the New York Central Park," *Atlantic Monthly* 7 (April 1861): 416–29; and "The Town-ward Tendency."

46. Kip, "The Building of Our Cities," p. 206.

47. Vandenburg, "The City of New York Ten Years Hence." Compare Amory D. Mayo, *Symbols of the Capital; or, Civilization in New York* (New York: Thatcher & Hutchinson, 1859), pp. 41–44.

48. The assessment of Olmsted's importance as an urban planner and theorist is from Albert Fein, "Introduction: Landscape into Cityscape," in *Landscape into Cityscape: Frederick Law Olmsted's Plans for a Greater New York City*, ed. Albert Fein (Ithaca, N.Y.: Cornell University Press, 1967), p. 42; the Olmsted quote is from his *Preliminary Report upon the Proposed Suburban Village at Riverside, Near Chicago* (1868), reprinted with an introduction by Theodora Kimball Hubbard in *Landscape Architecture* 21 (July 1931): 260.

49. Frederick Law Olmsted, "The Beginning of Central Park: A Fragment of Autobiography," in *Landscape into Cityscape*, ed. Fein, p. 52. A similar statement was quoted without identification of the author in a sermon by William Bannard in 1851: *A Discourse on the Moral Aspect and Destitution of the City of New York* (New York: Charles Scribner, 1851), p. 14.

50. Frederick Law Olmsted, "Public Parks and the Enlargement of Towns," *Journal of Social Science* 3 (1871): 4, 10.

51. Michael H. Cowan, *City of the West: Emerson, America, and Urban Metaphor* (New Haven, Conn.: Yale University Press, 1967), pp. 215, 183.

52. Nathaniel Hawthorne, *The Blithedale Romance* (New York: Dell, 1960), pp. 180–81. See also R. W. B. Lewis, *The American Adam* (Chicago: Phoenix Books, 1958), pp. 113–14; and Cowan, *City of the West*, p. 216.

53. Cornelius Mathews, *Big Abel and the Little Manhattan* (New York: Wiley and Putnam, 1845). For an assessment of Mathews and his place in New York literary circles, see Perry Miller, *The Raven and the Whale: The War of Words and Wits in the Era of Poe and Melville* (New York: Harcourt, Brace & World, 1956).

54. See Cornelius Mathews, *A Pen-and-Ink Panorama of New York City* (New York: John S. Taylor, 1853); and James T. Callow, *Kindred Spirits: Knickerbocker Writers and American Artists, 1807–1855* (Chapel Hill: University of North Carolina Press, 1967), pp. 149–50.

55. Miller, *The Raven and the Whale*, p. 142 and passim.

56. Herman Melville, *Pierre; or, The Ambiguities* (New York: Signet Classic, 1964), pp. 25–26.

57. F. O. Matthiessen, *American Renaissance: Art and Expression in the Age of Emerson and Whitman* (New York: Oxford University Press, 1968), p. 543. Compare David Weimer, *The City as Metaphor* (New York: Random House, 1966), p. 15.

58. Weimer, *The City as Metaphor*, p. 25.

59. Frederick Law Olmsted and Calvert Vaux, *Report of the Landscape Archi-*

tects and Superintendents to the President of the Board of Commissioners of Prospect Park, Brooklyn (1868), reprinted in *Landscape into Cityscape*, ed. Fein, p. 160.

60. Horace Binney Wallace, "Town and Country," in *Art and Scenery in Europe, with Other Papers*, 2d ed. (Philadelphia: J. B. Lippincott, 1868), pp. 329–30. This essay is undated, but it was written before December 1852, when Wallace died.

61. Andrew Jackson Downing, *Rural Essays*, ed. George William Curtis (New York: Leavitt & Allen, 1858, orig. ed. 1853), p. 148. See also ibid., p. 111.

62. Bellows, "The Townward Tendency," p. 40. See also Kip, "The Building of Our Cities," p. 212.

63. Walt Whitman, "Democratic Vistas," in *Whitman: Leaves of Grass and Selected Prose*, ed. Sculley Bradley (New York: Holt, Rinehart and Winston, 1949), p. 518.

64. Lewis Mumford, "The Megamachine–I," *New Yorker* (October 10, 1970), p. 66. See also Mumford, *The Brown Decades: A Study of the Arts in America, 1865–1895* (New York: Dover Publications, 1955).

II. *Agrarianism & Industrialism, 1800–1860*

Headquote from American Society for the Encouragement of Domestic Manufactures, *Address to the People of the United States* (New York: Van Winkle, Wiley & Co., 1817), pp. 12, 14.

1. For an early identification of agrarianism with Thomas Jefferson, see Brutus, "An Enquiry into the Causes of the Present Grievances of America [extract]," *American Museum* 5 (May 1789): 493–95.

2. Thomas Jefferson to Charles Bellini, Paris, September 30, 1785, *The Papers of Thomas Jefferson*, ed. Julian P. Boyd (Princeton, N.J.: Princeton University Press, 1950–   ), 8: 568–69.

3. Thomas Jefferson to Benjamin Rush, Monticello, September 23, 1800, *The Works of Thomas Jefferson*, ed. Paul L. Ford, 12 vols. (New York: G. P. Putnam's Sons, 1904–1905), 9: 147. See also Thomas Jefferson to Maria Cosway, New York, June 23, 1790, *Papers*, ed. Boyd, 16: 550; Thomas Jefferson to Anne Willing Bingham, Paris, February 7, 1787, ibid., 11: 122; Thomas Jefferson to Anne Willing Bingham, Paris, May 11, 1788, ibid., 13: 151–52; Thomas Jefferson to Maria Cosway, Paris, May 21, 1789, ibid., 15: 143; Thomas Jefferson to James Monroe, Paris, December 18, 1786, ibid., 10: 613. Compare Thomas Jefferson to Doctor Wistar, Washington, June 21, 1807, *Works*, ed. Ford, 10: 423.

4. Morton and Lucia White, *The Intellectual Versus the City* (New York: Mentor Book, 1964), p. 30.

5. Alfred F. Young, *The Democratic-Republicans of New York: The Origins, 1763–1797* (Chapel Hill: University of North Carolina Press, 1967), p. 550.

6. Thomas Jefferson to Thomas Pinckney, Philadelphia, September 7, 1793, *Works*, ed. Ford, 8: 26–27. Numerous letters show that Jefferson considered overseas commerce an agricultural and not a mercantile interest. For example, see Thomas Jefferson to Bernardo de Gálvez, Williamsburg, November 8, 1779, *Papers*, ed. Boyd, 3: 168; Jefferson to John Jay, Marseilles, May 4, 1787, ibid., 11: 338–39; Jefferson to George Washington, Paris, August 14, 1787, ibid., 12: 37–38; Jefferson to Charles L. Lewis, Paris, January 10, 1789, ibid., 14: 428; Jefferson to Gouverneur

Morris, Philadelphia, March 10, 1792, *Works*, ed. Ford, 6: 403; Jefferson to Dupont deNemours, Washington, February 1, 1803, ibid., 9: 438; Jefferson to James Madison, Monticello, April 17, 1812, ibid., 11: 232–35; Jefferson to John Adams, Monticello, June 10, 1815, *The Adams-Jefferson Letters*, ed. Lester J. Cappon, 2 vols. (Chapel Hill: University of North Carolina Press, 1959), 2: 442–43.

7. Thomas Jefferson to William H. Crawford, Monticello, June 20, 1816, *Works*, ed. Ford, 11: 537–38.

8. See Thomas Jefferson to Benjamin Stoddert, Washington, February 18, 1809, *Works*, ed. Ford, 11: 98; Jefferson to Thomas Leiper, Washington, January 21, 1809, ibid., 11: 90–91; and Jefferson to George Washington, Paris, August 14, 1787, *Papers*, ed. Boyd, 12: 37–38. The quotation is from the last letter cited.

9. Edmund S. Morgan, "The Puritan Ethic and the American Revolution," *William and Mary Quarterly* 24 (January 1967): 3–43.

10. The best example of this is Brutus, "An enquiry into the causes of the present grievances of America," pp. 493–95; but see also Tench Coxe, "An Address to an Assembly of the Friends of American Manufactures," *American Museum* 2 (September 1787): 253–54. Interior cities that were not engaged in foreign commerce provide a contrasting case. See Richard C. Wade, *The Urban Frontier: Pioneer Life in Early Pittsburgh, Cincinnati, Lexington, Louisville, and St. Louis* (Chicago: Phoenix Book, 1964), pp. 44–46.

11. Thomas Jefferson, *Notes on the State of Virginia*, ed. Thomas Perkins Abernthy (New York: Harper Torchbook, 1964), pp. 157–58; and Jefferson to Benjamin Austin, Monticello, January 9, 1816, *Works*, ed. Ford, 11: 504.

12. Thomas Jefferson to James Madison, Paris, December 20, 1787, *Papers*, ed. Boyd, 12: 442. See also Jefferson to Brissot de Warville, Paris, August 16, 1786, ibid., 10: 262.

13. It is true, however, as Samuel Rezneck points out, that Jefferson's acceptance of domestic manufactures was an important stage in the eventual development of an industrial consciousness in the United States. (See Samuel Rezneck, "The Rise and Early Development of Industrial Consciousness in the United States, 1760–1830," *Journal of Economic and Business History* 4 [1932]: 784–811.)

14. On Jefferson and his nail factory, see Thomas Jefferson to M. De Meusnier, Monticello, April 29, 1795, *Works*, ed. Ford, 8: 174–75; Jefferson to Archibald Stuart, Monticello, January 3, 1796, ibid., 8: 212–14; and Jefferson to John Adams, Monticello, May 27, 1795, *The Adams-Jefferson Letters*, ed. Cappon, 1: 258.

15. Thomas Jefferson to Mr. Lithson, Washington, January 4, 1805, *The Writings of Thomas Jefferson*, ed. Albert Ellery Bergh, 20 vols. (Washington, D.C.: Thomas Jefferson Memorial Association, 1907), 11: 55–56.

16. Alexander Hamilton, *Report on the Subject of Manufactures* in *The Papers of Alexander Hamilton,* ed. Harold C. Syrett (New York: Columbia University Press, 1961–), 10: 281, 294; and Hamilton, *Report on the Bank*, ibid., 7: 320–21; [George Logan,] *Letters Addressed to the Yeomanry of the United States . . .* (Philadelphia: Eleazer Oswald, 1791), pp. 26–27. See also Merrill D. Peterson, *Thomas Jefferson and the New Nation: A Biography* (New York: Oxford University Press, 1970), p. 459.

17. See Thomas Jefferson, "Notes on Prof. Ebeling's Letter of July 30, 1795," *Works*, ed. Ford, 8: 210.

18. Thomas Jefferson to James Jay, Monticello, April 7, 1809, *Writings*, ed. Bergh, 12: 271. See also Jefferson to William Short, September 8, 1823, ibid., 15: 469.

19. Tench Coxe, *A View of the United States of America* (Philadelphia: Hall and Wrigley & Merriman, 1794), pp. 23–24. This and similar passages are perceptively discussed in Leo Marx, *The Machine in the Garden* (New York: Oxford University Press, 1964), pp. 150–69.

20. Henry Clay, "On Domestic Manufactures [1810]," *The Works of Henry Clay*, ed. Calvin Colton, 10 vols. (New York: G. P. Putnam's Sons, 1904), 6: 8–9.

21. Thomas Jefferson to David Humphreys, Philadelphia, June 23, 1791, *Works*, ed. Ford, 6: 273. A description of this project may be found in Frank Landon Humphreys, *Life and Times of David Humphreys,* 2 vols. (New York: G. P. Putnam's Sons, 1917), 2: chapt. 17. Unless otherwise indicated, all information and quotes referring to Humphreysville are from this chapter.

22. It is difficult to determine the size of the workers' quarters. They are nowhere clearly described as dormitories, but neither are they ever described as family-style cottages. My statement is based upon the description in Timothy Dwight, *Travels in New-England and New-York,* 4 vols. (New Haven, Conn.: Timothy Dwight, 1821–1822), 3: 392.

23. Ibid., 3: 394; Tench Coxe, "Digest of Manufactures," in *American State Papers, Finance,* 2: 689. In 1810 Henry Clay made reference to Humphreysville in the same manner that he and others later would to Lowell–as the symbol of American industry. (*Works*, ed. Colton, 6: 10.)

24. Thomas Jefferson to Abraham Bishop, Washington, November 13, 1808, *Works*, ed. Ford, 11: 72–73; Humphreys, *Life and Times of David Humphreys,* 2: 375; and Jefferson to Colonel Humphreys, Washington, January 20, 1809, *Works*, ed. Ford, 11: 73. See also Joseph Dorfman, *The Economic Mind in American Civilization* (New York: Viking Press, 1946), 1: 442–43.

25. Internal evidence in the letter suggests this interpretation, and this view is confirmed by a second letter Jefferson wrote to Austin. See Thomas Jefferson to Benjamin Austin, Monticello, January 9, 1816, *Works*, ed. Ford, 11: 500–505; and Jefferson to Benjamin Austin, Monticello, February 9, 1816, ibid., 11: 505–6.

26. American Society for the Encouragement of Domestic Manufactures, *Address to the People of the United States* (New York: Van Winkle, Wiley & Co., 1817), pp. 7, 9, 10, 12, 14.

27. George Rogers Taylor, *The Transportation Revolution, 1815–1860* (New York: Harper Torchbook, 1968), pp. 210–11; and Kenneth Frank Mailloux, "The Boston Manufacturing Company of Waltham, Massachusetts, 1813–1848: The First Modern Factory in America" (Ph.D. diss., Boston University, 1957), p. 1.

28. Percy Wells Bidwell, "Rural Economy in New England at the Beginning of the Nineteenth Century," *Transactions of the Connecticut Academy of Arts and Sciences* 20 (April 1916): 266, 319.

29. See John P. Coolidge, *Mill and Mansion: A Study of Architecture and Society in Lowell, Massachusetts, 1820–1865* (New York: Russell & Russell, 1967), pp. 11–12; Caroline F. Ware, *The Early New England Cotton Manufacture* (New York: Johnson Reprint Corporation, 1966), chapt. 2 and passim; Robert K. Lamb, "The Entrepreneur and the Community," in *Men in Business: Essays in the History of Entrepreneurship*, ed. William Miller (Cambridge: Harvard University Press,

1952), p. 108; Peter J. Coleman, *The Transformation of Rhode Island, 1790–1860* (Providence, R.I.: Brown University Press, 1963), pp. 77–93; and George S. White, *Memoir of Samuel Slater*, 2d ed. (Philadelphia, 1836), p. 257 and passim.

30. Percy Wells Bidwell, "Population Growth in Southern New England, 1810–1860," *American Statistical Association Journal* 15 (December 1917): 814–15.

31. See Oliver Warner, *Abstract of the Census of Massachusetts, 1860* (n.p.: [1863?]), pp. 292–95; and Jeffrey G. Williamson and Joseph A. Swanson, "The Growth of Cities in the American Northeast, 1820–1870," *Explorations in Entrepreneurial History*, 2d ser., 4 (supplement, 1966): 3–101.

32. Henry A. Miles, *Lowell as It Was and as It Is*, 2d ed. (Lowell: Nathaniel L. Dayton, 1847), pp. 218–19; Douglass C. North, *The Economic Growth of the United States, 1790–1860* (New York: W. W. Norton, 1966), chapt. 12; Samuel Eliot Morison, *The Maritime History of Massachusetts, 1783–1860* (Boston: Sentry Edition, 1961), p. 214; Thomas C. Cochran, "Business Organization and the Development of an Industrial Discipline," in *Views of American Economic Growth: The Agricultural Era*, ed. Thomas C. Cochran and Thomas B. Brewer (New York: McGraw Hill, 1966), p. 220; Frederick W. Coburn, *History of Lowell and Its People*, 3 vols. (New York: Lewis Historical Publishing Company, 1920), 1: 104–31; Ware, *The Early New England Cotton Manufacture*, pp. 3, 17; and Paul F. McGouldrick, *New England Textiles in the Nineteenth Century: Profits and Investment* (Cambridge: Harvard University Press, 1968), pp. 12–18.

33. James Jackson, "Notes on the Life of P. T. Jackson" [1847] Ms (typescript), Houghton Library, Harvard University. For Jefferson's support of the tariff, see p. 35; for James Madison, see his "Seventh Annual Message," *Messages and Papers of the Presidents, 1789–1897*, comp. James D. Richardson, 10 vols. (Washington: Government Printing Office, 1896–1899), 1: 567. The characterization of Lowell is from Nathan Appleton, *Introduction of the Power Loom and the Origin of Lowell* (Lowell: B. H. Penhallow, 1858), p. 15. See also Theodore Edson, "Diary," March 1, 1876, Lowell Historical Society; Miles, *Lowell*, p. 22; and Coolidge, *Mill and Mansion*, pp. 18, 21–23, 165 n.

34. The best biographical account of Francis Cabot Lowell is Francis Cabot Lowell, "Address," in *Exercises at the Seventy-Fifth Anniversary of the Incorporation of the Town of Lowell* (Lowell: Courier-Citizen Company, Printers, 1901), pp. 42–49. See also Harold Kirker and James Kirker, *Bulfinch's Boston, 1787–1817* (New York: Oxford University Press, 1964), chapt. 1 and passim; Lamb, "The Entrepreneur and the Community," pp. 117–19, 319, 106–13; Edward Everett, "Memoir of John Lowell, Jun.," preface to John G. Palfrey, *Lowell Lectures on the Evidences of Christianity*, 2 vols. (Boston: James Munroe and Company, 1843), 1: xxv–xxvi; Mailloux, "The Boston Manufacturing Company," pp. 29–30; Walter Muir Whitehill, *Boston: A Topographical History*, 2d ed. (Cambridge: Harvard University Press, 1968), chapts. 3–4; and Robert Varnum Spalding, "The Boston Mercantile Community and the Promotion of the Textile Industry in New England, 1813–1860" (Ph.D diss., Yale University, 1963), p. 12 and passim.

35. Lamb, "The Entrepreneur and the Community," p. 319. Cabot's factory was prominently mentioned in Hamilton's report on manufactures, and George Washington visited it as president.

36. Appleton, *Introduction of the Power Loom*, p. 7.

37. Jackson, "Notes on the Life of P. T. Jackson," p. 5. See also Everett, "Memoir of John Lowell, Jun.," p. xxxii.

38. William R. Bagnall, "Contributions to American Economic History" (unpub. materials; 4 vols.; typed Ms, 1908) Baker Library, Harvard University, 3: 1991; and Ralph Waldo Emerson, *Journals of Ralph Waldo Emerson, 1820–1872,* ed. Edward Waldo Emerson and Waldo Emerson Forbes, 10 vols. (Cambridge, Mass.: Riverside Press, 1909–1914), 7: 145.

39. [Henry Lee,] "The Introduction of Cotton Manufactures into New England –No. 2," *Boston Daily Advertiser,* March 4, 1830 (for attribution of this article to Lee, see Miles, *Lowell,* p. 222); Appleton, *Introduction of the Power Loom,* p. 8.

40. Lamb, "The Entrepreneur and the Community," pp. 106–19, 319; Mailloux, "The Boston Manufacturing Company," pp. 45–48; and Everett, "Memoir of John Lowell, Jun.," p. xxxii.

41. See Samuel Batchelder to Jas. B. Durfee, Cambridge, December 18, 1877, typescript from Caroline Ware through Frances Gregory in Hamilton Manufacturing Company Collection, Baker Library, Harvard University, inventory folder; and Appleton, *Introduction of the Power Loom,* p. 8.

42. Mrs. Henry Lee to husband, August 17, 1813, in *The Jacksons and the Lees: Two Generations of Massachusetts Merchants, 1765–1844,* ed. Kenneth W. Porter, 2 vols. (Cambridge: Harvard University Press, 1937), 1: 747.

43. Appleton, *Introduction of the Power Loom,* pp. 9, 10.

44. Mailloux, "The Boston Manufacturing Company," pp. 88–89.

45. On this general problem, see Perry Miller, *The Life of the Mind in America* (New York: Harcourt, Brace & World, 1965), Book 3.

46. Franklin, "Letter to Agents of the Manufacturing Establishments of Lowell," *Lowell Journal,* June 15, 1827; and Miles, *Lowell,* p. 128. See also Norman Ware, *The Industrial Worker, 1840–1860* (Chicago: Quadrangle Books, 1964), p. 72; Ware, *The Early New England Cotton Manufacture,* pp. 8, 11; Charles L. Sanford, "The Intellectual Origins and New-Worldliness of American Industry," *Journal of Economic History* 18 (1958): 1–16; and Stuart Bruchey, *The Roots of American Economic Growth, 1607–1861* (New York: Harper & Row, 1965), p. 199.

47. Francis Cabot Lowell to Patrick T. Jackson, London, June 2, 1811, Lowell Papers (These papers were in the possession of Harriet Ropes Cabot when I examined them, but they will soon be transferred to the Massachusetts Historical Society.); Harriet Lowell to Mary Lee, London, June 6, 1811, ibid. See also Harriet Lowell to Mrs. Grant, London, June 2, 1811, ibid.; and Francis Cabot Lowell to Mrs. Samuel Gardner, London, June 5, 1811, ibid.

48. Francis Cabot Lowell to William Cabot, London, January 2, 1811, ibid.; Francis Cabot Lowell to Mary Lee, Edinburgh, April 6, 1811, ibid.; and Francis Cabot Lowell to William Cabot, London, May 29, 1811, ibid. Relying too heavily upon the published papers of Amos Lawrence, who was by far the most moralistic of the early industrialists, Charles L. Sanford has drawn the contrast between Europe and America in the minds of this group much too sharply. My examination of the papers of F. C. Lowell, Appleton, Abbott Lawrence, and other prominent Massachusetts industrialists suggests the more moderate view presented above. (Compare Sanford, "The Intellectual Origins and New-Worldliness of American Industry.")

49. Appleton, *Introduction of the Power Loom*, p. 15. See also Nathan Appleton to Editor, *Lowell Courier*, Boston, December 30, 1846, reprinted in *Correspondence between Nathan Appleton and John A. Lowell in Relation to the Early History of the City of Lowell* (Boston: Eastburn's Press, 1848), pp. 17–19; John A. Lowell, "Address," *Proceedings in the City of Lowell at the Semi-Centennial Celebration of the Town of Lowell, March 1, 1876* (Lowell: Penhallow, 1876), pp. 54–55; and John A. Lowell, "Memoir of Patrick Tracy Jackson," *Hunt's Merchants' Magazine* 18 (April 1848): 358.

50. Quotation from [Nathan Appleton,] "The New Tariff," *Boston Daily Advertiser*, February 1821, Appleton Papers, Scrapbook, 1: 5. Interestingly, one of the merchants opposing Lowell was Abbott Lawrence, who later founded the manufacturing city of Lawrence, Massachusetts. For a sample of the antitariff opinion, see *Massachusetts Spy*, May 1, 1816; "The Proposed New Tariff," *North American Review* 12 (January 1821): 85–86; [Boston] Committee of Merchants, *Report on the Tariff* (Boston: Wells and Lilly, 1820).

51. Nathan Appleton to Editor, *Lowell Courier*, Boston, December 30, 1846, reprinted in *Correspondence between Nathan Appleton and John A. Lowell*, p. 18; and Ware, *The Early New England Cotton Manufacture*, p. 8.

52. Actually, Slater developed a power loom in 1823, but did not put it into extensive use until 1827. (See Coleman, *The Transformation of Rhode Island*, p. 88.)

53. This would hold true whether weavers took yarn under contract to Slater or wove yarn purchased outright from him. This paragraph relies upon the works cited in note 29, above.

54. Samuel Batchelder, *Introduction and Early Progress of the Cotton Manufacture in the United States* (Boston: Little, Brown, 1863), p. 74. See also H. J. Habakkuk, *American and British Technology in the Nineteenth Century* (Cambridge, Eng.: University Press, 1967), pp. 113–14, 125–26.

55. Ware, *The Early New England Cotton Manufacture*, p. 64. Norman Ware and Vera Shlakman fail to see the greater demand for labor at Waltham as opposed to Rhode Island. (See Ware, *The Industrial Worker*, p. 75; and Shlakman, *Economic History of a Factory Town: A Study of Chicopee, Massachusetts* [Northampton, Mass.: Department of History of Smith College, 1935], p. 51.) On the quality of labor required, see Bagnall, "Contributions to American Economic History," 3: 2009; Charles Cowley, *Illustrated History of Lowell*, rev. ed. (Boston: Lee and Shepard, 1868), p. 38; and Ware, *The Early New England Cotton Manufacture*, p. 201.

56. Appleton, *Introduction of the Power Loom*, p. 15. See also [Nathan Appleton,] "The Cotton Manufacture–No. 5," *The Banner of the Constitution,* 1831, in Appleton Papers, Scrapbook, 1: 14. Even before Hamilton's report on manufactures, advocates of American manufacturing had been looking at this pool of unused labor. See "Essay on Manufactures," *American Museum* 7 (January 1790): 24–25. Edith Abbott discusses attitudes relating to the introduction of women into the factory labor force in her "The History of the Industrial Employment of Women in the United States: An Introductory Study," *Journal of Political Economy* 14 (1906): 490–501.

57. Harriet H. Robinson, *Loom and Spindle: Or, Life among the Early Mill Girls* (New York: Thomas Y. Crowell, 1898), pp. 61–62; Taylor, *The Transporta-*

tion Revolution, p. 275; Bagnall, "Contributions to American Economic History," 3: 2008–11; Mailloux, "The Boston Manufacturing Company," p. 100; Percy W. Bidwell, "The Agricultural Revolution in New England," *American Historical Review* 26 (July 1921): 683–702; and Cochran, "Business Organization and the Development of an Industrial Discipline," p. 222.

58. Miles, *Lowell,* p. 128. See also [Henry A. Miles,] "Cotton Manufactures," *North American Review* 52 (January 1841): 44, 52; the letter signed "J. R." in *Chelmsford Phenix,* August 5, 1825; Harriet H. Robinson, "The Life of Early Mill Girls," *Journal of Social Science* 16 (December 1882): 130. Howard Gitelman, "The Waltham System and the Coming of the Irish," *Labor History* 8 (Fall 1967): 227–53, considers this issue.

59. Hannah Josephson, *The Golden Threads: New England Mill Girls and Magnates* (New York: Duell, Sloan and Pearce, 1949), p. 74; P. T. Jackson to G. Gore, Boston, October 17, 1814, Lee Family Collection, Massachusetts Historical Society, Letterbook "B"; John A. Lowell, "Address," pp. 51–57; and Lowell, "Memoir of Patrick Tracy Jackson." Compare J. F. C. Harrison, *Quest for the New Moral World: Robert Owen and the Owenites in Britain and America* (New York: Scribner's, 1969), p. 52. Because of superficial similarities, some historians have speculated whether Lowell modeled his mill on New Lanark. Although there is little evidence on the point, what is available suggests that New Lanark was not Lowell's model and that it was not even one of the mills he inspected.

60. Coolidge, *Mill and Mansion,* p. 18.

61. Ware, *The Early New England Cotton Manufacture,* pp. 140–41; and Appleton, *Introduction of the Power Loom,* pp. 13–14.

62. Patrick Tracy Jackson, "Report on Manufactures of Cotton," in *General Convention of the Friends of Domestic Industry Assembled at New York, October 26, 1831,* p. 110.

63. William Tudor, *Letters on the Eastern States* (New York: Kirk and Mercein, 1820), p. 220. Tudor does not mention Waltham by name, but as a member of the Boston elite he must have had the factories there in mind when he prepared his discussion of manufactures.

64. "Application of Principles," *Niles' Weekly Register* 20 (June 23, 1821): 260; and U.S., Congress, House, Committee on Manufactures, "Protection to Manufactures," January 15, 1821, in *American State Papers, Finance,* 3: 601.

65. Cantel has been studied in Manning Nash, *Machine Age Maya: The Industrialization of a Guatemalan Community,* American Anthropological Association, *Memoir,* no. 87 (April 1958); and Manning Nash, *Primitive and Peasant Economic Systems* (San Francisco: Chandler Publishing Company, 1966), pp. 110–19. Nash cites studies in Pakistan, India, and Japan which indicate that Cantel is not unique. An important summary article on this general problem is Ian Weinberg, "The Problem of Convergence of Industrial Societies: A Critical Look at the State of a Theory," *Comparative Studies in Society and History* 11 (January 1969): 1–15. The expansionist and speculative character of the New England textile industry is the subject of a dissertation by Robert Spalding, "The Boston Mercantile Community and the Promotion of the Textile Industry in New England, 1813–1860."

66. On the shift of capital from commerce to manufacturing, see Mailloux, "The

Boston Manufacturing Company," chapt. 2; Lamb, "The Entrepreneur and the Community," pp. 106–7; Gregory, "Nathan Appleton," p. 429; and J. Herbert Burgy, *The New England Cotton Textile Industry: A Study in Industrial Geography* (Baltimore: Waverly Press, 1932), p. 21.

67. On Jackson, see Lowell, "Memoir of Patrick Tracy Jackson"; and *Dictionary of American Biography*.

68. On Appleton, see Josephson, *The Golden Threads*, chapt. 7; Gregory, "Nathan Appleton"; Frederic C. Jaher, "Businessman and Gentleman: Nathan and Thomas Gold Appleton–An Exploration in Intergenerational History," *Explorations in Entrepreneurial History*, 2d ser., 4 (Fall 1966): 17–39.

69. Appleton, *Introduction of the Power Loom*, pp. 17–20; "Sketch of the Town of Lowell," *Bowen's Boston News-Letter and City Record* 1 (March 25, 1826): 158.

70. Alfred Gilman, "Sketch of the Life of Kirk Boott," *Contributions of the Old Residents' Historical Association* 2 (1883): 3, 5. See also Theodore Edson, "Kirk Boott," ibid., 1 (1879): 87–97; Miles, *Lowell*, pp. 228–31; and *Dictionary of American Biography*.

71. Quoted in Bagnall, "Contributions to American Economic History," 3: 2157. See also Nathan Appleton to Samuel Appleton, Boston, September 22, 1823, Appleton Papers.

72. Bagnall, "Contributions to American Economic History," 3: 2162.

73. Rt. Reverend Thomas M. Clark, "Address," *Proceedings in the City of Lowell at the Semi-Centennial Celebration of the Incorporation of the Town of Lowell*, March 1, 1876, p. 60. On the instant establishment of western cities, see Daniel Boorstin, *The Americans: The National Experience* (New York: Vintage Books, 1965), pp. 113–23.

74. J. D. B. De Bow, *Statistical View of the United States* (Washington: A. O. P. Nicholson, 1854), p. 192.

75. Margaret Terrell Parker, *Lowell: A Study of Industrial Development* (New York: Macmillan, 1940), p. 1. See also James Montgomery, *The Cotton Manufacture of the United States of America . . . Contrasted and Compared with that of Great Britain* [1840] (New York: Johnson Reprint Corporation, 1968), p. 162; and "The Manufactures of the United States: No. 1. Lowell," *De Bow's Review* 16 (February 1854): 187–91.

76. See Spalding, "The Boston Mercantile Community and the Promotion of the Textile Industry in New England, 1813–1860."

77. Edward Everett, *Orations and Speeches on Various Occasions*, 2 vols. (Boston: Charles C. Little and James Brown, 1850), 2: 65; John Greenleaf Whittier, *The Stranger in Lowell* (Boston: Waite, Peirce and Company, 1845), p. 9. For the ethos of unreality surrounding Lowell, see Miller, *The Life of the Mind in America*, pp. 298–300.

78. Henry Clay to William Schouler, Ashland, November 10, 1843, James Schouler Papers, Massachusetts Historical Society; "New England Manufactories," *New York Statesman*, reprinted in *New England Farmer* 5 (December 22, 1826): 173.

79. Quoted phrase is from an account of Polk's visit to Lowell. See *Vox Populi* [Lowell], July 9, 1847.

80. George Lewis, *Impressions of America and the American Churches* (Edinburgh: W. P. Kennedy, 1845), p. 379. Americans used the same imagery, see White, *Memoir of Samuel Slater*, p. 168.

81. See Letter to editor, *Lowell Journal*, January 29, 1834.

82. *Lowell Times*, November 25, 1833; Henry A. Miles, *A Glance at Our History Prospects, and Duties* (Lowell: Stearns & Taylor, 1844), pp. 9–10. See also C. D. S., "Visit to Lowell," *New York Daily Tribune*, August 16, 1845.

83. Miles, *Lowell*, pp. 6, 61–63. See also F. Hedge, *The Pictoral Lowell Almanac for 1850* (Lowell: F. Hedge, 1849), pp. 22–23; and *Lowell Journal and Mercury*, December 18, 1835.

84. [Alexander Everett,] *America* (Philadelphia: H. C. Carey & I. Lea, 1827), pp. 156–62; Timothy Flint, Review of *America*, by Alexander Everett, *Western Monthly Review* 1 (July 1827): 170.

85. Bernard Whitman, *A Thanksgiving Discourse on the Means of Increasing Public Happiness* (Cambridge: Hilliard and Brown, 1828), pp. 26–32. Whitman had also supplied a Chelmsford pulpit in 1825, acted as editor of Lowell's first newspaper, and had been Lowell's Fourth of July Orator in 1825.

86. Miller, *The Life of the Mind in America*, p. 299.

87. Everett, *Orations and Speeches*, 2: 48–49, 65, 57–58.

88. This argument was repeated over and over by advocates of manufacturing who knew that they must win the support of farmers. For strong statements by the founders of Lowell, see Nathan Appleton to Editor of the *New York Evening Post*, reprinted in the *Lowell Courier*, April 13, 1844; and Jackson, "Report on Manufactures of Cotton," p. 111. For an especially interesting formulation by a Baltimore lawyer, see Daniel Raymond, *Thoughts on Political Economy* (Baltimore: Fielding Lucas, 1820), pp. 121–22.

89. Everett, *Orations and Speeches*, 2: 63, 56. Everett continued to use this bucolic imagery to describe Lowell even at mid-century. See Edward Everett to Abbott Lawrence, London, April 30, 1845, Edward Everett Papers, Massachusetts Historical Society; and Everett to Henry Holland, Cambridge, July 25, 1848, ibid. Everett's use of the word suburb here may be confusing. It differs from our own and mid nineteenth-century American usage. The explanation is that early British steam-powered factories were often built on the perimeter of existing towns and cities, and during the early nineteenth century *suburb* might refer to either the industrial or residential ring of a city. For a brief discussion of the use of *suburb* in England during the early nineteenth century, see Asa Briggs, *Victorian Cities*, Am. ed. (New York: Harper & Row, 1965), pp. 27–28.

90. See editorial "Influence of Manufacturing Institutions," *Lowell Mercury*, April 16, 1831.

91. Nathan Appleton, "Labor, Its Relations, in Europe and the United States Compared," *Hunt's Merchants' Magazine* 11 (September 1844): 220–21. This piece was also published separately as a pamphlet under the same title by Eastburn's Press in Boston. See also [Nathan Appleton,] "The New Tariff," *Boston Daily Advertiser*, February 1821, Appleton Papers, Scrapbook, 1: 5. Interestingly, Appleton and his associates also promoted a protective tariff for the *worker*—without realizing that the logic of a protective tariff for labor challenged the myth of free

land. The loss of his factory job as a result of European competition would be no disaster if the American worker could simply resort to a western farm. In fact, it was the capitalist who needed protection for his investment. For Appleton's ideas on the relationship of western land and the tariff, see Nathan Appleton to James Lloyd, August 1827 [draft], Appleton Papers; [Nathan Appleton,] "The Cotton Manufacture–No. 5," *The Banner of the Constitution,* 1831, Appleton Papers, Scrapbook, 1: 14. For the importance of the tariff in creating investor confidence, see McGouldrick, *New England Textiles,* p. 272 n; and D. A. White to Sam Lawrence, Salem, January 2, 1846, Charles Storrow Letters, Essex Company Collection, Merrimack Valley Textile Museum.

92. Helene S. Zahler, *Eastern Workingmen and National Land Policy, 1829–1862* (New York: Greenwood Press, 1969), pp. 85, 185, 193, and passim; Merrill D. Peterson, *The Jeffersonian Image in the American Mind* (New York: Oxford University Press, 1960), p. 85. Demands for cheap land and ten-hour legislation occurred with about equal frequency in the *Voice of Industry,* a labor newspaper published in Lowell during the mid-1840s.

93. Anon., *The Condition of Labor. An Address to Members of the Labor League of New England* (1847), quoted in Arthur M. Schlesinger, Jr., *The Age of Jackson* (Boston: Little, Brown, 1945), p. 345; [Orestes Brownson,] "The Laboring Classes," *Boston Quarterly Review* 3 (October 1840): 473. See also Charles A. Dana, Review of *American Factories and Their Female Operatives,* by the Rev. William Scoresby, *Lowell as It Was and as It Is,* by the Rev. Henry A. Miles, and *New York Daily Tribune,* August 16, 1845, in the *Harbinger* 1 (August 30, 1845): 185–88.

94. Andrews Norton to Nathan Appleton, November 11, 1844, Appleton Papers; Nathan Appleton to Andrews Norton, November 23, 1844, ibid.; Henry Nash Smith, *Virgin Land: The American West as Symbol and Myth* (New York: Vintage Book, 1950), p. 240.

95. *Register of Debates in Congress,* 21st Cong., 1st sess., 6 (January 18, 1830): 24. See also Schlesinger, *The Age of Jackson,* p. 347.

96. He gave this speech twice, and the reports of it differ slightly in language. See *Lowell Weekly Journal,* December 24, 1856; and ibid., January 23, 1857.

97. [Ezra Stiles Gannett,] Review of *Lowell as It Was and as It Is,* by Henry A. Miles, *Mind among the Spindles,* and *American Factories and Their Female Operatives,* by William Scoresby, in the *Christian Examiner* 29 (September 1845): 275–76. See also "Lowell and Its Manufactures," *Hunt's Merchants' Magazine* 16 (April 1847): 356–62.

98. [Amos A. Lawrence,] "Appendix," in *American Factories and Their Female Operatives,* by William Scoresby (Boston: William D. Ticknor and Co., 1845), p. 133; Elisha Huntington, *Address of the Mayor of Lowell* (Lowell: L. Huntress, 1841), p. 4. See also Anon., *Hand-Book for the Visiter* [*sic*] *to Lowell* (Lowell: A. Watson, 1848), p. 34.

99. Ware, *The Early New England Cotton Manufacture,* p. 118; Jesse Chickering, *A Statistical View of the Population of Massachusetts, from 1765–1840* (Boston: Charles C. Little and James Brown, [1847]), pp. 42–44, 73, 107; and Amos Blanchard, "Introduction," in *Lectures to Young People in Manufacturing Villages,* by Dorus Clarke (Boston: Perkins & Marvin, 1836), pp. ix–xxvii.

100. *Journals of Ralph Waldo Emerson*, 4: 207 (April 21, 1837). For an excellent study of Emerson's adjustment to a changing America, see Michael H. Cowan, *City of the West: Emerson, America, and Urban Metaphor* (New Haven, Conn.: Yale University Press, 1967).

101. Whittier, *The Stranger in Lowell*, p. 38. See also Miller, *The Life of the Mind in America*, p. 301; and [Harriet Farley,] "Editorial," *Lowell Offering* 3 (1843): 213.

102. Henry David Thoreau, *Walden and Other Writings of Henry David Thoreau*, ed. Brooks Atkinson (New York: Modern Library Edition, 1950), p. 24.

103. Miller, *The Life of the Mind in America*, p. 298.

104. Whittier, *The Stranger in Lowell*, pp. 21–22. See also Harriet Farley, *Operatives' Reply to Hon. Jere Clemens* (Lowell: S. J. Varney, 1850); and *Lowell Tri-Weekly American*, August 10, 1849. For a fine analysis of the free labor ideology, see Eric Foner, *Free Soil, Free Labor, Free Men: The Ideology of the Republican Party before the Civil War* (New York: Oxford University Press, 1967).

105. Batchelder, *Introduction and Early Progress of the Cotton Manufacture in the United States*, p. 94. See also Hugo A. Meier, "American Technology and the Nineteenth Century World," in *The American Culture*, ed. Hennig Cohen (Boston: Houghton Mifflin, 1968), p. 200.

106. I have examined five accounts of Lowell written between 1833 and 1880 in an effort to prepare an index showing the percentage of the total account devoted specifically to justifying the experiment at Lowell. In this rough content analysis I have considered only explicit statements, and the index is a percentage of pages (or lines) devoted to justification out of the total pages: 2: 53–113. 1833–21.0% [lines]; 1845–13.7%; 1856–3.5%; 1868–1.3%; 1880–0.0%. The five accounts that I have used are A. G. T., "Lowell," *New England Magazine* 4 (January 1833): 72–74; Henry A. Miles, *Lowell as It Was and as It Is* (Lowell: Powers and Bagley and N. L. Dayton, 1845); Charles Cowley, *A Handbook of Business in Lowell, with a History of the City* (Lowell: E. D. Green, 1856); Charles Cowley, *Illustrated History of Lowell*, rev. ed. (Boston: Lee and Shepard, 1868); and Alfred Gilman, "Lowell," in *History of Middlesex County*, ed. Samuel Adams Drake, 2 vols. (Boston: Estes and Lauriat, Publishers, 1880).

107. See J. Leander Bishop, *A History of American Manufactures* [1868 ed.], 3 vols. (New York: Johnson Reprint Corporation, 1967), 1: 7; Sanford, "The Intellectual Origins and New-Worldliness of American Industry," p. 14; and Meier, "American Technology and the Nineteenth Century World," p. 200.

108. Lawrence, *Letters . . . to Hon. William C. Rives of Virginia*, p. 18; Abbott Lawrence to Charles Storrow, London, October 4, 1850, reprinted in *Lowell Weekly Journal*, October 25, 1850; Meier, "American Technology and the Nineteenth Century World," p. 197; J. G. Dudley, "Growth, Trade and Manufacture of Cotton," *De Bow's Review* 16 (January 1854): 12; *Lowell Journal and Courier*, July 16, 1853; and E. H. Chapin, *The American Idea and What Grows Out of It: An Oration Delivered in the New York Crystal Palace, July 4, 1854* (Boston: Abel Tompkins, 1854), p. 17.

109. Eric Foner shows that many leaders of the emerging Republican party held similar views of American industrial development. (See *Free Soil, Free Labor, Free Men*, chapt. 1.)

III. Men, Machines & Factories: Toward Urban Industrialism

Headquote from Horace Bushnell, "The Age of Homespun [1851]," in *Work and Play* (New York: Charles Scribner, 1864), p. 376.

1. Samuel Miller, "Mechanic Arts," *Brief Retrospect of the Eighteenth Century* [1803], excerpted in *Of Men and Machines*, ed. Arthur O. Lewis, Jr. (New York: E. P. Dutton, 1964), pp. 114–25; "Preface," *Transactions of the American Philosophical Society* 1 (1771): i; and American Society for the Encouragement of Domestic Manufactures, *Address to the People of the United States* (New York: Van Winkle, Wiley & Co., 1817), p. 5. See also Hugo Meier, "Technology and Democracy, 1800–1860," *Mississippi Valley Historical Review* 43 (1957): 618–40.

2. Perry Miller, "The Responsibility of Mind in a Civilization of Machines," *American Scholar* 31 (Winter 1961): 60.

3. For a discussion of this Jeffersonian vocabulary, see Perry Miller, *The Life of the Mind in America* (New York: Harcourt, Brace & World, 1965), pp. 269–313.

4. Edward Everett, "The Importance of the Mechanic Arts," *Orations and Speeches on Various Occasions*, 2 vols. (Boston: Charles C. Little and James Brown, 1850), 2: 242, 247–48. See also Zachariah Allen, *The Science of Mechanics* (Providence, R.I.: Hutchens & Cory, 1829), pp. iii–v; G. W. Burnap, "The Influence of the Use of Machinery on the Civilization, Comfort, and Morality of Mankind," *American Museum* 2 (May 1839): 349–64; and Ezra Seaman, *Essays on the Progress of Nations* (New York: Baker & Scribner, 1846), p. 59.

5. See *Boston Daily Advertiser*, March 4, 1830; Edward Everett, "Memoir of John Lowell, Jun.," preface to John G. Palfrey, *Lowell Lectures on the Evidences of Christianity*, 2 vols. (Boston: James Munroe and Company, 1843), 1: xxx–xxxv; and Perry Miller, *The Life of the Mind in America*, p. 298.

6. Nathan Appleton, *Introduction of the Power Loom and the Origin of Lowell* (Lowell: B. H. Penhallow, 1858), p. 9; Henry A. Miles, *Lowell as It Was and as It Is*, 2d ed. (Lowell: Nathaniel L. Dayton, 1847), pp. 221–22 (second Appleton quote); [Benjamin Silliman,] "Lowell," *American Journal of Science and Arts* 27 (January 1835): 346; [Benjamin Silliman?] "An Analytical Examination of Prof. Babbage's 'Economy of Machinery and Manufactures,'" *American Journal of Science and Arts* 24 (July 1833): 105; and [Samuel Griswold Goodrich,] *Enterprise, Industry and Art of Man* (Philadelphia: Thomas, Cowperthwait & Co., 1845), pp. 327–28. See also S. G. B., "Pleasures of Factory Life," *Lowell Offering*, no. 2 (1840), p. 25; [Henry A. Miles,] "Cotton Manufactures," *North American Review* 52 (January 1841): 31–36; C. D. S., "Visit to Lowell," *New York Daily Tribune*, August 16, 1845; and Theo. Ledyard Cuyler, "A Day at Lowell," *Godey's Magazine and Lady's Book* 33 (1846): 184.

7. [Silliman,] "An Analytical Examination of Prof. Babbage's 'Economy of Machinery and Manufactures,'" p. 105; [Theodore Parker,] "Thoughts on Labor," *Dial* 1 (April 1841): 510.

8. Tench Coxe, "Digest of Manufactures," *American State Papers, Finance*, 2: 677.

9. [John Dix,] *Local Loitering and Visits in the Vicinity of Boston* (Boston: Redding & Co., 1846), p. 76. My interpretation of this passage follows Marvin Fisher, *Workshops in the Wilderness: The European Response to American In-*

dustrialization, 1830–1860 (New York: Oxford University Press, 1967), p. 154. On the concept of covert culture, see Bernard Bowron, Leo Marx, and Arnold Rose, "Literature and Covert Culture," *Studies in American Culture: Dominant Ideas and Images,* ed. Joseph J. Kwiat and Mary C. Turpie (Minneapolis: University of Minnesota Press, 1960), pp. 84–94.

10. See Leo Marx, *The Machine in the Garden* (New York: Oxford University Press, 1964), p. 219; and Oscar Handlin, "Man and Magic: First Encounters with the Machine," *American Scholar* 33 (Summer 1964): 419.

11. [Timothy Walker,] "Defence of Mechanical Philosophy," *North American Review* 33 (July 1831): 127. This debate had important philosophical implications which are discussed by Leo Marx in *The Machine in the Garden,* pp. 169–90.

12. Ralph Waldo Emerson, "Works and Days [1870]," in *Complete Works of Ralph Waldo Emerson,* ed. Edward W. Emerson, 12 vols. (Boston: Houghton Mifflin, 1912), 7: 164–65.

13. Edward Bellamy, *Looking Backward* (New York: Signet Classic, 1960), p. 164. Some city planners whose ideas were shaped in the mid-century were quite sensitive to the potentially dehumanizing implications of Bellamy's utopia. (See H. W. S. Cleveland to William W. Folwell, Minneapolis, May 14, 1889, Folwell Papers, Minnesota State Historical Society.)

14. Henry Adams, *The Education of Henry Adams* (Boston: Sentry Edition, 1961), p. 380.

15. Samuel Haber, *Efficiency and Uplift* (Chicago: University of Chicago Press, 1964), p. ix; and Frederick Winslow Taylor, *The Principles of Scientific Management* (New York: W. W. Norton & Company, 1967, orig. ed. 1911), p. 7. See the insightful discussion by John William Ward in his *Red, White and Blue: Men, Books, and Ideas in American Culture* (New York: Oxford University Press, 1969), pp. 227–94. On this same theme, see also Robert H. Wiebe, *The Search for Order, 1877–1920* (New York: Hill and Wang, 1967), pp. 145–63 and passim; Dwight Waldo, *The Administrative State* (New York: Ronald Press, 1948), passim, esp. pp. 19–20; and Joel H. Spring, *Education and the Rise of the Corporate State* (Boston: Beacon Press, 1972), chapts. 1–4, 8.

16. Lewis Mumford, *The Myth of the Machine: Technics and Human Development* (New York: Harcourt, Brace & World, 1967), p. 191.

17. Herman Melville, "The Tartarus of Maids," *Great Short Works of Herman Melville,* with an introduction by Jerry Allen (New York: Harper & Row, 1966), pp. 174, 180.

18. See Miller, "The Responsibility of Mind in a Civilization of Machines."

19. See, for example, the works cited in note 10, above.

20. Frederick Law Olmsted, *A Journey in the Seaboard Slave States* (New York: Dix & Edwards, 1856), pp. 214–15.

21. Lucy Larcom, *A New England Childhood: Outlined from Memory* (Boston: Houghton Mifflin, 1889), p. 226.

22. On this point, see Lewis Mumford, *Technics and Civilization* (New York: Harcourt, Brace & World, 1934), p. 10 and passim; and Thorstein Veblen, "The Discipline of the Machine," in *The Portable Veblen,* ed. Max Lerner (New York: Viking Press, 1948), pp. 335–48.

23. *Voice of Industry* [Lowell], June 19, 1846.

24. Ibid., February 20, 1846; *The Operative* [Lowell], January 25, 1845; and *Voice of Industry* [Lowell], June 19, 1846.

25. Blanchard Fosgate, "Social Influence of Manufacturing," *New World* 6 (June 3, 1843): 651; *Boston Daily Times*, July 16, 1839.

26. John Greenleaf Whittier, *The Stranger in Lowell* (Boston: Waite, Peirce and Company, 1845), p. 84; *Voice of Industry* [Lowell], April 3, 1846; ibid., September 11, 1846; and *Vox Populi* [Lowell,] July 16, 1847. See also *Voice of Industry* [Lowell], June 19, 1846; ibid., May 7, 1847; and Anon., *Corporations and Operatives* (Lowell: S. J. Varney, 1843), p. 16.

27. "The Factories of Lowell, and the Factory Girls," *New England Offering* (May 1848), p. 26; Whittier, *The Stranger in Lowell*, p. 24.

28. [Mathew Carey?] *Examination of the Pretensions of New England to Commercial Pre-eminence* (Philadelphia: M. Carey, 1814), p. 25. See also Alexis de Tocqueville, *Democracy in America*, ed. Phillips Bradley, 2 vols. (New York: Vintage Books, 1945), 2: 166; Julius Rubin, "Growth and Expansion of Urban Centers," in *The Growth of Seaport Cities, 1790–1825*, ed. David T. Gilchrist (Charlottesville: University Press of Virginia, 1967), pp. 3–31; Don Martindale, *Community, Character and Civilization: Studies in Social Behaviorism* (New York: Free Press, 1963), pp. 305, 318; and Adna F. Weber, *The Growth of Cities in the Nineteenth Century* (Ithaca, N.Y.: Cornell University Press, 1967; orig. ed., 1899), pp. 382–83.

29. On the function of rural survivals in an urbanizing society, see Gerald Breese, *Urbanization in Newly Developing Countries* (Englewood Cliffs, N.J.: Prentice-Hall, 1966), pp. 46, 87, 98.

30. For example, see Lucy Larcom, "Among the Lowell Mill Girls: A Reminiscence," *Atlantic Monthly* 48 (1881): 599; Adelia, "The Sister," *Lowell Offering* 4 (1844): 14–23.

31. See Susan, "Letters from Susan," *Lowell Offering* 4 (May 1844): 83–92.

32. Lucy Larcom, "Farewell to New England," *New England Offering* (September 1848), p. 126; Larcom, "Among the Lowell Mill Girls: A Reminiscence," p. 599. See also Larcom, *A New England Childhood*, p. 193; [Harriet Farley,] "Factory Girls," *Lowell Offering*, no. 2 (1840), pp. 17–19; Laura Currier to Harriette, Wentworth, November 2, 1845, Harriet (Hanson) Robinson Papers, Schlesinger Library for the History of Women, Radcliffe College, folder 67; and Laura Currier to Harriette, Wentworth, October 12, 1845, ibid.

33. Ralph Waldo Emerson, "Farming," in *Selected Writings of Emerson*, ed. Brooks Atkinson (New York: Modern Library, 1950), p. 750. See also Harriet H. Robinson, *Loom and Spindle: Or, Life among the Early Mill Girls* (New York: Thomas Y. Crowell, 1898), pp. 3–4. On the general theme of man's encounter with clock time in the industrial city, see Oscar Handlin, "The Modern City as a Field for Historical Study," *The Historian and the City*, ed. Oscar Handlin and John Burchard (Cambridge: M.I.T. Press, 1963), pp. 13–15; and E. P. Thompson, "Time, Work Discipline, and Industrial Capitalism," *Past and Present*, no. 38 (1967), pp. 56–97. Another fine appreciation of the significance of the clock in modern society is Lewis Mumford, *Technics and Civilization*, pp. 12–18.

34. George S. White, *Memoir of Samuel Slater*, 2d ed. (Philadelphia, 1836), p. 227; *Voice of Industry* [Lowell], March 27, 1846; and *Corporations and Operatives*,

p. 15. See also Albert Brisbane, "False and True Association Contrasted," *Harbinger* 3 (November 17, 1846): 366; and F., "Factory Bells (A Parody)," *Lowell Journal and Courier*, February 26, 1853.

35. Brisbane, "False and True Association Contrasted," p. 368; Melville, "The Tartarus of Maids," p. 174.

36. For a discussion of the shift from public definitions of the self to what he calls "introspective individualism," see Laurence Veysey, *Law and Resistance* (New York: Harper Torchbook, 1970), pp. 23–24.

37. Elisha Bartlett, *A Vindication of the Character and Condition of the Females in the Lowell Mills* (Lowell: Leonard Huntress, Printer, 1841), pp. 6, 13. For discussions of the extreme empiricism in the life sciences and the medical beliefs about the relation of outward morality and regularity of behavior to health that, in part, caused this failure of imagination, see George H. Daniels, "Finalism and Positivism in Nineteenth Century Physiological Thought," *Bulletin of the History of Medicine* 38 (July–August 1964): 343–63; and Barbara Gutmann Rosenkrantz, *Public Health and the State: Changing Views in Massachusetts, 1842–1936* (Cambridge: Harvard University Press, 1972), esp. pp. 5, 9–36. Bartlett is cited by [Miles,] "Cotton Manufactures," p. 40; and Miles, *Lowell*, p. 125.

38. "Duties and Rights of Mill Girls," *New England Offering* (July 1848), p. 79.

39. The phrase *industrial discipline* dates from the antebellum period. See, for example, Brisbane, "False and True Association Contrasted," p. 366.

40. *Lowell Gazette*, December 16, 1848; Charles A. Dana, Review of *American Factories and Their Female Operatives*, by the Rev. William Scoresby; *Lowell as It Was and as It Is*, by the Rev. Henry A. Miles; *New York Daily Tribune*, August 16, 1845, in the *Harbinger* 1 (August 30, 1845): 187; and Brisbane, "False and True Association Contrasted," p. 368. See also *Voice of Industry* [Lowell], March 20, 1846.

41. *Voice of Industry* [Lowell], June 18, 1846. On modern uses of machine metaphors, see Mumford, *The Myth of the Machine;* and "The Future of the Humanities," *Daedalus* (Summer 1969), pp. 795–99.

42. *The Operative* [Lowell], February 1, 1845; Almira, "The Spirit of Discontent," *Lowell Offering* 1 (1841): 111–14. The statewide average earnings of females in teaching for 1841 was $12.75 per month. Their earnings in Waltham-Lowell type mills were $12.42 per month. The source of the figure on teachers is H. Gitelman, "The Waltham System and the Coming of the Irish," *Labor History* 8 (Fall 1967): 238, who took it from the *Annual Report of the Secretary of the Board of Education*. I calculated the average earnings of the female operatives from data presented in Robert G. Layer, *Earnings of Cotton Mill Operatives* (Cambridge, Mass.: Committee on Research in Economic History, 1955), pp. 25, 51. It has been suggested that mill girls came to Lowell essentially on a lark, that there is no evidence that they were working out of necessity. (See Caroline Ware, *The Early New England Cotton Manufacture* [New York: Johnson Reprint Corporation, 1966], p. 217.) However, the short stories in the *Lowell Offering*–which must be considered largely autobiographical–suggest that real economic needs not easily met in any other way formed an important reason for working in the mills. See, for example, *Mind amongst the Spindles* (Boston: Jordan, Swift & Wiley, 1845), pp. 81–92, 108–17, 163–67; S. G. B., "Tales of Factory Life, No. 1," *Lowell*

Offering 1 (1841): 65–68; F. G. A., "Susan Miller," ibid., pp. 161–71; Adella, "The Affections Illustrated in Factory Life, No. III–The Daughter," ibid., 4 (1844): 83–92; and J. S. W., "The Mother and Daughter," ibid., pp. 126–28. See also Vera Shlakman, *Economic History of a Factory Town: A Study of Chicopee, Massachusetts* (Northampton: Department of History of Smith College, 1935), p. 50; and Harold F. Wilson, *The Hill Country of Northern New England: Its Social and Economic History, 1790–1930* (New York: AMS Press, 1967), pp. 7, 27–32, 66–72.

43. Examples of the use of the phrase *soulless corporation* may be found in the *Lowell Patriot*, July 7, 1836; and Hannah Josephson, *The Golden Threads: New England's Mill Girls and Magnates* (New York: Duell Sloan and Pearce, 1949), p. 247.

44. *Vox Populi* [Lowell], June 5, 1841; Massachusetts, *House Document* (1850), No. 153, reprinted in *A Documentary History of American Industrial Society*, ed. John R. Commons et al., 10 vols. (New York: Russell & Russell, 1958), 8: 176–77. See also Arthur M. Schlesinger, Jr., *The Age of Jackson* (Boston: Little, Brown, 1945), p. 335.

45. Tocqueville, *Democracy in America*, 2: 168–71.

46. Fosgate, "Social Influence of Manufacturing," pp. 651–54.

47. Thomas Jefferson to Eli Whitney, Germantown, November 16, 1793, *The Works of Thomas Jefferson*, ed. Paul L. Ford, 12 vols. (New York: G. P. Putnam's Sons, 1904–1905), 8: 70–71. My italics.

48. Thomas Jefferson to General Thaddeus Kosciusko, Monticello, June 28, 1812, ibid., 11: 260–61; and Jefferson to Du Pont de Nemours, Monticello, April 15, 1811, ibid., 9: 199–201. On cloth manufacturing at Monticello, see Jefferson to John T. Mason, Monticello, August 18, 1814, ibid., 11: 413–15; and Jefferson to Phillip Mazzei, Monticello, December 29, 1815, ibid., 11: 366.

49. Horace Bushnell, "The Age of Homespun," in *Work and Play* (New York: Charles Scribner, 1864), p. 376.

IV. Urban Industrialism & the American Landscape: Lowell

Headquote taken from the *Lowell Courier*, February 26, 1842.

1. Asa Briggs, *Victorian Cities*, Am. ed. (New York: Harper and Row, 1965), p. 51. See also Asa Briggs, "The Study of Cities," *Confluence* 7 (Summer 1958): 110.

2. Timothy Dwight, *Travels in New-England and New-York*, 4 vols. (New Haven, Conn.: Timothy Dwight, 1821–1822), 4: 516. See also ibid., 2: 141–42, 308–9; 4: 523–24.

3. Ibid., 2: 394.

4. *Essex Gazette*, August 12, 1825, quoted in John O. Green, "Historical Reminiscences," *Proceedings in the City of Lowell at the Semi-Centennial Celebration of the Incorporation of the Town of Lowell, March 1, 1876* (Lowell: H. Penhallow, 1876), pp. 67–68.

5. Anon., *Prospectus for a Manufacturing Establishment at Belvidere on Merrimack River* (n.p.; [1822]), 3–5.

6. Basing his statement upon an examination of the record of wills probated there, Frederick W. Coburn argues the general prosperity of preindustrial Lowell.

(See Frederick W. Coburn, *History of Lowell and Its People*, 3 vols. [New York: Lewis Historical Publishing Company, 1920], 1: 95–96.) Using architectural artifacts as evidence, John P. Coolidge concurs. (See John P. Coolidge, *Mill and Mansion: A Study of Architecture and Society in Lowell, Massachusetts, 1820–1865* [New York: Russell & Russell, 1967], p. 125.) Impressionistic evidence also conflicts with Everett's view. Writing a year before the Merrimack Manufacturing Company was established, Wilkes Allen portrays Chelmsford as a prosperous town. (See Wilkes Allen, *The History of Chelmsford* [Haverhill: P. N. Green, 1820], pp. 40–41 and passim.) Later historians, after about mid-century, also tend to reject Everett's view: see Henry A. Miles, *Lowell as It Was and as It Is,* 2d ed. (Lowell: Nathaniel L. Dayton, 1847), p. 19; Charles Cowley, *Illustrated History of Lowell,* rev. ed. (Boston: Lee and Shepard, 1868), pp. 69–70; Alfred Gilman, "Lowell," in *History of Middlesex County,* ed. Samuel Adams Drake, 2 vols. (Boston: Estes and Lauriat Publishers, 1880), 2: 53–56; and Charles C. Chase, "Lowell," in *History of Middlesex County, Massachusetts,* ed. D. Hamilton Hurd, 3 vols. (Philadelphia: J. W. Lewis, 1890), 1: 4.

7. Edward Everett, "Fourth of July at Lowell [1830]," in *Orations and Speeches on Various Occasions,* 2 vols. (Boston: Charles C. Little and James Brown, 1850), 2: 58, 65. It is interesting to contrast Henry David Thoreau's sharp response to this attitude toward the Merrimack River in *A Week on the Concord and Merrimack Rivers* (Boston: Houghton Mifflin, 1906), pp. 32, 89–90.

8. Everett, *Orations and Speeches,* 2: 56. One of the founders of Lowell, Patrick Tracy Jackson, expressed himself similarly in his "Report on Manufactures of Cotton," in *General Convention of the Friends of Domestic Industry Assembled at New York, October 26, 1831,* p. 110.

9. Charles Cowley, *A Handbook of Business in Lowell, with a History of the City* (Lowell: E. D. Green, 1856), p. 92; Green, "Historical Reminiscences," p. 68; Michel Chevalier, *Society, Manners, and Politics in the United States,* ed. John William Ward (Ithaca, N.Y.: Cornell University Press, 1969), p. 130.

10. "History of Lowell," *American Magazine of Useful and Entertaining Knowledge* 2 (November 1835): 98–99. Freeman Hunt was editor of the magazine during this period, and considering his later career as editor of *Hunt's Merchants' Magazine* in New York, it seems likely that he wrote this article.

11. Theodore Dwight, Jr., *The Northern Traveller,* 2d ed. (New York: A. T. Goodrich, 1826), p. 297; ibid., 6th ed. (New York: J. P. Haven, 1841), p. 187; and *Voice of Industry* [Lowell], November 7, 1845.

12. Marx, *The Machine in the Garden* (New York: Oxford University Press, 1964), pp. 114–16; and John William Ward, *Andrew Jackson: Symbol for an Age* (New York: Oxford University Press, 1955), p. 45.

13. *Lowell Mercury,* September 5, 1834; and *Lowell Journal and Mercury,* October 9, 1835.

14. A. R. A., "Pawtucket Falls," *Literary Repository* 1 (1840): 128. Pawtucket Falls provided water power at Lowell, and the text indicates that the writer lived in Lowell. See also John Greenleaf Whittier, *The Stranger in Lowell* (Boston: Waite, Peirce and Company, 1845), pp. 9, 13.

15. Adelaide, "Alone with Nature," *Operatives Magazine* (June 1841), p. 37. According to Harriet (Hanson) Robinson, the pseudonym "Adelaide" was used in

the *Lowell Offering* by Lydia S. Hall. (H. H. Robinson, *Names and Noms de Plume of Writers in the Lowell Offering* [Lowell, Mass.: n.p., 1902], p. ii.) Since it is known that Lydia S. Hall was associated with the *Operatives Magazine*, she was probably "Adelaide" in this case.

16. Ella, "The Window Darkened," *Lowell Offering* 5 (December 1845): 265–67. Harriet (Hanson) Robinson lists "Ella" as one of the pseudonyms of Harriet Farley. (Robinson, *Names and Noms de Plume of Writers in the Lowell Offering*, p. ii.)

17. This volume is in the Harriet (Hanson) Robinson Collection, Schlesinger Library, Radcliffe College. There is a notation inside the front cover by "H. R." dated 1886: "This book contains some of my earliest 'thoughts' scratched down while at my work in the mill." From this information, I have dated her markings between 1843, when the book was published in New York by Harper & Brothers, and 1848, when she left the mill to marry William S. Robinson, who later became a prominent Massachusetts newspaper editor and free-soil politician.

18. European visitors to Lowell, with Manchester in the back of their minds and with certain expectations of America, continued to place Lowell within the older rural imagery. (See Marvin Fisher, *Workshops in the Wilderness: The European Response to American Industrialization, 1830–1860* [New York: Oxford University Press, 1967], pp. 90–96 and passim.)

19. See Roger B. Stein, *John Ruskin and Aesthetic Thought in America, 1840–1900* (Cambridge: Harvard University Press, 1967), p. 48. It is interesting in this context to compare plates 3 and 4 with Thomas Cole's painting "The Architect's Dream" (1840).

20. Rural cemeteries were built in every major and most minor nineteenth-century American cities. A partial list of the more important cemeteries, with brief descriptions, may be found in *Spring Grove Cemetery: Its History and Improvements* (Cincinnati: Robert Clarke & Co., 1869), pp. 129–33.

21. Neil Harris's *The Artist in American Society: The Formative Years, 1790–1860* (New York: George Braziller, 1966), pp. 200–208, 377–80, is an exception.

22. John W. Reps, *The Making of Urban America: A History of City Planning in the United States* (Princeton, N.J.: Princeton University Press, 1965), p. 326.

23. On Bigelow, Mount Auburn, and their influence, see Hans Huth, *Nature and the American* (Berkeley: University of California Press, 1957), pp. 66–69; and Cornelia W. Walter, *Mount Auburn* (New York: R. Martin, 1847). At pages 33–35, Walter reprints a lecture that Bigelow used to promote Mount Auburn.

24. Quoted by Harris, *The Artist in American Society*, p. 201.

25. Reprinted in Joseph Story, *An Address Delivered on the Dedication of the Cemetery at Mount Auburn, September 24, 1831* (Boston: Joseph T. & Edwin Buckingham, 1831), appendix, p. 27. After describing Mount Auburn in 1845, Theodore Dwight wrote: "Cemeteries should be planed [sic] with reference to the living as well as the dead." (Theodore Dwight, *Travels in America* [Glasgow: R. Griffin & Co., 1848], p. 198.)

26. [Andrew Jackson Downing,] "Public Cemeteries and Public Gardens," *Horticulturist* 4 (July 1849): 10.

27. Story, *Address*, pp. 8, 12, 17–18, 20. The contrapuntal role is also explained by Henry Colman, *Fourth Report of the Agriculture of Massachusetts: Counties of*

Franklin and Middlesex (Boston: Dutton and Wentworth, 1841), pp. 440–41; and Stephen D. Walker, *Rural Cemetery and Public Walk* (Baltimore: Sands and Neilson, 1835), pp. iii–iv.

28. [Downing,] "Public Cemeteries and Public Gardens," pp. 9–12. See also Walker, *Rural Cemetery and Public Walk*, p. 7.

29. In 1842 there were also rural cemeteries in Salem, Worcester, Springfield, and Plymouth, Massachusetts; New Haven, Connecticut; and Nashua and Portsmouth, New Hampshire. See [J. Brazer,] "Rural Cemeteries," *North American Review* 53 (October 1841): 390.

30. C. C. Chase, "Brief Biographical Notices of Prominent Citizens of the Town of Lowell–1826–1836," *Contributions of the Old Residents' Historical Association* 4 (1891): 299; James S. Russell, "The Lowell Cemetery," ibid., pp. 272–81; and Amos Blanchard, *An Address Delivered at the Consecration of the Lowell Cemetery, June 20, 1841* (Lowell: Leonard Huntress, 1841), p. 8.

31. Cowley, *Illustrated History of Lowell*, p. 123.

32. Hans Huth, in *Nature and the American*, p. 67, makes this point in reference to Mount Auburn.

33. For a biographical sketch of Blanchard, see D. N. Patterson, "Rev. Amos Blanchard, D.D.," *Contributions of the Old Residents' Historical Association* 3 (1885): 169–86. As early as 1836, Blanchard perceived that industrial centers like Lowell were "cities, in all but the name." (See his "Introduction" in *Lectures to Young People in Manufacturing Villages*, by Dorus Clarke [Boston: Perkins & Marvin, 1836], p. ix.)

34. Blanchard, *Address*, pp. 7, 15. The issues of materialism and desecration are prominent in nearly all the rural cemetery commentaries of the time. See Story, *Address*, p. 12; F. W. S., "Rural Cemeteries," *Knickerbocker* 12 (December 1838): 538; and Anon., *The Cincinnati Cemetery of Spring Grove*, enl. ed. (Cincinnati: Bradley & Webb, Printers, 1862), p. 45.

35. Blanchard, *Address*, pp. 19, 8. See also ibid., p. 6.

36. *Lowell Courier*, December 9, 1841. Two years later, Henry A. Miles linked the newly established cemetery to the idea of a developing communal spirit in the hitherto volatile community. (See Henry A. Miles, *A Glance at Our History, Prospects, and Duties* [Lowell: Stearns & Taylor, 1844], pp. 11–12.) For more general comments on this point, see Story, *Address*, p. 5; Dwight, *Travels in America*, pp. 144–46; [Andrew Jackson Downing,] Review of *Designs for Monuments and Rural Tablets*, by J. J. Smith, in the *Horticulturist* 1 (January 1847): 329–30; and Harris, *The Artist in American Society*, pp. 205–6.

37. *The Operatives Magazine* (June 1841), p. 37.

38. Roderick Nash, *Wilderness and the American Mind* (New Haven, Conn.: Yale University Press, 1967), p. 44.

39. Andrew Jackson Downing emphatically makes this point in his "Public Cemeteries and Public Gardens," pp. 9–10.

40. Blanchard, *Address*, p. 8. For similar expressions with reference to Mount Auburn, see Dwight, *Travels in America*, p. 198; and Story, *Address*, pp. 12–16. All the consecration addresses that I have been able to read stress this point. A readily available sample of these addresses may be found in the excerpts reprinted in Brazer's review of several of them in his "Rural Cemeteries," pp. 385–412.

41. Blanchard, *Address*, pp. 13–14.

42. *Vox Populi* [Lowell], July 17, 24, 1841.

43. For comments on this "borrowing" tendency in the history of American environmental thought, see Ward, *Andrew Jackson*, pp. 30, 225 n; and Nash, *Wilderness and the American Mind*, pp. 44, 50.

44. See Perry Miller, "Nature and the National Ego," in *Errand into the Wilderness* (New York: Harper Torchbook, 1964), pp. 204–16, but especially pp. 215–16; Perry Miller, *The Raven and the Whale: The War of Words and Wits in the Era of Poe and Melville* (New York: Harcourt, Brace & World, 1956); and Harris, *The Artist in American Society*.

45. L. J. B. C., "Lowell Cemetery," *Eastern Argus,* reprinted in the *Lowell Patriot*, January 25, 1844; and Whittier, *The Stranger in Lowell*, pp. 42–43. For other treatments of the cemetery within this framework by Lowellians during the 1840s, see "Argus," *Norton: Or, The Lights and Shades of a Factory Village . . .* (Lowell: Vox Populi Office, 1849), p. 71; Elizabeth, "My First Independence Day in Lowell," *Lowell Offering* 5 (1845): 249–50; L. T. H., "A Letter to Cousin Lucy," ibid., pp. 109–12; and Anon., *A Handbook for the Visiter* [*sic*] *to Lowell* (Lowell: S. J. Varney, 1848), p. 33.

46. J. W. Meader, *The Merrimack* (Boston: B. B. Russell, 1869), pp. 274–75.

47. For example, see [Downing,] "Public Cemeteries and Public Gardens," p. 11.

48. Elisha Huntington, *Address of the Mayor of the City of Lowell, 1845* (Lowell: Stearns & Taylor, 1845), pp. 14–16. Quotations from pp. 14-15. This portion of the address is reprinted and accompanied by a favorable editorial in the *Vox Populi* [Lowell], April 11, 1845.

49. Frank P. Hill, *Lowell Illustrated* (Lowell: Huse, Goodwin & Co., 1884), p. 10; Anon., *A Handbook for the Visiter*, p. 33; and Miles, *Lowell*, pp. 43–44. North and South Commons were located at what were then considered the northern and southern ends of the city. They are shown on H. S. Bradley's map of Lowell (1848), which is printed in F. Hedge, *Pictoral Lowell Almanac, 1850* (Lowell: F. Hedge, 1849). Lowell's sister city of Lawrence laid out ten acres of land as a park a decade later. An account of it in the *Lawrence Courier* reveals motives similar to those in Lowell: "In the rapid development of our young community, in the midst of the material and moral changes taking place yearly and daily around us, it will surely hereafter be interesting to find one spot at least retaining most of its original features; one wooded summit, which while all around its base is undergoing transformation, shall remain sacred from the intrusion of the spade and shovel, and whose trees so lately waving over neglected farms, shall grow to adorn with the shade the abode of civilization and the arts." (Quoted in Michael B. Katz, *The Irony of Early School Reform: Educational Innovation in Mid Nineteenth-Century Massachusetts* [Cambridge: Harvard University Press, 1968], p. 111.)

50. Quotation from the *Lowell Daily Citizen*, May 22, 1886. The park is discussed in a pamphlet by Robert Boodey Caverly, *Parks and Progress and the Rogers Family* (Lowell: Vox Populi Press, 1882), esp. pp. 20–24.

51. For Thoreau on parks, see *The Journal of Henry D. Thoreau*, ed. Bradford Torrey and Francis H. Allen, 14 vols. (Boston: Houghton Mifflin, 1949), 12: 387; 14: 304.

52. Thoreau, *A Week on the Concord and Merrimack Rivers*, pp. 115–16, 117.

53. Ibid., p. 179.

54. Nash, *Wilderness and the American Mind*, chapt. 5, quotation from page 93. On this point, there is a suggestive letter from Thoreau to his father: Henry D. Thoreau to John Thoreau, June 8, 1843, Miscellaneous Mss, New York Historical Society. See also Russell B. Nye, *This Almost Chosen People: Essays in the History of American Ideas* ([East Lansing, Mich.:] Michigan State University Press, 1966), p. 284.

55. For a description of Lowell within this context by a visitor, see A Lady of N. York, "Description of Lowell," *American Penny Magazine* 2 (August 8, 1846): 421.

56. Lucy Larcom, *A New England Childhood: Outlined from Memory* (Boston: Houghton Mifflin, 1889), p. 163; Lucy Larcom to Charles Cowley, Boston, February 28, 1876, reprinted in *Proceedings in the City of Lowell at the Semi-Centennial Celebration of the Incorporation of the Town of Lowell*, p. 94; Lucy Larcom, "Lowell at Sunset," [undated Ms], Lucy Larcom Papers, Essex Institute.

57. Whittier, *The Stranger in Lowell*, p. 14. The original version, published in the *Middlesex Standard*, August 1, 1844, has the word ethics where he now uses *polemics*. In his collected works, the version quoted here is printed. (See *The Writings of John Greenleaf Whittier*, 7 vols. [Boston: Houghton Mifflin, 1893] 5: 355–56.)

58. Neil Harris has shown that American artists also took it upon themselves to provide urban Americans with natural landscapes through their artistic creations. (Harris, *The Artist in American Society*, pp. 186 and passim.)

59. Three examples, from among many, are Fiducia, "Fancy" [a poem], *Lowell Offering* 1 (1841): 117–18; T*******, "Factory Girl's Reverie," ibid., 5 (1845): 140–41; and L. T. H., "A Letter to Cousin Lucy," p. 109.

60. Ella [Harriet Farley], "A Weaver's Reverie," *Lowell Offering* 1 (1841): 188; *Middlesex Standard* [Lowell], August 15, 1844. The same point is made by Thoreau in *Walden and Other Writings of Henry David Thoreau*, ed. Brooks Atkinson (New York: Modern Library, 1950), p. 123.

61. L. T. H., "A Letter to Cousin Lucy," p. 110. A similar view is described by M. T., in "The Prospect from My Window in the Mill," *Lowell Offering* 3 (1842): 57–58. The view from a boardinghouse is described in a romance about Lowell: Day Kellogg Lee, *Merrimack, or Life at the Loom* (New York: Redfield, 1854), p. 78.

62. Uriah Clark, *Lectures on City Life and Character* (Lowell: Merrill & Heywood, 1849), p. 32; and Adelaide [Lydia S. Hall], "The Hill-Side and the Fountain Rill," *Lowell Offering*, (1840), p. 20. See also Everes, "American Forest Scenery," *Operatives' Magazine* (April 1841), pp. 1–2; T. W. P., "The Operative's Holiday Song," *Lowell Courier*, July 31, 1841; Whittier, *The Stranger in Lowell*, p. 106; and *A Handbook for the Visiter to Lowell*, p. 33. Donald B. Cole makes this point in reference to the city of Lawrence in his *Immigrant City: Lawrence, Massachusetts, 1845–1921* (Chapel Hill: University of North Carolina Press, 1963), p. 132.

63. The joy of these summer visits is revealed in H. E. Back to Harriet Hanson, Lowell, September 7, 1846, Harriet (Hanson) Robinson Collection, folder 67; Arial I. Cummings, *The Factory Girl or Gardez La Coeur* (Lowell: J. E. Short & Co., 1847), pp. 106–7; Eliza, "A Visit to the Country," *Lowell Offering*, no. 4 (March

1841), pp. 62–63; Susan, "Letters from Susan," ibid., 4 (August 1844): 237; and Lucy Larcom, "Among the Lowell Mill Girls: A Reminiscence," *Atlantic Monthly* 48 (1881): 600–601.

64. C. D. S., "Visit to Lowell," *New York Daily Tribune*, August 16, 1845.

65. See Appendix B.

66. *Lowell Weekly Journal*, August 4, 1848; *Spindle City and Middlesex Farmer* [Lowell], September 9, 1852; and Lowell School Committee, *Annual Report*, 1852, pp. 20–21.

67. On the place of summer vacations in turn-of-the-century urban culture, see Peter Schmitt, *Back to Nature: The Arcadian Myth in Urban America* (New York: Oxford University Press, 1969), especially chapt. 15; and Grace Peckham, "Influence of City Life on Health and Development," *Journal of Social Science* 21 (1886): 88.

68. A. F. D., "Life among Farmers," *Mind amongst the Spindles: A Miscellany Selected from the Lowell Offering* (Boston: Jordan, Swift & Wiley, 1845), pp. 138–47. See also Ms composition by Harriet Hanson, dated 1840 for High School, in Harriet (Hanson) Robinson Collection, folder 1; Laura Currier to Harriette, Wentworth, November 2, 1845, ibid., folder 67; and Laura Currier to Harriette, October 12, 1845, ibid.

69. See Thoreau, "Walking," in *Walden and Other Writings of Henry David Thoreau*, p. 603.

70. Anon., *The Boston Common, or Rural Walks in Cities* (Boston: George W. Light, 1838), pp. 19–23.

V. The Discovery of Urban Society: Lowell

Headquote from *Seventeenth Annual Report of the Minister at Large in Lowell*, 1862, p. 7.

1. William Ellery Channing, *The Obligation of a City to Watch over the Moral Health of Its Members* (Glasgow: J. Hedderwick, 1841), pp. 3–5. See also Joseph Tuckerman, *The Principles and Results of the Ministry at Large in Boston* (Boston: James Munroe & Co., 1838), p. 30; Edward Everett Hale, ed., *Joseph Tuckerman on the Elevation of the Poor: A Selection from His Reports as Minister at Large in Boston* (Boston: Roberts Brothers, 1874), pp. 28, 106–10, 133–39; Nathan I. Huggins, *Protestants against Poverty: Boston's Charities, 1870–1900* (Westport, Conn.: Greenwood Publishing Corporation, 1971), pp. 32–36 and passim; Daniel Walker Howe, *The Unitarian Conscience: Harvard Moral Philosophy, 1805–1861* (Cambridge: Harvard University Press, 1970), pp. 243–55; John S. Stone, *Considerations on the Care of the Poor in Large Cities* (Boston: William D. Ticknor, 1838), pp. 19–20; [George B. Arnold,] *Second Semi-Annual Report of . . . Minister at Large in New York* (New York: J. Van Norden, 1834), pp. 21–22; Orville Dewey, *A Sermon . . . on the Moral Importance of Cities, and the Moral Means for Their Reformation* (New York: David Felt & Co., 1836), pp. 3, 15; and Walter Channing, *An Address on the Prevention of Pauperism* (Boston: Office of the Christian World, 1843), esp. pp. 22–24, 67.

2. Lewis Mumford, *The City in History* (New York: Harcourt, Brace & World, 1961), p. 458.

3. Richard C. Wade, *The Urban Frontier: Pioneer Life in Early Pittsburgh, Cincinnati, Lexington, Louisville, and St. Louis* (Chicago: Phoenix Book, 1964), p. 39. See also Daniel J. Boorstin, *The Americans: The National Experience* (New York: Vintage Book, 1965), pp. 113–68.

4. I owe this insight to Sigmund Diamond's illuminating study of the Virginia Company, "From Organization to Society: Virginia in the Seventeenth Century," *American Journal of Sociology* 63 (1958): 457–75.

5. See Nathan Appleton to Samuel Appleton, Boston, May 1, 1824, Nathan Appleton Papers, Massachusetts Historical Society; William R. Bagnall, "Contributions to American Economic History" (unpub. materials, 4 vols.; typed Mss, 1908), Baker Library, Harvard University, 3: 2131; and Robert Varnum Spalding, "The Boston Mercantile Community and the Promotion of the Textile Industry in New England, 1813–1860" (Ph.D. diss., Yale University, 1963).

6. See Walter Muir Whitehill, *Boston: A Topographical History*, 2d ed. (Cambridge: Harvard University Press, 1968), chapt. 4; Harold Kirker and James Kirker, *Bulfinch's Boston, 1787–1817* (New York: Oxford University Press, 1964), chapts. 1, 2, 9; James Jackson, "Notes on the Life of Patrick Tracy Jackson," [1847] typed Mss, Houghton Library, Harvard University, pp. 15–16; Bagnall, "Contributions to American Economic History," 3: 1986–89; Spalding, "The Boston Mercantile Community," p. 12; and Samuel Eliot Morison, *Harrison Gray Otis: The Urbane Federalist, 1765–1848* (Boston: Houghton Mifflin, 1969), pp. 218–26. An essay by Gunther Barth alerted me to the possibility of gaining insights into attitudes toward the city through an investigation of approaches to urban development. (See Gunther Barth, "Metropolism and Urban Elites in the Far West," in *The Age of Industrialism in America: Essays in Social Structure and Cultural Values*, ed. Frederic Cople Jaher [New York: Free Press, 1968], pp. 158–87.)

7. Michel Chevalier, *Society, Manners, and Politics in the United States*, ed. John William Ward (Ithaca, N.Y.: Cornell University Press, 1969), pp. 131–32. See also Spalding, "The Boston Mercantile Community," chapt. 2.

8. Dr. John O. Green, who came to East Chelmsford in April 1822, recalled that "when I came here, it was said by those who thought themselves far-seeing men, that the village about to be begun would, in time, equal the then population of Waltham." ("Address of Dr. John O. Green," in Lowell School Committee, *Annual Report*, 1870, p. 57.) See also Victor S. Clark, *History of Manufactures in the United States,* 3 vols. (New York: Peter Smith, 1949), 1: 545; and Spalding, "The Boston Mercantile Community," pp. 43–44.

9. [Nathan Appleton,] "Lowell," in *Encyclopedia Americana*, ed. Francis Lieber (Philadelphia: Carey and Lea, 1831), 8: 132; and Nathan Appleton to Samuel Appleton, Boston, September 22, 1823, Appleton Papers.

10. John P. Coolidge, *Mill and Mansion: A Study of Architecture and Society in Lowell, Massachusetts, 1820–1865* (New York: Russell & Russell, 1967), pp. 26–27.

11. Jackson's failure to distinguish between city and company is revealed in P. T. Jackson to Hon. Senate & House of Representatives in General Court Assembled [March 3, 1834], copy in Proprietors of Locks and Canals Company, "Minutes of Directors," 9 vols. (microfilm typescript), Baker Library, Harvard University, 1: 334–36. On his prediction, see Samuel Batchelder, *Introduction and Early Progress*

of the Cotton Manufacture in the United States (Boston: Little, Brown, 1863), p. 69; and Nathan Appleton, *Introduction of the Power Loom and the Origin of Lowell* (Lowell: B. H. Penhallow, 1858), p. 19.

12. The effect of the landholding and selling policies of the corporations upon the physical development of Lowell is discussed in Coolidge, *Mill and Mansion*, pp. 22–24, 76–77, 206–7. On the hopes for speculative profits from the bourgeois section, see P. T. Jackson to Kirk Boott, January 18, 1830, in Locks and Canals Company, "Minutes of Directors," 1: 307. The substantial profits earned through land speculation in Lowell are suggested by Spalding, "The Boston Mercantile Community," pp. 56–57. The importance of the marketplace in the physical evolution of nineteenth-century American cities is emphasized by Sam Bass Warner, Jr., *The Private City: Philadelphia in Three Periods of Its Growth* (Philadelphia: University of Pennsylvania Press, 1968); and Seymour J. Mandelbaum, *Boss Tweed's New York* (New York: John Wiley & Sons, 1965), chapt. 7 and passim.

13. James Sterling Young, *The Washington Community, 1800–1828* (New York: Harcourt, Brace & World, 1966), p. 6; and Saul K. Padover, ed., *Thomas Jefferson and the National Capital* (Washington: Government Printing Office, 1946), pp. 290–91.

14. Harriet Hanson Robinson, *Loom and Spindle: Or, Life among the Early Mill Girls* (New York: Thomas Y. Crowell & Co., 1898), pp. 14–15; and Coolidge, *Mill and Mansion*, pp. 39, 176 n–177 n.

15. Hannah Josephson, *The Golden Threads: New England's Mill Girls and Magnates* (New York: Duell, Sloan and Pearce, 1949), pp. 51–52; and Coolidge, *Mill and Mansion*, p. 139.

16. Anon., *Hand-Book for the Visiter [sic] to Lowell* (Lowell: A. Watson, 1848), pp. 42–43; and *Lowell City Directory*, 1851, pp. 14–15.

17. Elisha Bartlett, "Mayor's Address," printed in the *Lowell Courier*, May 3, 1836; and Z. E. Stone, "Lowell's Once Popular Newspaper, Vox Populi–1841–1896," *Contributions of the Old Residents' Historical Association* 6 (1904): 173. See also *Vox Populi* [Lowell], June 5, 1841; clipping from *Vox Populi*, 1869, in *Selections, Historical and General* [scrapbook at Lowell Historical Society], 1: 59; and Benjamin F. Butler, "Oration," *Proceedings in the City of Lowell at the Semi-Centennial Celebration of the Incorporation of the Town of Lowell, March 1, 1876* (Lowell: H. Penhallow, 1876), pp. 41–43.

18. This is revealed in the rough content analysis summarized below. I have assumed that every theme covered in the histories could be fitted into the following four (after the Civil War, five) rubrics: 1. Preindustrial history of the site; 2. Manufacturing and business history of Lowell; 3. General history of Lowell; 4. Social history (principally schools, churches, and similar institutions); 5. History of Lowell in the Civil War, consisting primarily of accounts of Lowell men in the war. The four histories I have included in the analysis are A. G. T., "Lowell," *New England Magazine* 4 (January 1833): 72–74; Henry A. Miles, *Lowell as It Was and as It Is* (Lowell: Powers and Bagley and N. L. Dayton, 1845); Charles Cowley, *Illustrated History of Lowell*, rev. ed. (Boston: Lee and Shepard, 1868); and Alfred Gilman, "Lowell," in *History of Middlesex County*, ed. Samuel Adams Drake, 2 vols. (Boston: Estes and Lauriat, Publishers, 1880), 2: 53–113. Summary:

	1833 % lines	1845 % pages	1868 % pages	1880 % columns
1. Preindustrial	10.2	5.0	7.6	3.2
2. Manufacturing	61.0	80.0	20.7	18.3
3. General	17.1	9.5	45.9	46.5
4. Social	11.8	5.5	12.6	20.5
5. War	n.a.	n.a.	13.1	17.8

19. Frederick W. Coburn, *History of Lowell and Its People*, 3 vols. (New York: Lewis Historical Publishing Company, 1920), 1: 191; and [Wilson Waters,] *Saint Anne's Centennial Anniversary* ([Lowell] Courier Citizen Company, [1925]), p. 78. See also Alfred Gilman, "History of the Lowell Grammar Schools," *Contributions of the Old Residents' Historical Association* 4 (1888): 87–109; and C. C. Chase, "Address," *Exercises of the Fiftieth Anniversary Commemorative of the Incorporation of the City of Lowell, Thursday, April 1, 1886* (Lowell: Vox Populi Press: S. W. Huse & Co., 1886), pp. 21–29.

20. John A. Wright, "Effects of Internal Improvements on Commercial Cities: With Reference to the Pennsylvania Central Railroad," *Hunt's Merchants' Magazine* 16 (March 1847): 265, 267–68.

21. [Charles T. James,] *Strictures on Montgomery on the Cotton Manufactures of Great Britain and America* (Newburyport, Mass.: Morss and Brewster, 1841), pp. 20, 17, 52. Coolidge, *Mill and Mansion*, p. 204 n, identifies the writer as James. Stephan Thernstrom accepts this attribution in his *Poverty and Progress: Social Mobility in a Nineteenth Century City* (Cambridge: Harvard University Press, 1964), pp. 13, 243 n.

22. John W. Reps, *The Making of Urban America: A History of City Planning in the United States* (Princeton, N.J.: Princeton University Press, 1965), p. 420. Economic and technological factors were also involved in this changing locational pattern. See Allan Pred, "Manufacturing in the Mercantile City, 1800–1840," *Annals of the American Association of Geographers* 56 (June 1966): 307–25.

23. Henry A. Miles, *Lowell as It Was and as It Is*, 2d ed. (Lowell: Nathaniel L. Dayton, 1847), p. 76.

24. Foreigners made up one-third of Lowell's population in 1850 and by 1858 accounted for more than 54 percent. (See *Lowell Journal & Courier*, January 18, 1853; and Michael B. Katz, *The Irony of Early School Reform: Educational Innovation in Mid Nineteenth-Century Massachusetts* [Cambridge: Harvard University Press, 1968], pp. 173–74.) See Appendix B for percentage distribution of native and foreign-born operatives in the Hamilton Manufacturing Company of Lowell.

25. See Charles E. Persons, "The Early History of Factory Legislation in Massachusetts: From 1825 to the Passage of the Ten Hour Law in 1874," in *Labor Laws and Their Enforcement*, ed. Susan M. Kingsbury (London: Longman's, Green, 1911), p. 57; Caroline F. Ware, *The Early New England Cotton Manufacture* (New York: Johnson Reprint Corporation, 1966), pp. 230, 260; *Ninth Annual Report of the Minister at Large in Lowell*, 1853, p. 6; Paul F. McGouldrick, *New England Textiles in the Nineteenth Century: Profits and Investment* (Cambridge:

Harvard University Press, 1968), pp. 20, 41; and Josephson, *The Golden Threads*, p. 296.

26. *Boston Daily Times*, July 16, 1839.

27. William Austin to Henry Hall, Lowell, February 12, 1834, Lawrence Manufacturing Company Papers, Baker Library, Harvard University, v. MAB-1; William Austin to Henry Hall, Lowell, February 14, 15, 24, 1834, ibid.

28. See John Aiken to Henry Hall, Lowell, September 18, 22, 1837; ibid. Compare Amos Lawrence to John Aiken, May 1845, Lawrence Letterbooks, MHS, quoted in McGouldrick, *New England Textiles in the Nineteenth Century*, p. 274 n; Vera Shlakman, *Economic History of a Factory Town: A Study of Chicopee, Massachusetts* (Northampton: Department of History of Smith College, 1935), p. 140; and George Matley to T. G. Cary, Lowell, September 22, 1850, Appleton Company Letterbooks, 1844–1859, Merrimack Valley Textile Museum.

29. Coburn, *History of Lowell*, 1: 170–72; and *Portsmouth Journal*, reprinted in *Niles' Weekly Register* 40 (August 27, 1831): 452. See also C. C. Chase, "Address," pp. 19–20; and John F. McEvoy to Charles Cowley, Lowell, February 22, 1876, in *Proceedings in the City of Lowell, 1876*, pp. 132–36.

30. Seth Luther, *An Address to the Workingmen of New England* . . . (Boston: By the Author, 1832), p. 13. For other evidence of poverty in Lowell, see Josephson, *The Golden Threads*, pp. 215–17; and Theodore Sedgwick, *Public and Private Economy* (New York: Harper & Bros., 1836), p. 111.

31. "Riot," *Niles' Weekly Register* 40 (May 28, 1831): 221; and Luther, *Address*, p. 12 (where Selectmen are quoted). On this general point, see Robinson, *Loom and Spindle*, pp. 15–16; Coburn, *History of Lowell*, 1: 317; and George F. O'Dwyer, *Irish Catholic Genesis of Lowell* (Lowell: Sullivan Brothers, 1920).

32. *Lowell Journal*, August 23, 1832. See also *Lowell Journal and Mercury*, January 8, 1836.

33. See Secretary of the Commonwealth, *Abstract of the Returns of the Overseers of the Poor in Massachusetts* [title varies slightly] (Boston: 1837–1862); and *Semi-Annual Report of the Overseers of the Poor of the City of Lowell* (Lowell: Times Publishing Company, 1876), pp. 4–5.

34. *Twenty-fourth Annual Report of the Minister at Large in Lowell*, 1868, pp. 21–23; Henry A. Miles, *A Glance at Our History, Prospects, and Duties* (Lowell: Stearns & Taylor, 1844), pp. 13–14. During this period one finds the first references to beggars in the massive diary kept by the Reverend Theodore Edson from 1824 until his death. (See Theodore Edson, "Diary," Lowell Historical Society, September 6, 11, 1848, March 3, 1851.)

35. See *Lowell Weekly Journal*, January 26, 1848, April 18, 1851, December 3, 1852, January 13, July 28, 1854; and *Vox Populi* [Lowell], December 22, 1854, January 26, April 13, 1855.

36. Elisha Bartlett, *A Vindication of the Character and Condition of the Females in the Lowell Mills* . . . (Lowell: Leonard Huntress, Printer, 1841). On Crosby's testimony, see Katz, *The Irony of Early School Reform*, pp. 171–72.

37. Bartlett, *A Vindication*, pp. 9–13. Despite an immediate and well-argued refutation in Anon., *Corporations and Operatives* (Lowell: S. J. Varney, 1843), p. 63, Bartlett's claims were widely publicized by Miles, *Lowell*, pp. 116–27; and

"Lowell and Its Manufactures," *Hunt's Merchants' Magazine* 16 (April 1847): 356–62. See also George Rosen, "The Medical Aspects of the Controversy over Factory Conditions in New England, 1840–1850," *Bulletin of the History of Medicine* 15 (May 1944): 483–97.

38. John O. Green, *The Factory System in Its Hygienic Relations, An Address Delivered at Boston, at the Annual Meeting of the Massachusetts Medical Society* (Boston: Wm. S. Damrell, 1846), p. 25; Gilman Kimball, *Report of the Lowell Hospital from 1840 to 1849* (Lowell: n.p., 1849), pp. 10–11.

39. J. Curtis, "Public Hygiene of Massachusetts; But More Particularly of the Cities of Boston and Lowell," *Transactions of the American Medical Association* 2 (1849): 487–554. Portions of this report were previously published in the *Lowell Courier* in 1847.

40. Elisha Huntington, *Address of the Mayor of Lowell* (Lowell: S. J. Varney, 1852), pp. 7–8. See also Elisha Huntington, *Address of the Mayor of Lowell* (Lowell: L. Huntress, 1841), pp. 6–7; "Deterioration of American Labor," in *Lowell Weekly Journal*, July 28, 1854; *Vox Populi* [Lowell], September 15, 1854; and *Lowell Weekly Journal*, January 19, 1849.

41. Nathan Allen, "Report in Behalf of the Relief Association for the Poor, Presented May 1, 1858," reprinted in the *Lowell Weekly Journal*, May 7, 1858. See also Nathan Allen, *Annual Report of the City Physician . . . for the Year 1865* ([Lowell:] Knapp & Morey, 1866).

42. William R. Taylor provides a stimulating discussion of antebellum ideas about status and leadership in his *Cavalier and Yankee* (Garden City, N.Y.: Anchor Books, 1963).

43. Coolidge, *Mill and Mansion*, pp. 32, 183.

44. Quote from Bagnall, "Contributions to American Economic History," 3: 2161. See also Robinson, *Loom and Spindle*, pp. 14–15; Coolidge, *Mill and Mansion*, p. 33; and Miles, *Lowell*, 2d ed., pp. 64–65, 75.

45. Robinson, *Loom and Spindle*, pp. 14–15.

46. On Jacksonian individualism, see John William Ward, *Andrew Jackson: Symbol for an Age* (New York: Oxford University Press, 1955).

47. Ithamar A. Beard, *An Address Delivered before the Middlesex Mechanic Association at Their Anniversary, Oct. 4, 1827* (Lowell: Printed at the Journal Office, 1827), pp. 4, 7, 8, 9.

48. Amos Blanchard, "Introduction," in *Lectures to Young People in Manufacturing Villages*, by Dorus Clarke (Boston: Perkins & Marvin, 1836), pp. ix–x, xii–xiii.

49. John Aiken, *Labor and Wages, at Home and Abroad* (Lowell: D. Bixby & Co., 1849), pp. 17–21.

50. See C. Wright Mills, "The American Business Elite: A Collective Portrait," *Journal of Economic History* 5 (supplement December 1945): 20–44; William Miller, "American Historians and the Business Elite," ibid., 8 (1949): 184–208; Reinhard Bendix and Frank W. Howton, "Social Mobility and the American Business Elite," in *Social Mobility in Industrial Society*, ed. Seymour Martin Lipset and Reinhard Bendix (Berkeley: University of California Press, 1959), pp. 114–43; P. M. G. Harris, "Social Origins of American Leaders: The Demographic Foundations," *Perspectives in American History* 3 (1969): 159–344; Frances W. Gregory

and Irene D. Neu, "The American Industrial Elite in the 1870's," in *Men in Business: Essays in the History of Entrepreneurship*, ed. William Miller (Cambridge: Harvard University Press, 1952), p. 202; and Thernstrom, *Poverty and Progress*, pp. 163–65.

51. For biographical material on Bancroft, see "The Mayors of the City of Lowell," *Contributions of the Old Residents' Historical Association* 1 (1879): 147–51; and Coburn, *History of Lowell*, 1: 221–22.

52. Jefferson Bancroft, *Address of the Mayor of the City of Lowell* (Lowell: Joel Taylor, Printer, 1846), p. 5.

53. Bancroft's address can be found in the *Lowell Weekly Journal*, July 2, 1847. A reporter's transcription of Polk's was printed in *Vox Populi* [Lowell], July 9, 1847. For another example of the symbolic importance of Bancroft's career, see the *Lowell Weekly Journal*, November 22, 1861.

54. [Orestes Brownson,] "The Laboring Classes," *Boston Quarterly Review* 3 (October 1840): 462–66; Richard Weiss, *The American Myth of Success: From Horatio Alger to Norman Vincent Peale* (New York: Basic Books, 1969), p. 7; and Thernstrom, *Poverty and Progress*, pp. 72–79.

55. See C. S. Griffin, *The Ferment of Reform, 1830–1860* (New York: Thomas Y. Crowell, 1967), chapt. 1.

56. I was first made aware of this distinction by Thernstrom's discussion of mobility in *Poverty and Progress*, pp. 69–70, 115–37.

57. See *Eighth Annual Report of the Minister at Large in Lowell*, 1852, p. 19. Thernstrom's study of Newburyport's unskilled workers suggests that this was the most important means of upward social mobility for the Irish working class. (See Thernstrom, *Poverty and Progress*, chapt. 5.)

58. See Stephan Thernstrom and Peter R. Knights, "Men in Motion: Some Data and Speculations about Urban Population Mobility in Nineteenth-Century America," *Journal of Interdisciplinary History* 1 (Autumn 1970): 7–35.

59. My use of city directories for this purpose raises the question of their reliability. Although they do not provide a perfectly accurate enumeration of the population, these directories are almost as accurate as the nineteenth-century censuses. Their greatest weakness is a systematic bias against lower economic groups and recent migrants to the city. To the extent that this bias operated in the Lowell directories, the point being made here is strengthened rather than weakened. The reliability of the directories is discussed in Peter R. Knights, "City Directories as Aids to Ante-Bellum Urban Studies: A Research Note," *Historical Methods Newsletter* 2 (September 1969): 1–10. I did not compare my list with the mortality data available for Lowell, and this introduces a bias in the opposite direction.

60. Thernstrom and Knights, "Men in Motion," p. 34.

61. *Seventh Annual Report of the Minister at Large in Lowell*, 1851, pp. 3–4; *Twenty-Third Annual Report of the Minister at Large in Lowell*, 1867, pp. 3–7. See also Eric Foner, *Free Soil, Free Labor, Free Men: The Ideology of the Republican Party before the Civil War* (New York: Oxford University Press, 1970), p. 32; and Carter Goodrich and Sol Davidson, "The Wage-Earner in the Westward Movement," *Political Science Quarterly* 51 (March 1936): 61–116. The high level of working class geographical mobility is stressed in Thernstrom and Knights,

"Men in Motion." Caroline Ware has estimated the turnover rate for eight Lowell mills in 1845 at 25 percent annually. (Ware, *The Early New England Cotton Manufactures*, p. 224.)

62. For an example of the continued belief in geographical mobility (not necessarily back to the farm) as a safety valve, see *Eighteenth Annual Report of the Minister at Large in Lowell*, 1863, p. 6.

63. Charles Cowley, *A Handbook of Business in Lowell, with a History of the City* (Lowell: E. D. Green, 1856), p. 4; Cowley, *Illustrated History of Lowell*, p. 165; and Elisha Huntington, *Address of the Mayor of Lowell* (Lowell: Stearns & Taylor, 1844), pp. 4–5. See also Miles, *A Glance at Our History*, pp. 11–12; Miles, *Lowell*, pp. 44–45; *Vox Populi* [Lowell], August 13, 1847; and *Lowell Weekly Journal*, January 16, 1857, December 2, 1864.

64. Huntington, *Address of the Mayor of Lowell*, 1844, p. 5; Miles, *A Glance at Our History*, p. 12. For evidence showing positive correlations among property, social mobility, and residential persistence, see Thernstrom, *Poverty and Progress*, pp. 89–90, 118.

65. Huntington, *Address of the Mayor of Lowell*, 1841, p. 6.

66. Elisha Bartlett, *Address of the Mayor of Lowell* (Lowell: Huntress, 1837), p. 7; See also Bartlett, *Communication from the Mayor Concerning the City Almshouse, Poor Farm, Support of Paupers, Etc., Oct. 9, 1837*. The average number of inmates in 1837 was 76.

67. See *Annual Reports of the Receipts and Expenditures of the City of Lowell* (Lowell, 1837–1862). On this general issue see Robert W. Kelso, *The History of Poor Relief in Massachusetts, 1620–1920* (Boston: Houghton Mifflin, 1922), chaps. 6–8; and David Rothman, *The Discovery of the Asylum: Social Order and Disorder in the New Republic* (Boston: Little, Brown, 1971), chapt. 8.

68. Elisha Huntington, *Address of the Mayor of Lowell* (Lowell: J. T. Chesley, 1856), p. 11. See also Huntington, *Address of the Mayor of Lowell*, 1852, pp. 6–9.

69. Coburn, *History of Lowell*, 1: 380. Earlier charities included the Lowell Hospital (financed by corporations), the Lowell Dispensary, the Howard Benevolent Society, the Irish Benevolent Society, and societies attached to the various churches.

70. Lowell Unitarian Missionary Society, *Second Annual Reports of the Treasurer and Secretary* (Lowell: Joel Taylor, 1845), pp. 22, 15; [Horatio Wood, Jr.,] "Memoir of Horatio Wood, by his Son," *Contributions of the Old Residents' Historical Association*, 4 (1891): 381–84; and *First Annual Report of the Minister at Large in Lowell*, 1845, p. 16.

71. "Memoir of Horatio Wood," p. 385; *Second Annual Report of the Minister at Large in Lowell*, 1846, p. 7; and *Twenty-Fourth Annual Report of the Minister at Large in Lowell*, 1868, p. 26. See also *Fourth Annual Report of the Minister at Large in Lowell*, 1848, p. 13.

72. *Fifth Annual Report of the Minister at Large in Lowell*, 1849, p. 7; and *Second Annual Report of the Minister at Large in Lowell*, 1846, pp. 9, 12–13. See also *Fourth Annual Report of the Minister at Large in Lowell*, 1848, p. 8; *Fifth Annual Report of the Minister at Large in Lowell*, 1849, pp. 7, 18; *Ninth Annual Report of the Minister at Large in Lowell*, 1853, pp. 9–10; and *Eleventh Annual Report of the Minister at Large in Lowell*, 1855, p. 8.

73. *Fifteenth Annual Report of the Minister at Large in Lowell*, 1860, pp. 8–9.

74. *Twenty-Fourth Annual Report of the Minister at Large in Lowell*, 1868, p. 26; *Second Annual Report of the Minister at Large in Lowell*, 1846, p. 14; and *First Annual Report of the Minister at Large in Lowell*, 1845, p. 20. See also *Third Annual Report of the Minister at Large in Lowell*, 1847, p. 9.

75. Fourth Congregational Society of Lowell, *The Importance and Means of Evangelizing Manufacturing Cities* (n.p.: n.p., 1854), p. 4. On the development of permanent resident operatives, see Ware, *The Early New England Cotton Manufacture*, pp. 109, 219.

76. William Barry, *Moral Exposure and Spiritual Wants of Manufacturing Cities* (Lowell: n.p., 1850), p. 8.

77. *Fourth Annual Report of the Minister at Large in Lowell*, 1848, p. 17; and Blanchard, "Introduction," pp. xi–xii. On this general issue in educational thought, see Daniel Calhoun, "The City as Teacher: Historical Problems," *History of Education Quarterly* 9 (Fall 1969): 312–25.

78. Fourth Congregational Society of Lowell, *The Importance and Means of Evangelizing Manufacturing Cities*, p. 6; Barry, *Moral Exposure and Spiritual Wants of Manufacturing Cities*, p. 8; Clarke, *Lectures to Young People in Manufacturing Villages*, p. 59; and Ambrose Lawrence, *Address of the Mayor of Lowell* (Lowell: Z. E. Stone, 1855), p. 4. One of the leading historians of religion in America has argued that during the nineteenth century the public school system became the equivalent of an established religion in America. (See Sidney E. Mead, *The Lively Experiment: The Shaping of Christianity in America* [New York: Harper & Row, 1963], pp. 67–68.)

79. For a study of this aspect of the Massachusetts public school system, see Katz, *The Irony of Early School Reform*.

80. Lowell School Committee, *Annual Report*, 1846, p. 3. See also ibid., 1853, p. 45; ibid., 1845, p. 14; ibid., 1839, p. 5; and ibid., 1847, p. 27.

81. Quotation from ibid., 1841, p. 4.

82. William G. McLoughlin, *The Meaning of Henry Ward Beecher: An Essay on the Shifting Values of Mid-Victorian America, 1840–1870* (New York: Alfred A. Knopf, 1970), p. 173.

83. Calls for a more efficient police force began appearing in Lowell at mid-century. See Josiah B. French, *Address of the Mayor of Lowell* (Lowell: S. J. Varney, 1850), p. 20; James H. B. Ayer, *Address of the Mayor of Lowell* (Lowell: S. J. Varney, 1851), p. 14; Sewell G. Mack, *Address of the Mayor of Lowell* (Lowell: S. J. Varney, 1853), p. 8; and Lawrence, *Address of the Mayor of Lowell*, 1855, p. 11. Civic leaders looked upon the developing Boston police force as a model for their own efforts. This department has been studied by Roger Lane, *Policing the City: Boston, 1822–1885* (Cambridge: Harvard University Press, 1967). On the preference for schools, see *The Republic and the School: Horace Mann on the Education of Free Men*, ed. Lawrence A. Cremin (New York: Teachers College, 1957), pp. 98–101.

84. Lowell School Committee, *Annual Report*, 1851, p. 16; and ibid., 1841, p. 4.

85. Ibid., 1853, pp. 42–45; and Katz, *The Irony of Early School Reform*, p. 88 and passim.

86. Lowell School Committee, *Annual Report*, 1855, p. 10.

87. Ibid., 1835, quoted in Louis S. Walsh, *The Early Irish Catholic Schools of Lowell, Massachusetts, 1835–1852* (Boston: Press of Thomas A. Whalen & Co., 1901), pp. 9–10.

88. Lowell School Committee, *Annual Report*, 1835, quoted in ibid., 1851, p. 11; ibid., 1835, quoted in Walsh, *The Early Irish Catholic Schools of Lowell*, p. 11; and Amos Lawrence to Amos A. Lawrence, October 11, 1840, Amos A. Lawrence Papers, Massachusetts Historical Society, quoted in Ware, *The Early New England Cotton Manufacture*, p. 229. See also Lowell School Committee, *Annual Report*, 1840, p. 7.

89. Walsh, *The Early Irish Catholic Schools of Lowell*, pp. 16–17. The special schools were followed, however, by the establishment of "Intermediate Schools," which provided educational opportunities to Irish youth whose school careers were irregular. They were abolished when the system was bureaucratized. The flexibility and adaptation represented by the Intermediate School was apparently perceived as an organization anomaly. It seems to have been more than a coincidence that the first permanent superintendent was hired and the entire system through the high school was "graded" at the same time that the Intermediate Schools were abolished in the early 1860s.

For a powerful criticism of this trend toward bureaucratic uniformity in the Lowell school system, see the Reverend William R. Huntington's oration before the members of the High School Association printed in the *Lowell Weekly Journal*, July 26, 1867.

90. Lowell School Committee, *Annual Report*, 1839, pp. 4–5.

91. Ibid., 1836, p. 6. See also ibid., 1840, pp. 6–7.

92. Ibid., 1848, p. 24.

93. Ibid., 1846, p. 17. In this year, only 61 percent of Lowell's children between 4 and 16 years were in schools. See also ibid., 1848, pp. 28–30; and ibid., 1851, p. 11.

94. The origin and early operation of the Lowell Reform School is described in Massachusetts, Board of State Charities, *Second Annual Report*, 1865, in *Massachusetts Public Documents*, 1866, Doc. No. 19, pp. 105–8. For a general account of the treatment of urban delinquents in Massachusetts, see Katz, *The Irony of Early School Reform*, pp. 162–211.

95. Ayer, *Address of Mayor of Lowell*, 1851, p. 9. About this time a movement was commenced to remove the insane from the almshouse where "there is no suitable provision for the proper treatment, or even safe-keeping of such persons" and to "provide for them in some public asylum." (Huntington, *Address of the Mayor of Lowell*, 1844, p. 7.)

96. Ayer, *Address of the Mayor of Lowell*, 1851, pp. 9–10; Huntington, *Address of the Mayor of Lowell*, 1856, p. 10.

97. See Oscar Handlin, "The Horror," in his *Race and Nationality in American Life* (Garden City, N.Y.: Anchor Book, 1957), pp. 111–32; Katz, *The Irony of Early School Reform*, pp. 117–24 and passim; and Richard Sennett, *Families against the City: Middle Class Homes of Industrial Chicago, 1872–1890* (Cambridge: Harvard University Press, 1970), pp. 110–13 and passim.

98. See George F. Kenngott, *The Record of a City: A Social Survey of Lowell, Massachusetts* (New York: Macmillan, 1912).

99. *Fifteenth Annual Report of the Minister at Large in Lowell*, 1860, pp. 12–13.

See also *Twelfth Annual Report* . . . , 1857, p. 22; and *Twenty-Second Annual Report* . . . , 1867, p. 17–18. Wood's early praise for reformatories is in his *Fifth Annual Report* . . . , 1850, p. 26.

100. *Twentieth Annual Report of the Minister at Large in Lowell*, 1865, appendix, pp. 37–38. See also Massachusetts, Board of State Charities, *Second Annual Report*, 1865.

VI. The Idea of Community & the Problem of Organization in Urban Reform

Headquotes from "Natural Science: With a Comparison between the Lessons of the Country and the Town," *Knickerbocker* 6 (August 1840): 99; and Charles Loring Brace, *The Dangerous Classes of New York and Twenty Years' Work among Them* [1872] (New York: Wynkoop & Hallenbeck, Publishers, 1880), pp. 371–72.

1. My thinking on this issue was clarified by Michael H. Frisch, *Town into City: Springfield, Massachusetts, and the Meaning of Community, 1840–1880* (Cambridge: Harvard University Press, 1972), passim, but esp. pp. 48–49.

2. On this characteristic of industrial cities, see especially Sam B. Warner, Jr.'s studies of Philadelphia: "If All the World Were Philadelphia: A Scaffolding for Urban History, 1774–1930," *American Historical Review* 74 (October 1968): 26–43; *The Private City: Philadelphia in Three Periods of Its Growth* (Philadelphia: University of Pennsylvania Press, 1968).

3. C. L. B., "Children's Lodging-Houses," *New York Times*, December 20, 1868, p. 3; and Children's Aid Society, *Thirty-Fifth Annual Report*, 1887, p. 8.

4. C. L. B., "The Industrial School and Its Benefits," *New York Times*, November 14, 1868, p. 8. See also Charles L. Brace, *Address on Industrial Schools, Delivered to the Teachers of the Schools* (New York: Wynkoop & Hallenbeck, 1868), pp. 4, 17; C. L. B., "A Gospel to the Rich," *Independent* 7 (May 24, 1855): 161; C. L. B., "Work for Young Men," ibid., 8 (May 29, 1856): 170; and C. L. B., "The Industrial School," ibid., 6 (January 12, 1854): 9.

5. David J. Rothman, *The Discovery of the Asylum: Social Order and Disorder in the New Republic* (Boston: Little, Brown, 1971).

6. *Reformatory Education*, ed. Henry Barnard (Hartford, Conn.: F. C. Brownell, 1857), p. 354; Rothman, *The Discovery of the Asylum*, p. 207; Joseph M. Hawes, *Children in Urban Society: Juvenile Delinquency in Nineteenth Century America* (New York: Oxford University Press, 1971), chaps. 3, 5; and Orlando F. Lewis, *The Development of American Prisons and Prison Customs, 1776–1845* ([Albany:] Prison Association of New York, 1922), chapt. 24.

7. State of New York, *Messages from the Governors*, ed. Charles Z. Lincoln, 11 vols. (Albany: J. B. Lyon Company, 1909), 2: 551.

8. Robert S. Pickett, *House of Refuge: Origins of Juvenile Reform in New York State, 1815–1857* (Syracuse, N.Y.: Syracuse University Press, 1969), p. 26; Rothman, *The Discovery of the Asylum*, pp. 225–26; David M. Schneider, *The History of Public Welfare in New York State, 1609–1866* (Montclair, N.J.: Patterson Smith, 1969), pp. 324–25; *Documents Relative to the House of Refuge*, ed. Nathaniel C. Hart (New York: Mahlon Day, 1832), pp. 23–24, 275–87; Hawes, *Children in*

Urban Society, pp. 47–49; Bradford K. Peirce, *A Half-Century with Juvenile Delinquents* (New York: D. Appleton, 1869), pp. 81–85, 103–6, 174, 244, 247; and *Reformatory Education*, p. 354.

9. For his criticism of the New York House of Refuge, see [Charles L. Brace,] "The Science of Charity," *Nation* 8 (June 10, 1869): 457–58.

10. Brace, *The Dangerous Classes of New York*, pp. 236–37. See also Brace, *Short Sermons to News Boys* (New York: Charles Scribner, 1866), p. 33.

11. Society for the Reformation of Juvenile Delinquents, *Twenty-Eighth Annual Report*, 1852, p. 23; *Documents Relative to the House of Refuge*, ed. Hart, p. 84; Peirce, *Juvenile Delinquents*, pp. 103–6, 248–71; Anon., *The Picture of New York* (New York: A. T. Goodrich, 1828), pp. 448–49; and George P. Jacoby, *Catholic Child Care in Nineteenth Century New York* (Washington: Catholic University of America Press, 1941), p. 68.

12. See Schneider, *The History of Public Welfare in New York State*, pp. 333, 344; and Frank J. Bruno, *Trends in Social Work, 1874–1956*, 2d ed. (New York: Columbia University Press, 1957), pp. 56–57.

13. See Rothman, *The Discovery of the Asylum*, chaps. 3–4 and passim.

14. On the importance of Brace, see Schneider, *The History of Public Welfare in New York State*, p. 334; Henry W. Thurston, *The Dependent Child* (New York: Columbia University Press, 1930), p. 92; Edith Abbott, *Some American Pioneers in Social Welfare* (New York: Russell & Russell, 1963), p. 131; Robert H. Bremner, *From the Depths: The Discovery of Poverty in the United States* (New York: New York University Press, 1956), pp. 40–41; Rothman, *The Discovery of the Asylum*, pp. 258–60; and Hawes, *Children in Urban Society*, pp. 87–89, 108.

15. Charles L. Brace to Miss Flower, January 16, 1887, in Emma Brace, *The Life and Letters of Charles Loring Brace* (New York: Charles Scribner's Sons, 1894), p. 433. See also Charles L. Brace to his father, December 11, 1842, in ibid., p. 9; and ibid., pp. 7–8.

16. Horace Bushnell, *Sermons for the New Life*, rev. ed. (New York: Charles Scribner's Sons, 1899), pp. 186, 192, 195–96.

17. Horace Bushnell, *Christian Nurture*, with an introduction by Luther A. Weigle (New Haven, Conn.: Yale University Press, 1967), pp. 76, 88, 99–100.

18. See Daniel H. Calhoun, "From Noah Webster to Chauncey Wright: The Intellectual as Prognostic," *Harvard Educational Review* 36 (1966): 435–38.

19. Barbara Cross, *Horace Bushnell: Minister to a Changing America* (Chicago: University of Chicago Press, 1958), pp. 21–30; and William G. McLoughlin, *The Meaning of Henry Ward Beecher: An Essay on the Shifting Values of Mid-Victorian America, 1840–1870* (New York: Alfred A. Knopf, 1970), pp. 40–42.

20. H. Shelton Smith, ed., *Horace Bushnell* (New York: Oxford University Press, 1965), pp. 34–35; and Horace Bushnell, "Preliminary Dissertation on the Nature of Language, as Related to Thought and Spirit," in his *God in Christ* (Hartford, Conn.: Brown and Parsons, 1849), p. 46. See also Cross, *Horace Bushnell*, chapt. 7; and Charles Feidelson, Jr., *Symbolism and American Literature* (Chicago: University of Chicago Press, 1953), pp. 151–57.

21. Bushnell, *Christian Nurture*, p. 20.

22. [Charles L. Brace,] "Literary Notices," *Knickerbocker* 35 (March 1850):

254–63; Charles L. Brace to Theodore Parker, New York, February 16, 1853, in Brace, *Life*, p. 177; and Charles L. Brace to Ralph Waldo Emerson, New York, November 24, 1853, Emerson Papers, Houghton Library, Harvard University.

23. On his concern about finding a satisfactory social role in the metropolis, see Charles L. Brace to John C. Olmsted, February 6, 1851, in Brace, *Life*, p. 114.

24. Brace, *Short Sermons*, pp. 5–9; Brace, *Life*, p. 156; Brace, *Dangerous Classes of New York*, p. 75; and Charles L. Brace to George and Elizabeth Bushnell, Southside, [May 21, 1852], Blake Family Papers, Yale University. See also Frederick Law Olmsted to Charles L. Brace, Southside, March 25, 1848, Frederick Law Olmsted Papers, Library of Congress; and Charles L. Brace to Theodore Parker, New York, July 28, 1853, in Brace, *Life*, p. 181.

25. On Brace's commitment to "man-helping," see Charles L. Brace to his father [1853], in Brace, *Life*, pp. 156–57; Charles L. Brace to F. J. Kingsbury, June 23, 1848, May 25, 1849, November 29, 1850, in ibid., pp. 57, 66–67, 100–101; and Charles L. Brace to his father, September 29, 1850, in ibid., p. 93.

26. The phrase *subjective necessity* is borrowed from the title of an essay Jane Addams wrote explaining why she established Hull House. (Jane Addams, *Twenty Years at Hull House* [New York: Signet Classic, 1961], chapt. 6.)

27. Charles L. Brace to Bill Colt, [New Haven], December 22, 1845, Brace papers in possession of Gerald Brace, Belmont, Mass.; Charles L. Brace to his father, October 31, 1849, in Brace, *Life*, pp. 75–76; and Charles L. Brace to Emma Brace, [February 15, 1850], in ibid., pp. 82–83.

28. Brace, *Dangerous Classes of New York*, p. 78. See also Charles L. Brace, *Address to the Theological Students of Harvard University* (n.p.: n.p., 1881), p. 5; Charles L. Brace, *Home-Life in Germany* (New York: Charles Scribner, 1853), esp. pp. 61–66; Charles L. Brace to Mary Elizabeth Bushnell, London, June 29, 1850, Blake Family Papers; and Brace, *Life*, p. 153. He had not, however, completely abandoned his earlier ministerial ambitions.

29. See Charles L. Brace to Theodore Parker, July 26, 1853, in Brace, *Life*, pp. 180–81. On the Five Points Mission, see Carroll Smith Rosenberg, *Religion and the Rise of the American City: The New York City Mission Movement, 1812–1870* (Ithaca, N.Y.: Cornell University Press, 1971), chapt. 8.

30. Brace, *Dangerous Classes of New York*, pp. 43–44; and Children's Aid Society, *Twenty-Third Annual Report*, 1875, pp. 5–7. The findings of Dugdale's impressive effort in empirical social research are reported in Robert L. Dugdale, *The Jukes: A Study in Crime, Pauperism, Disease, and Heredity*, 4th ed. (New York: G. P. Putnam's Sons, 1910).

31. Children's Aid Society, *Second Annual Report*, 1855, p. 4. My italics.

32. Brace, *Dangerous Classes of New York*, p. 57; Children's Aid Society, *Twenty-Fifth Annual Report*, 1877, p. 3; Children's Aid Society, *Third Annual Report*, 1856, p. 5. Brace was also sensitive to the special problems of adjustment faced by the immigrants. (See Brace, *Dangerous Classes of New York*, pp. 34–35.) For a useful historical account, see Robert Ernst, *Immigrant Life in New York City, 1825–1863* (New York: King's Crown Press, 1949).

33. *New York Daily Times*, October 18, 1852, p. 2.

34. Brace, *Dangerous Classes of New York*, p. 25; Children's Aid Society, *Third*

Annual Report, 1856, p. 3; and Children's Aid Society, *Second Annual Report*, 1855, p. 4. On the general increase of awareness of urban poverty at this time, see Rosenberg, *Religion and the Rise of the American City*, chapt. 6.

35. Brace, *Dangerous Classes of New York*, pp. 26, 29–30.

36. Ibid., pp. 26–27. For his admiration of the traits of street boys, see ibid., pp. 97–100.

37. *Joseph Tuckerman on the Elevation of the Poor: A Selection from His Reports as Minister at Large in Boston*, ed. Edward Everett Hale (Boston: Roberts Brothers, 1874), p. 103. See also *Mr. Tuckerman's Fourth Quarterly, or First Annual Report* (Boston, 1827), pp. 4–7.

38. Children's Aid Society, *Fifth Annual Report*, 1858, p. 11; and Brace, *Dangerous Classes in New York*, p. 47.

39. Ibid., pp. 48–49. On this general topic, see Charles L. Brace, "The Best Method of Founding Children's Charities in Towns and Villages," National Conference of Charities and Correction, *Proceedings* 7 (1880): 227–37. Hereafter cited as NCCC, *Proceedings*.

40. Brace, *Dangerous Classes of New York*, p. 46.

41. Brace, *Short Sermons*, pp. 12–13; Charles L. Brace to George and Elizabeth Bushnell, Southside, [May 21, 1852], Blake Family Papers; and Brace, *Dangerous Classes of New York*, p. ii. See also ibid., pp. 77–79; and C. L. B., "Vagrant Children," *New York Daily Times*, December 6, 1852, p. 3.

42. This circular is reprinted as an appendix in Brace, *Life*, pp. 489–92. Brace expressed this combination of motives throughout his life. For example, see his "Walks among the New York Poor," in the *New York Daily Times*, October 11, 18, November 2, December 6, 1852; Children's Aid Society, *First Annual Report*, 1854, p. 12; Children's Aid Society, *Second Annual Report*, 1855, pp. 18–19; Children's Aid Society, *Thirty-Sixth Annual Report*, 1888, p. 76.

43. Brace, *Dangerous Classes of New York*, p. 77; Charles L. Brace, *The Best Method of Disposing of Our Pauper and Vagrant Children* (New York: Wynkoop, Hallenbeck & Thomas, 1859), p. 4; and Children's Aid Society, *Fifth Annual Report*, 1858, p. 7.

44. Brace, *The Best Method*, p. 13; Brace, *Dangerous Classes of New York*, pp. 398–99; and Brace, *The Best Method*, p. 3.

45. Brace, *Dangerous Classes of New York*, p. 381; Brace, *Address to the Theological Students of Harvard University*, p. 3; Brace, *Life*, p. 202; Children's Aid Society, *Fifth Annual Report*, 1858, p. 7.

46. Brace, *Address to the Theological Students of Harvard University*, p. 3; Brace, *The Best Method*, pp. 9–11; and Children's Aid Society, *Twenty-Second Annual Report*, 1874, p. 3. See also Brace, *Home-Life in Germany*, pp. 92–96.

47. Children's Aid Society, *Twenty-Second Annual Report*, 1874, p. 4; and Brace, *The Best Method*, pp. 9–11.

48. Brace, *Life*, p. 491. On the Children's Aid Society's emigration work, see Miriam Z. Langsam, *Children West: A History of the Placing-Out System of the New York Children's Aid Society, 1853–1890* (Madison: State Historical Society of Wisconsin, 1964); Hawes, *Children in Urban Society*, chapt. 6; Thurston, *The Dependent Child*, pp. 92–160; and Charles L. Brace, Jr., "The Children's Aid Society of New York: Its History, Plans, and Results," in Twentieth National

Conference of Charities and Correction, *History of Child Saving* (Boston: George H. Ellis, 1893), pp. 1–36. "Homeless" did not necessarily mean orphaned. About one half of the children placed were orphans; most of the remainder had one parent living, although a significant number had both parents living. If it was determined that at least one parent was living, the Society was generally careful to obtain permission before sending a child out of the city.

49. Brace, *The Best Method*, pp. 11–13.

50. See, for example, *Transactions of the Fourth National Prison Reform Congress*, 1876, pp. 585–93; *Journal of Social Science* 11 (1880): 98–103; and Massachusetts, Board of State Charities, *Second Annual Report*, 1865, in *Massachusetts Public Documents*, 1866, Doc. No. 19.

51. New York Catholic Protectory, *First Annual Report*, 1864, pp. 42–44. See also Schneider, *The History of Public Welfare in New York State*, p. 335. A brief history of the Protectory may be found in Jacoby, *Catholic Child Care in Nineteenth Century New York*, chapt. 5.

52. L. P. Alden, "Letter on Mr. Brace's Paper," *Journal of Social Science* 11 (1880): 99–101. Incidentally, the birthplace of boys in the Michigan State Reform School is readily available, and the figures hardly suggest a flood of New York criminals. In 1878, the year preceding Alden's remarks, only six of 166 boys in the State Reform School were born in New York. Ninety-eight were born in Michigan, suggesting that the midwestern state was capable of rearing its own criminals without any help from New York. However, it should be noted that New York was disproportionately represented in comparison with other noncontiguous states. (See *Report of Superintendent of the [Michigan] State Reform School, in Documents Accompanying the Report of the Superintendent of Public Instruction*, 1878, p. 51.)

53. Massachusetts, Board of State Charities, *Second Annual Report*, pp. xliv and passim.

54. Laura E. Richards, ed., *Letters and Journals of Samuel Gridley Howe* (Boston: Dana Estes & Company, 1909), p. 48; and Massachusetts, Board of State Charities, *Second Annual Report*, p. lxxvii.

55. This interpretation is suggested by the comments on the symbolic functions of institutions contained in ibid., pp. xli, lxii. However, if Edward Eggleston's portrait of an Indiana "charitable institution" in the *Hoosier School-Master* (1871) can be believed, the institutions that men like Alden were building to replace "pioneer" institutions in the newly settled Midwest must be granted more than symbolic importance.

56. Alden, "Letter on Mr. Brace's Paper." Alden describes his own work in *Third Biennial Report of the Board of State Commissioners for the General Supervision of Charitable, Penal, Pauper, and Reformatory Institutions [in Michigan]*, 1876, pp. 63–69. For a characterization of the pedagogical theories of mid-century reformers as either "hard" or "soft," see Michael B. Katz, *The Irony of Early School Reform: Educational Innovation in Mid-Nineteenth Century Massachusetts* (Cambridge: Harvard University Press, 1968), pp. 132–51.

57. Children's Aid Society, Board of Trustees, "Minutes," 1853–1873, September 21, 1858 (These "Minutes" are in the files of the Children's Aid Society in New York.); and Children's Aid Society, *Seventh Annual Report*, 1860, pp. 6–7.

58. During its first three years of operation, nearly half of the children served by its programs were transported to new homes in the West. This percentage steadily declined over the years. By 1881 less than one in seven of all children helped was sent west. The remainder were served by new programs established in the city. These percentages are derived from the figures presented in Children's Aid Society, *Second Annual Report*, 1855, *Third Annual Report*, 1856, and *Twenty-Ninth Annual Report*, 1881. Figures from the *Seventeenth Annual Report*, 1869, reveal about one in nine children being sent west in that year.

The shifting distribution of expenditures better reveals the pattern of the transition. The amount of money spent on emigration work in 1870 (which subsequently remained constant) was about $30,000 per year while the annual budget of the Society increased from $150,000 in 1871 to $234,000 in 1881, and to $366,000 in 1890. This data taken from Nineteenth, Twenty-Ninth, and Thirty-Eighth *Annual Reports*, respectively.

For Brace's assessment of this new direction, see Children's Aid Society, *Eleventh Annual Report*, 1864, p. 11; Children's Aid Society, *Twenty-Sixth Annual Report*, 1878, pp. 6–7; Brace, *Address on Industrial Schools*, p. 4; Children's Aid Society, *Thirty-Second Annual Report*, 1884, p. 2; Charles L. Brace, "Child-Helping as a Means of Preventing Crime in the City of New York," *Journal of Social Science* 17 (May 1884): 289–305; and Children's Aid Society, *Thirty-Seventh Annual Report*, 1889, pp. 9–12.

59. Children's Aid Society, *Fifteenth Annual Report*, 1868, p. 10. See also Charles L. Brace to Charles Eliot Norton, New York, October 24, 1866, Charles Eliot Norton Papers, Houghton Library, Harvard University.

60. Quote from *New York Times*, February 27, 1887, p. 8. (This editorial was probably drafted by Brace.) Important exceptions to this educational thrust include a Model Tenement proposal and suggestions for sanitary legislation on the British model.

61. C. L. B., "The Industrial Day School," *New York Times,* June 12, 1876, p. 3; and Brace, *Dangerous Classes of New York*, p. 221.

62. Charles L. Brace to Teachers of the Industrial Schools, February 1865, reprinted in Children's Aid Society, *Twelfth Annual Report*, 1865, p. 61; Fourth Ward Industrial School Association, *Second Annual Report*, 1855, p. 6; and Brace, *Dangerous Classes of New York*, p. 96. See also Children's Aid Society, *Twenty-Seventh Annual Report*, 1879, pp. 4–5; *Twenty-First Annual Report*, 1871, p. 44; *Thirty-Seventh Annual Report,* 1889, p. 11; and Brace, *Address on Industrial Schools*, pp. 2–3.

63. Brace, *Dangerous Classes of New York*, p. 179.

64. *New York Times*, November 10, 1872; Children's Aid Society, *The Crusade for Children* (New York: Children's Aid Society, [1928]), pp. 24, 50; C. L. Brace to Editor, *New York Times*, July 22, 1874, July 11, 1876; Brace, *Dangerous Classes of New York*, pp. 457–59; Brace, *Life*, pp. 338–39; Children's Aid Society, *Twenty-Ninth Annual Report*, 1881, pp. 40–41; and Charles L. Brace, "Model Tenement Houses," *Plumber and Sanitary Engineer* 1 (February 1878): 47–48. The "poor people's levees" were reported in the *New York Times*, April 28, 1872, p. 5, and were designed to help kindle self-respect in the poorer neighborhoods.

65. Brace, *Dangerous Classes of New York*, p. 45.

66. Children's Aid Society, *Eleventh Annual Report*, 1864, p. 44. See also Brace, *Short Sermons*, p. v.

67. Children's Aid Society, *Eleventh Annual Report*, 1864, pp. 44–47; and Brace, *Dangerous Classes of New York*, p. 193. See also C. L. B., "The Object System of Teaching in an Industrial School," *New York Times*, January 24, 1864, p. 5; and Charles L. Brace, *The New West: Or, California in 1867–1868* (New York: G. P. Putnam & Son, 1869), p. 75.

68. See Daniel Calhoun, ed., *The Educating of Americans: A Documentary History* (Boston: Houghton Mifflin, 1969), pp. 295, 315–16.

69. Brace, *Dangerous Classes of New York*, pp. 184 and passim.

70. Ibid., p. iii. See also Herbert B. Adams, "Personal Philanthropy: Illustrated by the Life of Charles Loring Brace," *Charities Review* 1 (April 1892): 243.

71. Children's Aid Society, *Second Annual Report*, 1855, p. 11.

72. Children's Aid Society, *Fourth Annual Report*, 1857, p. 14; and Brace, *Life*, p. 194. See also C. L. B., "Industrial Schools," *New York Times*, October 30, 1868, p. 4.

73. The breakdown of the staffing in the industrial schools for 1883 reveals only forty-eight volunteer teachers and eighty-nine salaried teachers. The basic education was clearly in the hands of professional teachers. (Brace, "Child-Helping as a Means of Preventing Crime," p. 292.) See also Brace, "The Best Method of Founding Children's Charities," p. 231; Brace, *Dangerous Classes of New York*, p. 175; Children's Aid Society, *Seventeenth Annual Report*, 1869, p. 23; and Charles L. Brace, "The Industrial Day School," *Transactions of the Fourth National Prison Reform Congress*, 1876, p. 486.

74. Brace, *Dangerous Classes of New York*, pp. 49–50; and "The Science of Charity," p. 457.

75. Brace, *Dangerous Classes of New York*, p. 137; Children's Aid Society, *Third Annual Report*, 1856, p. 13; Children's Aid Society, *Twenty-Sixth Annual Report*, 1878, p. 7; Brace, "The Best Method of Founding Children's Charities," p. 231; and Children's Aid Society, *Seventeenth Annual Report*, 1869, p. 4.

76. Brace, *Dangerous Classes of New York*, pp. 280–83. See also Charles L. Brace, *Address upon the Industrial School Movement* (New York: Wynkoop, Hallenbeck & Thomas, 1857), p. 12; and Brace, "The Industrial Day School," p. 487. By 1870 from one-third to half of the budget came from state and local authorities. (See Brace, *Dangerous Classes of New York*, pp. 284–85; and Langsam, *Children West*, p. 39.) Detailed budgets published with each annual report indicate that the proportion of public support remained at about this level through 1890.

77. Brace, *Dangerous Classes of New York*, p. 379.

78. By the late 1880s, this generalization falters. Even in the early years there are exceptions. See Marvin Gettleman, "Charity and Social Classes in the United States, 1874–1900," *American Journal of Economics and Sociology* 22 (1963): 321.

79. Charles S. Fairchild, "The Objects of Charity Organization," NCCC, *Proceedings* 11 (1885): 65; and Hawes, *Children in Urban Society*, p. 109.

80. Fairchild, "Objects of Charity Organization," pp. 66–68. Other nineteenth-century reformers who expressed similar views include Robert Treat Paine, "The Work of Volunteer Visitors of the Associated Charities among the Poor," *Journal of Social Science* 12 (1880): 101–16; Oscar C. McCulloch, "The Personal Element

in Charity," NCCC, *Proceedings* 22 (1895): 340–47; Zilpha D. Smith, "Volunteer Visiting: The Organizing Necessity to Make It Effective," ibid., 11 (1884): 69–72; Josephine Shaw Lowell, "Charity Organization," *Lend-a-Hand* 3 (February 1888): 81–87. On the Charity Organization Society in New York, see Dorothy G. Becker, "The Visitor to the New York City Poor, 1843–1920: The Role and Contributions of the Volunteer Visitors of the New York Association for the Improvement of the Condition of the Poor, State Charities Aid Association, and New York Charity Organization Society" (D.S.W. thesis, Columbia University, 1960).

81. See Roy Lubove, *The Professional Altruist: The Emergence of Social Work as a Career, 1880–1930* (New York: Atheneum, 1969), chaps. 1–2; Nathan I. Huggins, *Protestants against Poverty: Boston's Charities, 1870–1900* (Westport, Conn.: Greenwood Publishing Company, 1971), chapt. 7 and passim; Gettleman, "Charity and Social Classes in the United States, 1874–1900"; Jane Addams, "The Subtle Problems of Charity," *Atlantic Monthly* 83 (February 1899): 163–78.

82. See Allen F. Davis, *Spearheads for Reform: The Social Settlements and the Progressive Movement, 1890–1914* (New York: Oxford University Press, 1967), chapt. 1; Lubove, *The Professional Altruist*, pp. 23, 35; and Huggins, *Protestants against Poverty*, pp. 12, 31.

83. Addams, "The Subtle Problems of Charity," p. 164; Jane Addams, *Democracy and Social Ethics* (New York: Macmillan, 1905), p. 38; and Addams, "The Subtle Problems of Charity," p. 163. See also Addams, *Twenty Years at Hull House*, chaps. 4, 6; and Alice Miller, "Hull House," *Charities Review* 1 (February 1892): 167–73. Her motivation and the remaining contradictions in her reform style are variously analyzed by Christopher Lasch, *The New Radicalism in America: The Intellectual as a Social Type* (New York: Vintage Book, 1967), chapt. 1; Allen F. Davis, *American Heroine: The Life and Legend of Jane Addams* (New York: Oxford University Press, 1973), esp. chaps. 3–7; and Daniel Levine, *Varieties of Reform Thought* (Madison: State Historical Society of Wisconsin, 1964), chapt. 1.

84. Addams, *Twenty Years at Hull House*, pp. 92, 97–98.

85. Roy Lubove apparently believes that this vision was utopian and not really a serious alternative to the welfare bureaucracy. (See Lubove, *The Professional Altruist*, pp. 173–80, 220–21.)

86. Children's Aid Society, *Twenty-Eighth Annual Report*, 1880, pp. 4–5; Children's Aid Society, *Thirty-Fourth Annual Report*, 1886, p. 5; and Children's Aid Society, *Thirty-Seventh Annual Report*, 1889, p. 13.

87. Richard Sennett, *Families against the City: Middle Class Homes of Industrial Chicago, 1872–1890* (Cambridge: Harvard University Press, 1970), chaps. 1–3, quote from pp. 23–24.

88. See Becker, "The Visitor to the New York City Poor, 1843–1920," pp. 292, 333, 388, 447–48; Lubove, *The Professional Altruist*, passim; and Samuel Mencher, "The Future for Voluntarism in American Social Welfare," in *Issues in American Social Work*, ed. Alfred J. Kahn (New York: Columbia University Press, 1959), pp. 219–41.

89. For some interesting theoretical arguments on this point, see Gideon Sjoberg, Richard A. Brymer, and Buford Farris, "Bureaucracy and the Lower Class," *Sociology and Social Research* 50 (1966): 325–37.

90. Lubove, *The Professional Altruist*, pp. 157–59 and passim; Brace, *Dangerous*

Classes of New York, pp. 366–72; and Children's Aid Society, *Third Annual Report*, 1856, p. 10.

91. "Natural Science: With a Comparison between the Lessons of the Country and the Town," *Knickerbocker* 6 (August 1840): 99. The phrase *factual generation* is from Bremner, *From the Depths*, chapt. 9. For a consideration of some mid-century charity leaders within the context of "romantic reform," see John L. Thomas, "Romantic Reform in America, 1815–1865," *American Quarterly* 17 (Winter 1965): 656–81.

92. Brace, *Dangerous Classes of New York*, p. 371.

VII. Cityscape & Landscape in America: Frederick Law Olmsted

The headquotes are from Frederick Law Olmsted to Charles L. Brace, July 1847, quoted in Broadus Mitchell, *Frederick Law Olmsted: A Critic of the Old South* (Baltimore: Johns Hopkins Press, 1924), p. 39; Frederick Law Olmsted, "Auto-biographical Passages," in *Frederick Law Olmsted: Landscape Architect, 1822–1903*, ed. Frederick Law Olmsted, Jr., and Theodora Kimball, 2 vols. in one (New York: Benjamin Blom, 1970, orig. ed. 1922–1928), 1: 43; and Henry W. Bellows, "Cities and Parks: with special reference to the New York Central Park," *Atlantic Monthly* 7 (April 1861): 423.

1. Herman Melville, *Pierre; Or, The Ambiguities* (New York: Signet Classic, 1964), p. 266.

2. Quoted in John William Ward, "The Politics of Design," in *Who Designs America?* ed. Laurence B. Holland (Garden City, N.Y.: Anchor Book, 1966), p. 64.

3. See Neil Harris, *The Artist in American Society: The Formative Years, 1790–1860* (New York: Braziller, 1966), esp. chapts. 6–8. Perry Miller offers an important assessment of American romantic art in this context in "Nature and the National Ego," in his *Errand into the Wilderness* (New York: Harper Torchbook, 1964), pp. 204–16.

4. Andrew Jackson Downing, *Rural Essays* (New York: Leavitt and Allen, 1858, orig. ed. 1853), pp. 13–15. It is impossible in what follows to do more than touch upon a few pertinent themes in Downing's thought. A comprehensive study of Downing's ideas is long overdue. The following brief discussions, however, were exceptionally perceptive and useful: Ward, "The Politics of Design"; Harris, *The Artist in American Society*, pp. 208–16; Roger B. Stein, *John Ruskin and Aesthetic Thought in America, 1840–1900* (Cambridge: Harvard University Press, 1967), pp. 46–56. George W. Curtis's introduction to Downing's *Rural Essays* is valuable and although it is restricted to Downing's architectural criticism so is James Early, *Romanticism and American Architecture* (New York: A. S. Barnes, 1965), chapt. 2.

5. Andrew Jackson Downing, *A Treatise on the Theory and Practice of Land-scape Gardening* (New York: C. M. Saxton and Company, 1856, orig. ed. 1841), p. ii.

6. See Early, *Romanticism and American Architecture*, pp. 60, 66–67.

7. See, for example, Wayne Andrews, *Architecture, Ambition and Americans* (New York: Free Press, 1964), p. 208. Downing could accept the Greek revival style in public buildings.

8. Andrew Jackson Downing, *The Architecture of Country Houses* (New York: Da Capo Press, 1968, orig. ed. 1850), pp. v, 257–58. See also Ward, "The Politics of Design," pp. 64–66.

9. Downing, *A Treatise of the Theory and Practice of Landscape Gardening*, esp. section 9. The quoted phrase is from p. 371. See also Ward, "The Politics of Design," p. 66. Compare Downing's essay on "Public Cemeteries and Public Gardens" (in *Rural Essays*, pp. 154–59) with Joseph Story, *An Address Delivered on the Dedication of the Cemetery at Mount Auburn* (Boston: Joseph T. & Edwin Buckingham, 1831). The difference between Olmsted and Downing on parks may be illustrated in a brief example. Olmsted opposed the introduction of museums, statues, or any architectural features in the hope that their absence would strengthen the contrast between the landscape and the surrounding cityscape. Downing, in contrast, tended to ignore the cityscape in his discussions of the proposed New York park. Focusing narrowly upon the park, he presented it as a setting for "noble works of art, statues, monuments, and buildings commemorative at once of the great men of the nation, of the history of the age and country, and the genius of our highest artists." Parks and cemeteries would thus provide within themselves "the united charm of nature and art." (*Rural Essays*, pp. 150, 155.)

10. Frederick Law Olmstead, "Autobiographical Passages," in *Frederick Law Olmsted: Landscape Architect, 1822–1903*, ed. Frederick Law Olmsted, Jr., and Theodora Kimball, 2 vols. in one (New York: Benjamin Blom, 1970, orig. ed. 1922–1928), 1: 46–47. Hereafter cited as Olmsted and Kimball, *Olmsted*.

11. On Olmsted's interest in Bushnell's ideas, see Frederick Law Olmsted to Charles L. Brace, Hartford, January 27, 1846, Olmsted Papers, Library of Congress; Frederick Law Olmsted to Frederick Kingsbury, Sachem's Head, September 23, 1847, ibid.; Frederick Law Olmsted to Charles L. Brace, [July 1851], ibid. (hereafter cited as Olmsted Papers). This aspect of Bushnell's intellectual style is most apparent in his pamphlet *California: Its Characteristics and Prospects* (San Francisco: Whitton, Town & Co., 1858).

12. Albert Fein, "The American City: The Ideal and the Real," in *The Rise of an American Architecture*, ed. Edgar Kaufmann, Jr. (New York: Praeger, 1970), p. 57.

13 Olmsted, "Autobiographical Passages," in Olmsted and Kimball, *Olmsted*, 1: 61.

14. Downing, *Rural Essays*, p. 386; and Frederick Law Olmsted to John Olmsted, Waterbury, June 23, 1845, Olmsted Papers. See also Frederick Law Olmsted to Charles L. Brace [Waterbury, January 1845], ibid.; and Frederick Law Olmsted to Charles L. Brace, Waterbury, June 22, 1845, ibid.

15. Frederick Law Olmsted to Frederick Kingsbury, June 1846, in Olmsted and Kimball, *Olmsted*, 1: 77.

16. Albert Fein, "Introduction: Landscape into Cityscape," in *Landscape into Cityscape: Frederick Law Olmsted's Plans for a Greater New York City*, ed. Albert Fein (Ithaca, N.Y.: Cornell University Press, 1967), pp. 29, 15.

17. Frederick Law Olmsted to Charles L. Brace, Southside, July 26, 1852, Olmsted Papers.

18. Frederick Law Olmsted, *The Cotton Kingdom*, ed. Arthur M. Schlesinger, Sr. (New York: Alfred A. Knopf, 1953), p. xv. Compare Charles E. Beveridge,

"Frederick Law Olmsted: The Formative Years, 1822–1865" (Ph.D. diss., University of Wisconsin, 1966), chapt. 7.

19. On the influence of Olmsted's articles and books during the 1850s, see Eric Foner, *Free Soil, Free Labor, Free Men: The Ideology of the Republican Party before the Civil War* (New York: Oxford University Press, 1970), pp. 42–43. Evidence of their enduring importance and a challenge to Olmsted's interpretation may be found in Robert W. Fogel and Stanley Engerman, *Time on the Cross* (Boston: Little, Brown, 1974), pp. 172–81, 191–246.

20. This implicit judgment forms a systematic bias throughout the series, but Olmsted is more or less explicit in Frederick Law Olmsted, *A Journey in the Seaboard Slave States* (New York: Dix & Edwards, 1856), pp. 13, 19, 135–36, 140, 164–306, 366; and Frederick Law Olmsted, *A Journey in the Backcountry* (New York: Mason Brothers, 1860), pp. 184, 280, 455.

21. In a preface to a condensed version of the three-volume series, Olmsted wrote: "One system or the other is to thrive and extend, and eventually possess and govern this whole land." (Olmsted, *The Cotton Kingdom*, p. 4.) See also Frederick Law Olmsted to John Olmsted [his father], Fairmount, August 12, 1846, Olmsted Papers.

22. Frederick Law Olmsted to Charles L. Brace, Richmond, [December 22, 1852], Olmsted Papers.

23. Olmsted, *Seaboard Slave States*, pp. 479, 490. See also ibid., p. 199. For a general discussion, see Foner, *Free Soil, Free Labor, Free Men.*

24. Olmsted, *Seaboard Slave States*, p. x. He makes a similar point in his preface to *Backcountry*, p. vi.

25. Ibid., pp. 117–18. See also Olmsted, *Seaboard Slave States*, pp. 259–69; Olmsted, *Backcountry*, p. 280. For an excellent study of this myth, see William R. Taylor, *Cavalier and Yankee* (Garden City, N.Y.: Anchor Book, 1963).

26. Frederick Law Olmsted to Charles L. Brace, Southside, November 12, 1850, Olmsted Papers; *New York Times*, January 12, 1854, reprinted in Olmsted, *The Cotton Kingdom*, p. 620.

27. Olmsted, *Backcountry*, p. 416.

28. Frederick Law Olmsted to Charles L. Brace and Charles Elliott, Cumberland River, December 1, 1853, Olmsted Papers. See also Olmsted, *The Cotton Kingdom*, pp. 17–18, 620–21.

29. Frederick Law Olmsted, "Public Parks and the Enlargement of Towns," *Journal of Social Science* 3 (1871): 4–5.

30. Olmsted, "Autobiographical Passages," in Olmsted and Kimball, *Olmsted*, 1: 43.

31. Olmsted, "Public Parks and the Enlargement of Towns," p. 2; Frederick Law Olmsted, *A Few Things to be Thought of before Proceeding to Plan Buildings for the National Agricultural Colleges* (New York: American News Company, 1866), pp. 10–14. Olmsted again expresses his concern for bringing culture to the countryside in a letter to Charles Eliot Norton, Washington, January 22, 1880, Norton Papers, Houghton Library, Harvard University; hereafter cited as Norton Papers.

32. Olmsted, "Public Parks and the Enlargement of Towns," pp. 5, 6, 10. See also Frederick Law Olmsted and Calvert Vaux, *Report of the Landscape Architects and Superintendents to the President of the Board of Commissioners of Prospect*

Park, Brooklyn (1868), reprinted in *Landscape into Cityscape*, ed. Fein, p. 138 (hereafter cited as Olmsted, *Brooklyn*); Frederick Law Olmsted, *Preliminary Report in Regard to a Plan of Public Pleasure Grounds for the City of San Francisco* (New York: Wm. C. Bryant & Co., 1866), p. 13 (hereafter cited as Olmsted, *San Francisco*); and Frederick Law Olmsted, "Urban and Pagan Changes," undated Ms, Olmsted Papers.

33. Frederick Law Olmsted, "The Justifying Value of a Public Park," *Journal of Social Science* 12 (1880): 163.

34. Olmsted, *Brooklyn*, p. 145. See also ibid., pp. 146–48.

35. Olmsted, "Justifying Value of a Public Park," p. 163. See also Olmsted, "Public Parks and the Enlargement of Towns," p. 11; Olmsted, *Brooklyn*, p. 150; and Frederick Law Olmsted, "To Those Having the Care of Young Children" [handbill dated 1872], reprinted in Olmsted and Kimball, *Olmsted*, 2: 417. For a complementary analysis by a contemporary New York psychiatrist, see George M. Beard, *American Nervousness: Its Causes and Consequences* (New York: G. P. Putnam's Sons, 1881).

36. These ideas run through all his writings, but are most clearly stated in Olmsted, *Brooklyn;* and Frederick Law Olmsted and J. James Croes, *Document No. 72 of the Board of the Department of Public Parks: 1. Preliminary Report of the Landscape Architect and the Civil and Topographical Engineer, upon the Laying Out of the Twenty-third and Twenty-fourth Wards; 2. Report Accompanying a Plan for Laying Out that Part of the Twenty-fourth Ward, Lying West of the Riverdale Road* (1876), reprinted in *Landscape into Cityscape*, ed. Fein, pp. 349–73; hereafter cited as Olmsted, *Twenty-third and Twenty-fourth Wards*. For two historical assessments of the impact of economic privatism upon the nineteenth-century American city, see Sam Bass Warner, Jr., *The Private City: Philadelphia in Three Periods of Its Growth* (Philadelphia: University of Pennsylvania Press, 1968); and Seymour J. Mandelbaum, *Boss Tweed's New York* (New York: John Wiley & Sons, 1965).

37. Frederick Law Olmsted, "The Beginning of Central Park: A Fragment of Autobiography," reprinted in *Landscape into Cityscape*, ed. Fein, p. 53; and Frederick Law Olmsted, "The Yosemite Valley and the Mariposa Big Tree Grove" (1865), ed. Laura Wood Roper in *Landscape Architecture* 42 (October 1952): 17.

38. Frederick Law Olmsted to Parke Godwin, Central Park, August 1, 1858, Bryant-Godwin Collection, New York Public Library. See also Henry W. Bellows, "Cities and Parks: With special reference to the New York Central Park," *Atlantic Monthly* 7 (April 1861): 421.

39. Olmsted, *Brooklyn*, p. 160. See also Frederick Law Olmsted, "Instructions to the Keepers of the Central Park [1873]," in Olmsted and Kimball, *Olmsted*, 2: 458.

40. *Walden and Other Writings of Henry David Thoreau*, ed. Brooks Atkinson (New York: Modern Library, 1950), p. 613. See Hugh H. Iltis, Orie L. Loucks, and Peter Andrews, "Criteria for an Optimum Human Environment," *Bulletin of the Atomic Scientists* 26 (January 1970): 2–6; and René Dubos, *A God Within* (New York: Charles Scribner's Sons, 1972), chapt. 3.

41. William Bridges, *Map of the City of New-York and Island of Manhattan;*

With Explanatory Remarks and References (New York: T. & J. Swords, 1811), pp. 24–25. For Olmsted's most important criticism of the gridiron plan, see his *Brooklyn*, pp. 134–44, 149–64.

42. Allan Nevins, *The Evening Post: A Century of Journalism* (New York: Boni and Liverright, 1922), pp. 192–93.

43. Olmsted and Kimball, *Olmsted*, 2: 18–40; Nevins, *Evening Post*, chapt. 8.

44. Frederick Law Olmsted to John Olmsted, September 11, 1857, Olmsted Papers.

45. Frederick Law Olmsted to Parke Godwin, January 29, 1856, Bryant-Godwin Collection.

46. Horace Bushnell, "City Plans," in his *Work and Play* (New York: Charles Scribner, 1864), p. 336; Frederick Law Olmsted to Calvert Vaux, March 12, 1865, Calvert Vaux Collection, New York Public Library; Frederick Law Olmsted to Calvert Vaux, August 1, 1865, ibid. For Olmsted's search for a career, see Beveridge, "Frederick Law Olmsted"; and the recent biography by Laura Wood Roper, *FLO: A Biography of Frederick Law Olmsted* (Baltimore: Johns Hopkins University Press, 1973).

47. Roper, *FLO*, pp. 138 n, 262–63, 291–93, 342–43, provides the best discussion of this issue. See also *Landscape into Cityscape*, ed. Fein, p. 43. On the question of credit, see Frederick Law Olmsted to Charles L. Brace, Park, December 8, 1860, Olmsted Papers; Frederick Law Olmsted to Henry W. Bellows, New York, December 24, 1879, Bellows Papers; Frederick Law Olmsted to Mariana G. Van Rensselaer, Chicago, June 11, 1893, Olmsted Papers; Frederick Olmsted to Mariana G. Van Rensselaer, Brookline, May 22, 1893, ibid.; and Frederick Law Olmsted to Calvert Vaux, November 1863, reprinted in Olmsted and Kimball, *Olmsted*, 2: 78.

48. Frederick Law Olmsted and Calvert Vaux, *Description of a Plan for the Improvement of the Central Park: "Greensward"* (1858), reprinted in *Landscape into Cityscape*, ed. Fein, p. 64; hereafter cited as Olmsted, *Greensward*. For Olmsted's view on the significance of rural cemeteries, see Olmsted, "Public Parks and the Enlargement of Towns," p. 19; Olmsted, *San Francisco*, p. 11; Frederick Law Olmsted, "Report of Mr. Olmsted," in *Mountain View Cemetery* (San Francisco: M. D. Carr & Company, 1865); and Olmsted and Kimball, *Olmsted*, 1: 125–26.

49. "Communication from Hon. Fred. Law Olmsted," in *The Development of Golden Gate Park* (San Francisco: Bacon & Company, 1886), p. 22; Frederick Law Olmsted and Calvert Vaux, *Two Letters to the President [of the Department of Public Parks] on Recent Changes and Projected Changes in the Central Park* (New York: n.p., 1872), p. 15; Frederick Law Olmsted and Calvert Vaux, *Preliminary Report to the Commissioners for Laying Out a Park in Brooklyn, New York: Being a Consideration of Circumstances of Site and Other Conditions Affecting the Design of Public Pleasure Grounds* (1866), reprinted in *Landscape into Cityscape*, ed. Fein, p. 98; hereafter cited as Olmsted, *Preliminary Report for Brooklyn;* and Frederick Law Olmsted, "Superintendent of Central Park to Gardeners" [ca. 1873], in Olmsted and Kimball, *Olmsted*, 2: 356. See also ibid., 2: 250–51, 514.

50. Olmsted, "The Justifying Value of a Public Park," p. 163.

51. On the importance of these memories, see Olmsted, "Autobiographical Pas-

sages," in Olmsted and Kimball, *Olmsted*, 1: 59–60; Fein, "Introduction: Landscape into Cityscape," pp. 3–5; and Beveridge, "Frederick Law Olmsted," pp. 1–2.

52. Olmsted, "Public Parks and the Enlargement of Towns," p. 11.

53. Ibid., p. 22; Olmsted, *Preliminary Report for Brooklyn*, p. 101. See also ibid., p. 104.

54. Ibid., pp. 100–101. See also Olmsted, *San Francisco;* and Frederick Law Olmsted and J. C. Olmsted, *Plan of Public Recreation Grounds for the City of Pawtucket* (Boston: T. R. Martin & Son, 1888), p. 7.

55. Olmsted, *San Francisco*, p. 10; Olmsted, "Public Parks and the Enlargement of Towns," pp. 32, 35. See H. W. S. Cleveland, *Suggestions for a System of Parks and Parkways, for the City of Minneapolis* (Minneapolis: Johnson, Smith & Harrison, 1883), p. 3. For Cleveland's use of this argument in a more general context, see H. W. S. Cleveland, *Landscape Architecture as Applied to the Wants of the West*, ed. Roy Lubove (Pittsburgh: University of Pittsburgh Press, 1965, orig. ed. 1873), p. 38.

56. Olmsted, *San Francisco*, p. 14. Using city directories in a similar, if more statistically sophisticated, manner, Stephan Thernstrom and Peter R. Knights have arrived at similar conclusions. See their "Men in Motion: Some Data and Speculations about Urban Population Mobility in Nineteenth-Century America," *Journal of Interdisciplinary History* 1 (Autumn 1970): 7–35.

57. Olmsted, *San Francisco*, p. 17.

58. Olmsted, "Public Parks and the Enlargement of Towns," pp. 18–19. For Downing's earlier expression, see his *Rural Essays*, pp. 142–43, 151.

59. See Mandelbaum, *Boss Tweed's New York*, pp. 74–75. Jacob Riis, in his *How the Other Half Lives* (New York: Hill and Wang, 1957, orig. ed. 1890), p. 137, pointed out in 1890 that few slum children ever saw Central Park. It should be noted that by 1881, when he wrote a polemic on New York politics, Olmsted regretfully admitted that the wealthier classes seemed to be using the park more than the poor he had hoped would benefit from it. (See Frederick Law Olmsted, *The Spoils of the Park: With a Few Leaves from the Deep-laden Notebooks of "A Wholly Unpractical Man"* [1882], reprinted in *Landscape into Cityscape*, ed. Fein, pp. 422–23.)

60. Olmsted, "Public Parks and the Enlargement of Towns," p. 17. Olmsted's earliest statements on the value of a park system appear in Olmsted, *San Francisco*, pp. 25–31; Olmsted, *Preliminary Report for Brooklyn*, p. 99.

61. See Frederick Law Olmsted, "Plan to Organize Keepers for Union Square," Ms in Olmsted Papers, Box 29; Frederick Law Olmsted to W. R. Martin, August 9, 1876, ibid.; Frederick Law Olmsted, "Report on Parade Ground, 1874," Ms in ibid., Box 44; Frederick Law Olmsted, "Preliminary Study of a Design for the Laying Out of Morningside Park," Board of the Department of Public Parks [1873], Doc. No. 50, pp. 2–3; Frederick Law Olmsted, "Parks, Parkways and Pleasure-Grounds," *Engineering Magazine* 9 (May 1895): 253–60; and Lewis Mumford, *The Brown Decades: A Study of the Arts in America, 1865–1895* (New York: Dover Publications, 1955), p. 90. George F. Chadwick, in *The Park and the Town: Public Landscape in the 19th and 20th Centuries* (New York: Frederick A. Praeger, 1966),

p. 191, points out that the idea of a park system, dating from Olmsted's statement of 1870, is an American contribution to the park movement.

62. Frederick Law Olmsted, "Designers' Report as to the Proposed Modification in the Plan" [May 31, 1858], in Olmsted and Kimball, *Olmsted*, 2: 239. See also Frederick Law Olmsted to S. H. Wales, December 26, 1873, reprinted in Olmsted and Kimball, *Olmsted*, 2: 481. For the original intentions regarding the park and the poor, see ibid., 2: 24–26.

63. Olmsted, "Report of Mr. Olmsted," in *Mountain View Cemetery*, p. 53. These ideas are also expressed in Olmsted, *San Francisco;* Frederick Law Olmsted, "History of Civilization in the United States" Ms written between 1860 and 1870 in Olmsted Papers; and [Frederick Law Olmsted to Miss W.], n.d., Olmsted Papers, Box 45. This approach to American society taken by Olmsted seems to have been greatly influenced by Horace Bushnell, especially Bushnell's discourse *Barbarism the First Danger* (New York: American Home Missionary Society, 1847).

64. See Paul Shepard, *Man in the Landscape* (New York: Alfred A. Knopf, 1967), p. 93.

65. Downing, *Rural Essays*, p. 152. See also ibid., p. 81; Harris, *The Artist in American Society*, esp. chapts. 6 and 8; and Henry P. Tappan, *The Growth of Cities: A Discourse Delivered before the New York Geographical Society* (New York: R. Craighead, 1855), pp. 35–36. See Stephan D. Walker, *Rural Cemetery and Public Walk* (Baltimore: Sands and Neilson, 1835), pp. 5–6, for one of the earliest expressions of this point of view.

66. Olmsted, "Public Parks and the Enlargement of Towns," p. 34. See also Olmsted and Kimball, *Olmsted*, 2: 175 n; and Bellows, "Cities and Parks," pp. 428–29.

67. See Stein, *John Ruskin and Aesthetic Thought in America;* Daniel Walker Howe, *The Unitarian Conscience: Harvard Moral Philosophy, 1805–1861* (Cambridge: Harvard University Press, 1970), pp. 185–89; and Harris, *The Artist in American Society*, pp. 180–86 and passim.

68. Olmsted, *San Francisco*, p. 15. For an early (1848) statement on this theme within a rural context, see Olmsted and Kimball, *Olmsted*, 1: 86.

69. Frederick Law Olmsted, "Scenery, Society, and Gardening," undated Ms, Olmsted Papers, Box 41; [Frederick Law Olmsted to Miss W., 1890], ibid., Box 45. See also Roper, *FLO*, pp. 251–57.

70. Olmsted, *San Francisco*, pp. 10–11. See also Olmsted, *Preliminary Report for Brooklyn*, pp. 124–25.

71. Frederick Law Olmsted, "Of the Villagizing Tendency," undated Ms, Olmsted Papers, Box 41; Frederick Law Olmsted to Francis G. Newlands, November 16, 1891, ibid.

72. Frederick Law Olmsted to Charles L. Brace, March 7, 1882, ibid. See Frederick Law Olmsted, *Report upon a Projected Improvement of the Estate of the College of California, at Berkeley, near Oakland* (New York: Wm. C. Bryant, 1886), esp. pp. 4–24 (hereafter cited as Olmsted, *College of California*); and Frederick Law Olmsted, *Preliminary Report upon the Proposed Suburban Village at Riverside, near Chicago* (1868), reprinted with an introduction by Theodora

Kimball Hubbard in *Landscape Architecture* 21 (July 1931): 257–91 (hereafter cited as Olmsted, *Riverside*).

73. Olmsted, *Riverside*, pp. 261–62. See also Olmsted, *Twenty-third and Twenty-fourth Wards*, p. 364; and Frederick Law Olmsted, *Report to the Staten Island Improvement Commission of a Preliminary Scheme of Improvements* (1871), reprinted in *Landscape into Cityscape*, ed. Fein, pp. 178–80 (hereafter cited as Olmsted, *Staten Island*).

74. Olmsted, "Public Parks and the Enlargement of Towns," p. 9; Olmsted, *Staten Island*, p. 183; Frederick Law Olmsted, "The Future of New York," *New York Daily Tribune*, December 28, 1879, p. 5; and Olmsted, *Twenty-third and Twenty-fourth Wards*, p. 352. See also Olmsted, *Riverside*, p. 262; and Frederick Law Olmsted to Francis G. Newlands, November 16, 1891, Olmsted Papers.

75. Frederick Law Olmsted, "Of the Villagizing Tendency," undated Ms, Olmsted Papers, Box 41. The critics I have in mind are Paul and Percival Goodman, *Communitas*, 2d ed. (New York: Vintage Book, 1960); Lewis Mumford, *The City in History* (New York: Harcourt, Brace & World, 1961); Jane Jacobs, *The Death and Life of Great American Cities* (New York: Vintage Book, 1961); and Herbert J. Gans, *The Urban Villagers* (New York: Free Press, 1962). For other comments linking Olmsted to these critics, see Fein, "Introduction: Landscape into Cityscape," p. 37 n.

76. Olmsted, *Staten Island*, p. 183; Frederick Law Olmsted to Mariana G. Van Rensselaer, Chicago, June 11, 1893, Olmsted Papers. See also Olmsted, *Brooklyn*, pp. 150, 161–62; and Frederick Law Olmsted to Francis G. Newlands, November 16, 1891, Olmsted Papers.

77. On Los Angeles, see Robert M. Fogelson, *The Fragmented Metropolis: Los Angeles, 1850–1930* (Cambridge: Harvard University Press, 1967).

78. Olmsted, *Twenty-third and Twenty-fourth Wards*, p. 364; Olmsted, *Staten Island*, p. 193. See also Olmsted, *Brooklyn*, p. 155.

79. John Burchard and Albert Bush-Brown, *The Architecture of America: A Social and Cultural History*, abridged ed. (Boston: Little, Brown, 1966), p. 72.

80. Olmsted, *Riverside*, p. 262. For a brief discussion of the romantic suburb, which began with Andrew J. Davis's Lewellyn Park in 1852 and includes Olmsted's work, see Christopher Tunnard, *The City of Man* (New York: Charles Scribner's Sons, 1953), chapt. 8; and Christopher Tunnard, "The Romantic Suburb in America," *Magazine of Art* 40 (May 1947): 184–87.

81. Olmsted, *Riverside*, p. 266, 275.

82. Ibid., pp. 275, 276. Olmsted sometimes wrote of suburban homes for workingmen, but he never planned such a suburb. (See Olmsted, *Twenty-third and Twenty-fourth Wards*, p. 353.)

83. Olmsted, *Staten Island*, p. 200; Olmsted, *College of California*, pp. 10–11. See also Olmsted, *Brooklyn*, p. 157.

84. Olmsted, *College of California*, p. 13.

85. Mumford, *The Brown Decades*, p. 88.

86. See, for example, Frederick Law Olmsted to Charles Eliot Norton, Brookline, October 19, 1881, Norton Papers; Frederick Law Olmsted to Professor C. S. Sargent, February 7, 1891, Olmsted Papers; Olmsted and Kimball, *Olmsted*, 1: 127–28; and Olmsted, *Spoils of the Park*, pp. 423, 427.

87. See Ward, "The Politics of Design"; Frederick W. Coburn, "The Five-Hundred-Mile City," *World To-Day* 11 (December 1906): 1251–60; and Charles N. Glaab, "Metropolis and Suburb: The Changing American City," in *Change and Continuity in Twentieth Century America: The 1920's*, ed. John Braeman et al. (Columbus: Ohio State University Press, 1968), p. 437. On this general theme, I found Tunnard, *The City of Man*, chapt. 10, quite illuminating.

88. See Frederick Law Olmsted, Jr., Harland Bartholomew, and Charles Henry Cheney, *A Major Street Plan for Los Angeles* (Los Angeles: n.p., 1924).

89. On the planning of the Exposition, see David H. Crook, "Louis Sullivan, the Columbian Exposition and American Life" (Ph.D. diss., Harvard University, 1963); Charles Moore, *Daniel Burnham: Architect-Planner of Cities*, 2 vols. (Boston: Houghton Mifflin, 1921), 1: 31–81; and Maurice F. Neufield, "The Contribution of the World's Columbian Exposition in 1893 to the Idea of a Planned Society in the United States" (Ph.D. diss., University of Wisconsin, 1935).

90. On the significance of the Exposition for the planning movement during the Progressive Era, see John W. Reps, *The Making of Urban America: A History of City Planning in the United States* (Princeton, N.J.: Princeton University Press, 1965), chapt. 18; Mel Scott, *American City Planning since 1890* (Berkeley: University of California Press, 1969), chapts. 1–2; Crook, "Louis Sullivan, The Columbian Exposition and American Life"; and Moore, *Daniel Burnham*. Compare William H. Wilson, *The City Beautiful Movement in Kansas City* (Columbia: University of Missouri Press, 1964), pp. xii–xvii.

91. Frederick Law Olmsted to Mr. Stiles, October 7, 1892, Olmsted Papers. See also Charles C. McLaughlin, "Selected Letters of Frederick Law Olmsted" (Ph.D. diss., Harvard University, 1960), p. 92.

92. Frederick Law Olmsted to Lyman J. Gage, Chicago, August 18, 1890, Olmsted Papers; Frederick Law Olmsted to H. S. Codman, November 4, 1891, ibid. See also Frederick Law Olmsted to H. S. Codman, September 16, 1890, ibid.; and Frederick Law Olmsted to H. S. Codman, Salisbury [England], April 20, 1892, ibid.

93. Frederick Law Olmsted to Mr. Ulrich, Brookline, March 11, 1893, Olmsted Papers; Frederick Law Olmsted to Daniel Burnham, Biltmore, N.C., June 20, 1893, ibid.

94. Frederick Law Olmsted, "The Landscape Architecture of the World's Columbian Exposition," *Inland Architect and News Record* 22 (September 1893): 20.

95. Peter J. Schmitt, *Back to Nature: The Arcadian Myth in Urban America* (New York: Oxford University Press, 1969), chapts. 5, 6, and passim. For an example of Olmsted's growing despair on this point, see "Communication from Hon. Fred. Law Olmsted," in *The Development of Golden Gate Park*, p. 24; and Frederick Law Olmsted, *Spoils of the Park*, pp. 431–32.

96. H. W. S. Cleveland to Frederick Law Olmsted, Minneapolis, June 6, 1893, Olmsted Papers. See also Olmsted and Kimball, *Olmsted*, 1: 127–28.

97. On the reorientation of city planning in the Progressive Era, see Scott, *American City Planning*, chapts. 2–3; Ward, "Politics of Design." For more general assessments, see Robert H. Wiebe, *The Search for Order, 1877–1920* (New York: Hill and Wang, 1967), chapt. 6 and passim; and Samuel Haber, *Efficiency and Uplift* (Chicago: University of Chicago Press, 1964), chapt. 6.

Epilogue

1. See Lynn L. Marshall, "The Strange Stillbirth of the Whig Party," *American Historical Review* 72 (January 1967): 445–68; Michael B. Katz, *The Irony of Early School Reform: Educational Innovation in Mid-Nineteenth Century Massachusetts* (Cambridge: Harvard University Press, 1968); Michael B. Katz, "From Voluntarism to Bureaucracy in American Education," *Sociology of Education* 44 (Summer 1971): 297–332; David Rothman, *The Discovery of the Asylum: Social Order and Disorder in the New Republic* (Boston: Little, Brown, 1971); Daniel Calhoun, *The American Civil Engineer* (Cambridge: Technology Press, 1960); and Daniel Calhoun, *Professional Lives in America: Structure and Aspiration, 1750– 1850* (Cambridge: Harvard University Press, 1965). Compare Stanley M. Elkins, *Slavery: A Problem in American Institutional and Intellectual Life* (Chicago: University of Chicago Press, 1959); R. Jackson Wilson, *In Quest of Community: Social Philosophy in the United States, 1860–1920* (New York: Oxford University Press, 1970), chapt. 1; and George M. Fredrickson, *The Inner Civil War: Northern Intellectuals and the Crisis of the Union* (New York: Harper Torchbook, 1968).

2. See Allan Nevins, *The War for the Union*, 4 vols. (New York: Charles Scribner's Sons, 1959–1971), 1: v.

3. The reference here is to Fredrickson's excellent book *The Inner Civil War*.

4. Accounts of the New York Association for Improving the Condition of the Poor may be found in Robert Bremner, *From the Depths: The Discovery of Poverty in the United States* (New York: New York University Press, 1965), pp. 31–38; Roy Lubove, "The New York Association for Improving the Condition of the Poor: The Formative Years," *New York Historical Society Quarterly* 43 (1959): 307–27; Dorothy G. Becker, "The Visitor to the New York City Poor, 1843–1920: The Role and Contributions of the Volunteer Visitors of the New York Association for the Improvement of the Condition of the Poor, State Charities Aid Association, and New York Charity Organization Society" (D.S.W. diss., Columbia University, 1960); Carroll Smith Rosenberg, *Religion and the Rise of the American City: The New York City Mission Movement, 1812–1870* (Ithaca, N.Y.: Cornell University Press, 1971), chapt. 9. However, none of these studies communicate the tenor of the organization's social philosophy as effectively as do the annual reports, which are available at the New York Public Library.

5. Henry W. Bellows to Charles Stillé, New York, November 15, 1865, Henry W. Bellows Papers, Massachusetts Historical Society. Hereafter cited as Bellows Papers. Compare Fredrickson, *The Inner Civil War*, chapt. 7, where, inexplicably, this long and important letter is not mentioned; and John Higham, *From Boundlessness to Consolidation: The Transformation of American Culture, 1848–1860* (Ann Arbor, Mich.: William L. Clements Library, 1969). Bellows's study of poverty during the 1850s is discussed briefly in Clifford E. Clark, Jr., "Religious Beliefs and Social Reform in the Gilded Age: The Case of Henry Whitney Bellows," *New England Quarterly* 43 (March 1970): 59–78.

6. Henry W. Bellows to Charles Stillé, November 15, 1865, Bellows Papers.

7. Frederick Law Olmsted to Charles L. Brace, On board the *Wilson Small* [1862], in *The Life and Letters of Charles Loring Brace*, ed. Emma Brace (New York: Charles Scribner's Sons, 1894), p. 298.

8. Frederick Law Olmsted, "Sanitary Commission," undated Ms, Frederick Law Olmsted Papers, Library of Congress, Box 41. Hereafter cited as Olmsted Papers. See also [Frederick Law Olmsted,] *What They Have to Do Who Stay at Home* (U.S. Sanitary Commission, Doc. No. 50, 1862), pp. 5–6.

9. Lewis Mumford, "The Fallacy of Systems," *Saturday Review of Literature* 32 (October 1, 1949): 8.

10. Henry W. Bellows, "Cities and Parks: With Special Reference to the New York Central Park," *Atlantic Monthly* 7 (April 1861): 423.

11. Frederick Law Olmsted to Board of Commissioners of Central Park, January 22, 1861, Olmsted Papers.

12. This paragraph and the two following it are based primarily upon my understanding of the following studies: John Higham, "The Reorientation of American Culture in the 1890's," in *The Origins of Modern Consciousness*, ed. John Weiss (Detroit: Wayne State University Press, 1965), pp. 25–48; Wilson, *In Quest of Community*; Henry F. May, *The End of American Innocence* (Chicago: Quadrangle Books, 1964); and Robert H. Wiebe, *The Search for Order, 1877–1920* (New York: Hill and Wang, 1967).

13. Wiebe, *The Search for Order*, p. 170.

14. I am using *rationalization* in the sense developed by Max Weber.

15. Randolph S. Bourne, *War and the Intellectuals*, ed. Carl Resek (New York: Harper Torchbook, 1964), p. 59.

16. See, for example, Higham, *From Boundlessness to Consolidation*; Wiebe, *The Search for Order*; Marvin Lazerson, *Origins of the Urban School: Public Education in Massachusetts, 1870–1915* (Cambridge: Harvard University Press, 1971); and the works cited in note 1.

17. Higham, *From Boundlessness to Consolidation*.

Bibliographical Essay

Since I have drawn upon a wide variety of primary and secondary material in this study, my footnotes provide a better indication of the type and scope of materials consulted than any formal bibliography could. In this essay, therefore, I have simply listed the manuscript collections cited and have written briefly about some of the most important materials used, particularly the most useful secondary works.

Manuscripts

Appleton Company Letterbooks, Merrimack Valley Textile Museum

Nathan Appleton Papers, Massachusetts Historical Society

Henry W. Bellows Papers, Massachusetts Historical Society

Blake Family Papers, Yale University

Charles Loring Brace Papers, in the possession of Gerald Brace, Belmont, Massachusetts

Bryant-Godwin Papers, New York Public Library

Theodore Edson "Diary," Lowell Historical Society

Ralph Waldo Emerson Papers, Houghton Library, Harvard University

Essex Company Collection, Merrimack Valley Textile Museum

Edward Everett Papers, Massachusetts Historical Society

William W. Folwell Papers, Minnesota State Historical Society

James Jackson, "Notes on the Life of Patrick Tracy Jackson," (1847), Houghton Library, Harvard University

Hamilton Manufacturing Company Collection, Baker Library, Harvard University

Lucy Larcom Papers, Essex Institute

Lawrence Papers, Massachusetts Historical Society

Lawrence Manufacturing Company Collection, Baker Library, Harvard University

Lee Family Collection, Massachusetts Historical Society

Francis Cabot Lowell Papers, in the possession of Harriet Ropes
    Cabot, Boston
Merrimack Manufacturing Company Collection, Baker Library,
    Harvard University
Miscellaneous Manuscripts, New York Historical Society
New York Children's Aid Society, files, New York City
Charles Eliot Norton Papers, Houghton Library, Harvard
    University
Frederick Law Olmsted Papers, Library of Congress
Proprietors of the Locks and Canals Company Collection, Baker
    Library, Harvard University
Harriet (Hanson) Robinson Papers, Schlesinger Library on the
    History of Women in America, Radcliffe College
James Schouler Papers, Massachusetts Historical Society
Calvert Vaux Papers, New York Public Library

General

The best survey of American urban history is Charles N. Glaab and
A. Theodore Brown, *A History of Urban America* (New York,
1967). My sense of the general shape of nineteenth-century Amer-
ican urban history has also been significantly influenced by Sam
Bass Warner, Jr., *The Private City: Philadelphia in Three Periods
of Its Growth* (Philadelphia, 1968); Seymour J. Mandelbaum, *Boss
Tweed's New York* (New York, 1965); Stephan Thernstrom, *Pov-
erty and Progress: Social Mobility in a Nineteenth Century City*
(Cambridge, Mass., 1964); Richard C. Wade, "The City in History
–Some American Perspectives," in *Urban Life and Form,* ed.
Werner Z. Hirsch (New York, 1963), pp. 59–77; and *Nineteenth-
Century Cities,* ed. Stephan Thernstrom and Richard Sennett (New
Haven, 1969). I offer some speculations on the study of our urban
past in "Studying Nineteenth-Century Cities," *History of Educa-
tion Quarterly* 12 (Spring 1972): 89–96. On the role of earlier
American cities, I relied upon Carl Bridenbaugh, *Cities in Revolt:
Urban Life in America, 1743–1776* (New York, 1964); Arthur M.
Schlesinger, "The City in American Civilization," in his *Paths to
the Present* (New York, 1949), pp. 210–33; and the essays in *The*

Growth of the Seaport Cities, 1790–1825, ed. David T. Gilchrist (Charlottesville, Va., 1967).

There are now several historiographical essays dealing with American urban history; among the most useful are Charles N. Glaab, "The Historian and the American City: A Bibliographical Survey," in *The Study of Urbanization,* ed. Philip M. Hauser and Leo F. Schnore (New York, 1965), pp. 52–80; Roy Lubove, "The Urbanization Process: An Approach to Historical Research," *Journal of the American Institute of Planners* 33 (January 1967): 33–39; Allen F. Davis, "The American Historian vs. the City," *Social Studies* 56 (1965): 91–96, 127–35; and Dwight Hoover, "The Diverging Paths of American Urban History," *American Quarterly* 20 (Summer 1968): 296–317.

My understanding of urban culture has been especially influenced by the work of Paul Goodman, particularly *Communitas,* rev ed. (New York, 1960), written with Percival Goodman; Lewis Mumford's *The City in History* (New York, 1961); and *The Death and Life of Great American Cities* (New York, 1961), by Jane Jacobs.

Nearly all studies in nineteenth-century cultural history make some effort to describe ideas about the city, but I found three works by Perry Miller particularly useful: "Nature and the National Ego," in his *Errand into the Wilderness* (New York, 1964, orig. ed. 1956), pp. 204–16; *The Raven and the Whale: The War of Words and Wits in the Era of Poe and Melville* (New York, 1956); and *The Life of the Mind in America* (New York, 1965). Neil Harris's study of American artists, *The Artist in American Society: The Formative Years* (New York, 1966) is also perceptive in its consideration of the relationship among ideas of nature, nationalism, and urbanization. I found John Higham's *From Boundlessness to Consolidation: The Transformation of American Culture, 1848–1860* (Ann Arbor, 1969) to be quite stimulating. Although he is concerned with the antipode of the city, Roderick Nash's *Wilderness and the American Mind* (New Haven, 1967) is suggestive for the student of urbanism.

The most important study specifically examining the city in American thought is Morton and Lucia White, *The Intellectual Versus the City* (New York, 1964, orig. ed. 1962). According to the Whites, American intellectuals have been traditionally antiurban.

This assertion drew a quick counterstatement from Charles N. Glaab in "The Historian and the American Urban Tradition," *Wisconsin Magazine of History* 46 (Autumn 1963): 13–35. Glaab argued there that a pro-urban interpretation could be presented. More recently, historians have begun to move beyond the limiting framework accepted by both the Whites and Glaab. They are beginning to ask how Americans learned to cope with the city. Michael H. Cowan's study of Emerson, in *City of the West: Emerson, America, and Urban Metaphor* (New Haven, 1967), is a notable interpretation of an American literary man within this broader conceptual framework. Other departures from the framework assumed by the Whites include David R. Weimer, *City as Metaphor* (New York, 1966); and Thomas Bender, "James Fenimore Cooper and the City," *New York History* 51 (April 1970): 287–305.

Agrarianism, Industrialism, and the Machine

The relation of agrarian ideals to emerging American nationalism has been treated in a number of studies. The most useful to me were Chester E. Eisinger, "The Freehold Concept in Eighteenth Century American Letters," *William and Mary Quarterly* 4 (January 1947): 42–59; Eisinger, "Land and Loyalty: Literary Expressions of Agrarian Nationalism in the Seventeenth and Eighteenth Centuries," *American Literature* 21 (1949): 160–78; Ralph N. Miller, "American Nationalism as a Theory of Nature," *William and Mary Quarterly* 12 (January 1955): 74–95; A. Whitney Griswold, *Farming and Democracy* (New York, 1948); Henry Nash Smith, *Virgin Land: The American West as Symbol and Myth* (New York, 1950); Richard Hofstadter, *The Age of Reform* (New York, 1955), chapt. 1; Charles L. Sanford, *The Quest for Paradise: Europe and the American Moral Imagination* (Urbana, Ill., 1961); Edmund S. Morgan, "The Puritan Ethic and the American Revolution," *William and Mary Quarterly* 24 (January 1967): 3–43; and Gordon S. Wood, *The Creation of the American Republic, 1776–1787* (Chapel Hill, 1969).

Leo Marx's important book *The Machine in the Garden* (New York, 1964) probes the Jeffersonian and other American responses to industrialism with great sensitivity. On Jefferson himself, I have benefited from Merrill Peterson's scholarship. *Thomas Jefferson and the New Nation: A Biography* (New York, 1970) is bulky, but I found it concise and reliable. Peterson's earlier study, *The Jeffersonian Image in the American Mind* (New York, 1960), was useful in following the Jeffersonian tradition into the nineteenth century. Linda Kerber's *Federalists in Dissent: Imagery and Ideology in Jeffersonian America* (Ithaca, 1970) provides an introduction to the Federalist mind. Despite the recent resurgence of interest in the Federalists, we still need to know more about their ideas of industrialism and urbanism. In pursuing the themes of industrialism and agrarianism into the early nineteenth century, I was guided by the works of Perry Miller and Leo Marx cited above and by John William Ward's *Andrew Jackson: Symbol for an Age* (New York, 1955).

The transformation of the economy between 1800 and 1860 is described by George Rogers Taylor, *The Transportation Revolution, 1815–1860* (New York, 1968, orig. ed. 1951); Douglass C. North, *The Economic Growth of the United States, 1790–1860* (New York, 1966, orig. ed. 1961); and Stuart Bruchey, *The Roots of American Economic Growth, 1607–1861* (New York, 1965). The best survey of the development of the textile industry in New England is still Caroline F. Ware, *The Early New England Cotton Manufacture* (New York, 1966, orig. ed. 1931). *The Golden Threads: New England's Mill Girls and Magnates* (New York, 1949), by Hannah Josephson is brilliantly conceived, but is somewhat marred in execution.

Perry Miller's "The Responsibility of Mind in a Civilization of Machines," *American Scholar* 31 (Winter 1961): 51–69, and the works already mentioned by Miller and Marx are the most sophisticated studies of American attitudes toward the technology that underlay this economic transformation. I also found Oscar Handlin's essay, "Man and Magic: First Encounters with the Machine," *American Scholar* 33 (Summer 1964): 408–19, useful. Two essays by Hugo Meier, "American Technology and the Nineteenth-Century World," *American Quarterly* 10 (Summer 1958): 116–30; and "Technology and Democracy, 1800–1860," *Mississippi Valley Historical Review* 43 (1957): 618–40, provide conventional introductions to the topic. Marvin Fisher's book *Workshops in the*

Wilderness: The European Response to American Industrialism, 1830–1860 (New York, 1967) concentrates upon European reactions to American developments, but his methods of analysis are suggestive for the student of American attitudes. John A. Kouwenhoven's *Made in America: The Arts in American Civilization* (Garden City, 1962, orig. ed. 1948) is an arresting, if controversial, interpretation of the place of the machine in American culture.

John W. Ward's *Red, White and Blue: Men, Books, and Ideas in American Culture* (New York, 1969) contains two thoughtful essays examining the use of machine metaphors in American social thought. *Efficiency and Uplift* (Chicago, 1964) by Samuel Haber and Joel Spring's *Education and the Rise of the Corporate State* (Boston, 1972) are both important in this context.

My own understanding of the complexities of man's relationship with the machine has been enhanced by the works of Lewis Mumford, especially "The Megamachine," *New Yorker* (October 10, 17, 24, 31, 1970); *The Myth of the Machine: Technics and Human Development* (New York, 1967); and *Technics and Civilization* (New York, 1934). Arthur O. Lewis, Jr., has edited a useful anthology on this topic under the title *Of Men and Machines* (New York, 1963).

Lowell

It has been Lowell's good fortune to have had capable amateur historians among its residents. Frederick W. Coburn's *History of Lowell and Its People*, 3 vols. (New York, 1920), is especially good, but even the mid nineteenth-century historians are creditable. Henry A. Miles's *Lowell as It Was and as It Is* (Lowell, 1845) and Charles Cowley's *Illustrated History of Lowell* (Boston, 1868) are "booster" histories, but they are also occasionally perceptive. It is interesting and revealing to compare Miles's study with that of another Lowell minister a half-century later: George F. Kenngott's *The Record of a City: A Social Survey of Lowell, Massachusetts* (New York, 1912) exposes the failure of Lowell as an industrial city. The articles in the *Contributions of the Old Residents' Historical Society* 6 (1879–1904) and *Contributions of the Lowell Historical Society*, 2 vols. (1907–1926) are of extremely uneven quality, but they contain some invaluable material, particularly biographical information on early leaders in Lowell and data on early urban institutions in Lowell.

The best study of Lowell by a professional scholar is John P. Coolidge's *Mill and Mansion: A Study of Architecture and Society in Lowell, Massachusetts, 1820–1865* (New York, 1967, orig. ed. 1942). Coolidge wisely places his architectural history within the larger social context of the city so the value of the book extends beyond architectural history.

Nearly all studies of the textile industry contain substantial discussions of Lowell. The books noted above by Caroline Ware and Hannah Josephson have important information on Lowell. Robert V. Spalding's dissertation, "The Boston Mercantile Community and the Promotion of the Textile Industry in New England, 1813–1860" (Yale University, 1963), has an excellent chapter on Lowell. William R. Bagnall, "Contributions to American Economic History: Sketches of Manufacturing Establishments," a massive unpublished study compiled during the late nineteenth century and now housed at Baker Library, Harvard University, is invaluable. Norman Ware covers the labor movement in Lowell in *The Industrial Worker, 1840–1860* (Chicago, 1964, orig. ed. 1924). Public health in Lowell is examined in George Rosen, "The Medical Aspects of the Controversy over Factory Conditions in New England, 1840–1850," *Bulletin of the History of Medicine* 15 (May 1944): 483–97; it is placed in broader perspective in Barbara Gutmann Rosenkrantz, *Public Health and the State: Changing Views in Massachusetts, 1842–1936* (Cambridge, Mass., 1972).

The great value of Lowell to the historian, however, is the wealth of contemporary opinions of the place that he has to work with. The papers of the men who established America's first industrial city do not have as much self-conscious speculation on the significance of what they were doing as the historian might hope for, but there is some of this, particularly in the Nathan Appleton Papers. Moreover, Appleton and Patrick Tracy Jackson published statements on the issue of American manufactures. The records of the Lowell textile corporations run to several thousand volumes in Baker Library, Harvard University. Most of this material is of no value to a study like the present one, but the minutes of the Boards of Directors and the almost daily letters between the Lowell mill agents and the treasurer at the central office in Boston repay investigation.

Research in newspapers is a time-consuming, inefficient, and dirty business, but for a study like this one newspapers are invaluable. One finds very little "city news" in them, but editorials, poems, and letters to the editor can be very revealing. Between the Lowell Public Library, the Lowell Historical Society, the Boston Public Library, the Library of Congress, the State Historical Society of Wisconsin, and the American Antiquarian Society, substantial runs of Lowell's newspapers, including the *Voice of Industry*, a radical labor newspaper, are preserved. Official city documents, I discovered, can be of immense value to the student of urban attitudes. After the Civil War, the Lowell records become increasingly technical, but earlier I found the Mayor's Annual Addresses, the School Committee Reports, and other miscellaneous city documents to be discursive and speculative.

Lowell was very much in the spotlight during the antebellum years, and many travelers' accounts of the place were published. One also finds numerous articles on Lowell in the American periodical press.

The minds of the working classes are usually closed to the historian. In Lowell, however, representatives of the working class put their ideas in print in the *Lowell Offering*, a literary magazine published by the female operatives. Since the editor, Harriet Farley, refused to publish direct critcism of the factory system, labor historians looking to the *Lowell Offering* for prolabor and anticapitalist expressions by mill operatives have been disappointed. Yet the largely autobiographical and artless stories that were published in the magazine provide a wealth of material for the historian concerned with how rural migrants to the city adjusted to urban and industrial conditons. Moreover, two operatives, Lucy Larcom and Harriet (Hanson) Robinson later wrote autobiographical accounts of their experiences as Lowell "mill girls." And the Harriet (Hanson) Robinson papers at the Schlesinger Library for the History of Women in America include a few letters between Harriet and other "mill girls" during the 1840s.

My discussion of the problem of society and social change in

Lowell should be placed against the background of other studies in the nineteenth-century social history of Massachusetts. The ones I found most helpful are Stephan Thernstrom, *Poverty and Progress: Social Mobility in a Nineteenth-Century City* (Cambridge, Mass., 1964); Oscar Handlin, *Boston's Immigrants: A Study in Acculturation*, rev. ed. (New York, 1959); and Michael B. Katz, *The Irony of Early School Reform: Educational Innovation in Mid Nineteenth-Century Massachusetts* (Cambridge, Mass., 1968). Michael H. Frisch's thoughtful book, *Town into City: Springfield, Massachusetts and the Meaning of Community, 1840–1880* (Cambridge, Mass., 1972), was published too late to be of use in shaping my discussion of Lowell, but it was valuable in the final stages of writing. Nathan I. Huggins's *Protestant against Poverty: Boston's Charities, 1870–1900* (Westport, Conn., 1971) was also useful. The conceptual framework within which I consider social change in Lowell has been shaped in part by Sigmund Diamond's argument in "From Organization to Society: Virginia in the Seventeenth Century," *American Journal of Sociology* 63 (1958): 457–75.

Charles L. Brace, Charity Organization, & the Problem of Community

There is no modern biography of Brace, and the *Life and Letters of Charles Loring Brace* (New York, 1894), by his daughter, Emma Brace, is inadequate. It is valuable, however, for the early letters reprinted in it. R. Richard Wohl has written a suggestive piece on Brace's attitude toward city and country: "The 'Country Boy' Myth and Its Place in American Urban Culture: The Nineteenth-Century Contribution," ed. Moses Rischin in *Perspectives in American History* 3 (1969): 77–158.

The only aspect of Brace's career that has received significant attention from historians is his placing-out system: Miriam Z. Langsam, *Children West: A History of the Placing-Out System of the New York Children's Aid Society, 1853–1890* (Madison, 1964); and Henry W. Thurston, *The Dependent Child: A Story of Changing Aims and Methods in the Care of Dependent Children* (New York, 1930). Carroll Smith Rosenberg provides a useful discussion of a charity movement that attracted Brace's early attention in her *Religion and the Rise of the American City: The New York City Mission Movement, 1812–1870* (Ithaca, 1971)–although I think she errs in stressing the evangelical or revivalistic basis of urban reform to the exclusion of liberal religion.

I relied upon Robert S. Pickett, *House of Refuge: Origins of Juvenile Reform in New York State, 1815–1857* (Syracuse, 1969); and David M. Schneider, *History of Public Welfare in New York State, 1609–1866* (Montclair, N.J., 1969, orig. ed. 1938), for guidance in assessing the treatment of dependent children in New York before Brace founded the Children's Aid Society. David J. Rothman's *The Discovery of the Asylum: Social Order and Disorder in the New Republic* (Boston, 1971) was published as I was completing my work. It completely supercedes both Pickett and Schneider and is an excellent study of the ideas Brace challenged at mid-century. Joseph M. Hawes, *Children in Urban Society: Juvenile Delinquency in Nineteenth Century America* (New York, 1971), is less imaginative but it does introduce the major issues and characters, including Brace. Late nineteenth-century developments are interpreted in Anthony M. Platt's thought-provoking book *The Child Savers: The Invention of Juvenile Delinquency* (Chicago, 1968). Jack M. Holl reveals that Brace's romantic style of reform was not completely eclipsed by the turn of the century in a book on *Juvenile Reform in the Progressive Era: William R. George and the Junior Republic Movement* (Ithaca, 1971).

Recent work in American educational history has been useful in placing Brace in cultural context. I found Katz's *Irony of Early School Reform* particularly helpful. Two articles by Daniel Calhoun also suggested fruitful approaches to the problem of community and organization in the mid-century city: "From Noah Webster to Chauncey Wright: The Intellectual as Prognostic," *Harvard Educational Review* 36 (1966): 427–46; and "The City as Teacher: Historical Problems," *History of Education Quarterly* 9 (Fall 1969): 312–25.

More generally, my understanding of the idea of community and the problem of organization in nineteenth-century America has been informed by Frisch, *Town into City*; George M. Fredrickson, *The Inner Civil War: Northern Intellectuals and the Crisis of the Union* (New York, 1965); Robert Wiebe, *The Search for Order*,

1877–1920 (New York, 1967); and R. Jackson Wilson, *In Quest of Community: Social Philosophy in the United States, 1860–1920* (New York, 1968).

My interpretation of the professionalization of welfare work has been guided by Roy Lubove, *The Professional Altruist: The Emergence of Social Work as a Career, 1880–1930* (New York, 1969, orig. ed. 1965). I also found Huggins, *Protestants against Poverty* useful. The shift from voluntarism to professionalism in New York City is the subject of a dissertation by Dorothy G. Becker, "The Visitor to the New York City Poor, 1843–1920: The Role and Contributions of the Volunteer Visitors of the New York Association for the Improvement of the Condition of the Poor, State Charities Aid Association, and New York Charity Organization Society" (Columbia University, 1960). A more general discussion is available in Samuel Mencher, "The Future of Voluntaryism in American Social Welfare," in *Issues in American Social Work*, ed. Alfred J. Kahn (New York, 1959), pp. 219–41. The consequences of bureaucracy are described in Gideon Sjoberg, Richard A. Brymer, and Buford Farris, "Bureaucracy and the Lower Class," *Sociology and Social Research* 50 (1966): 325–37. The best introduction to Jane Addams's criticism of the main trends of charity work is her own writings.

Source material on Brace is ample. With the exception of two significant letters in the Blake Family Papers at Yale University and some personal papers in the possession of Gerald Brace of Belmont, Massachusetts, I was unable to locate any important collection of Brace manuscripts. However, his published writings are voluminous. As head of the Children's Aid Society, Brace wrote thirty-eight annual reports. These documents, all of which were published, are immensely informative. The "Minutes" of the Trustees of the Children's Aid Society, presently in the files of the Society, are also informative. During the 1850s, he wrote regularly for the *Independent* on poverty. He later wrote numerous pamphlets and articles on child-saving. Most important of all, however, is *The Dangerous Classes of New York and Twenty Years' Work among Them* (New York, 1880, orig. ed. 1872). This autobiographical book, a minor classic in its time, provides a clear picture of Brace's thought and work.

Frederick Law Olmsted & Environmental Design

My ideas on the relations of architecture, urban and environmental design, and American culture have been influenced by Vincent Scully, *American Architecture and Urbanism* (New York, 1969); John Burchard and Albert Bush-Brown, *The Architecture of America* (Boston, 1966); and Christopher Tunnard and Henry Hope Reed, *American Skyline* (New York, 1956). In a more general way, Sigfried Giedion's *Space, Time and Architecture*, 5th ed. (Cambridge, Mass., 1967), stimulated my thinking about the relationship between urban aesthetics and intellectual style. On the history of American city planning, John Reps, *The Making of Urban America: A History of City Planning in the United States* (Princeton, N.J., 1965); and Mel Scott, *American City Planning since 1890* (Berkeley, 1969), are indispensable. Norman T. Newton, *Design on the Land* (Cambridge, Mass., 1971), provides a comprehensive history of landscape design while William H. Whyte, in *The Last Landscape* (Garden City, N.Y., 1970), synthesizes some of the best contemporary thinking on environmental planning.

Since I completed this manuscript, Olmsted has finally found his biographer in Laura Wood Roper, whose *FLO: A Biography of Frederick Law Olmsted* (Baltimore, 1973) provides a complete map of his life and work. For biographical data I relied primarily upon *Frederick Law Olmsted: Landscape Architect, 1822–1903*, ed. Frederick Law Olmsted, Jr., and Theodora Kimball (New York, 1970, orig. ed. 1922–1928). Written with Olmsted's cooperation, Mariana G. Van Rensselaer's "Frederick Law Olmsted," *Century Magazine* 46 (October 1893): 860–67, is short but extremely informative. Charles E. Beveridge's dissertation, "Frederick Law Olmsted: The Formative Years, 1822–1865" (University of Wisconsin, 1966), offers a wealth of detail on Olmsted's early life. Arthur M. Schlesinger, Sr.'s introduction to a modern edition of *The Cotton Kingdom* (New York, 1953) is useful for both biographical information and Olmsted's view of southern and northern society. Relying upon both textual analysis and econometrics, Robert W. Fogel and Stanley Engerman, in *Time on the Cross* (Boston, 1974), offer a sharp challenge to Olmsted's interpretation of the southern economy.

Lewis Mumford's excellent chapter on Olmsted in *The Brown Decades* (New York, 1955, orig. ed. 1931) is the first attempt to place Olmsted, the environmental designer, within the broad context of American cultural history. Recent studies have gone more deeply into the artistic and cultural traditions of Olmsted's generation. I found three of these works particularly useful: Neil Harris, *The Artist in American Society*; Roger B. Stein, *John Ruskin and Aesthetic Thought in America, 1840–1900* (Cambridge, Mass., 1967); and John William Ward, "The Politics of Design," in *Who Designs America?* ed. Laurence B. Holland (Garden City, N.Y., 1966), pp. 51–85.

The work of Albert Fein is important. His introduction to *Landscape into Cityscape: Frederick Law Olmsted's Plans for a Greater New York City* (Ithaca, 1967), a collection of Olmsted's reports relating to New York, is brief but often perceptive. He has attempted, less successfully, to place Olmsted into a larger context in his essay "The American City: The Ideal and the Real," in *The Rise of an American Architecture*, ed. Edgar Kaufmann, Jr. (New York, 1970), pp. 50–105. His recent book, *Frederick Law Olmsted and the American Environmental Tradition* (New York, 1972), is valuable for its pictorial data on Olmsted's plans and works, but it is ultimately disappointing.

Because of the peculiar problems posed by California's climate and landscape, Olmsted was forced in his work there to articulate his philosophy of environmental design more fully than elsewhere. Moreover, his first independent work in landscape design was done there. This makes his California experience especially interesting, and Diane Kostial McGuire has written a useful M.A. thesis on the topic: "Frederick Law Olmsted in California: An Analysis of His Contributions to Landscape Architecture and City Planning" (University of California, Berkeley, 1956).

Olmsted left a wealth of source material for the historian. Although often severely damaged by later development, many of his important works in environmental design still exist. He also wrote dozens of reports (many published) for cities throughout the nation. The second volume of *Frederick Law Olmsted: Landscape Architect* reprints many of Olmsted's reports relating to Central Park. Recently several more of Olmsted's reports have been reprinted. Albert Fein has done an excellent job of selecting and editing the more important reports on New York City in *Landscape into Cityscape*. In *Civilizing American Cities: A Selection of Frederick Law Olmsted's Writings on City Landscapes* (Cambridge, Mass., 1971), S. B. Sutton has chosen her documents well, but has seriously limited the usefulness of the collection by failing to reproduce each document in full. Although it "necessarily sacrifices some historical content," she decided to edit the reports in order to "sharpen the focus upon Olmsted's understanding of and solutions for urban spaces."

The Olmsted Papers in the Library of Congress contain over 24,000 items. One cannot examine this collection without sensing the extraordinary significance of Olmsted in nineteenth-century American culture. A few of the more important Olmsted letters have been reprinted in an unpublished dissertation by Charles Capen McLaughlin, "Selected Letters of Frederick Law Olmsted" (Harvard University, 1960). McLaughlin is editing a five volume selection of Olmsted's papers. Although they contain fewer than a hundred Olmsted letters, the Charles Eliot Norton Papers at Houghton Library, Harvard University, should not be overlooked. This correspondence, covering nearly fifty years, shows in brief compass the many sides of Olmsted's character and thought.

Index

*This book has been composed & printed
by Heritage Printers in Granjon, a
type named after Robert Granjon,
a French type designer. It is one
of the finest versions of Garamond
available. It was cut for the Linotype
by George W. Jones. Bembo
has been used for display.*

Book design by Jonathan Greene